Char-Broil

GRILLING
FOR THE FAMILY

Char-Broil®

GRILLING
FOR THE FAMILY

300 DELICIOUS RECIPES
to Satisfy Every Member of the Family

CREATIVE
HOMEOWNER®

Recipes on the following pages were provided by G&R Publishing DBA CQ Products: 45, 49, 59–60, 64, 66–67, 78, 86, 89, 98, 101, 103, 105–106, 114, 117, 136–137, 139–140, 144, 147–149, 152, 176–177, 179, 181, 186–187, 189, 217, 223, 228–237, 239–243, 245, 256, 258–260, 264–266

Char-Broil® Grilling for the Family

Vice President-Content: Christopher Reggio; Editor: Laura Taylor; Copy Editor: Amy Deputato;
Designer: Wendy Reynolds; Indexer: Jay Kreider

ISBN 978-1-58011-832-3

Library of Congress Cataloging-in-Publication Data

Names: Creative Homeowner.
Title: Char-broil grilling for the family / editors of Creative Homeowner.
Description: Mount Joy, PA : Creative Homeowner, [2019] | Includes index.
Identifiers: LCCN 2018054571 (print) | LCCN 2018058567 (ebook) | ISBN 9781607656548 (e-book) | ISBN 9781580118323 (pbk.)
Subjects: LCSH: Broiling. | Barbecuing. | Outdoor cooking. | Cookbooks.
Classification: LCC TX840.B3 (ebook) | LCC TX840.B3 C47566 2018 (print) | DDC 641.7/6–dc23
LC record available at https://lccn.loc.gov/2018054571

We are always looking for talented authors. To submit an idea, please send a brief inquiry to acquisitions@foxchapelpublishing.com.

Printed in Singapore

Current Printing (last digit)
10 9 8 7 6 5 4 3 2 1

Creative Homeowner, www.creativehomeowner.com, is an imprint of New Design Originals Corporation and distributed exclusively in North America by Fox Chapel Publishing Company, Inc., 800-457-9112, 903 Square Street, Mount Joy, PA 17552, and in the United Kingdom by Grantham Book Service, Trent Road, Grantham, Lincolnshire, NG31 7XQ.

Photo Credits

Photos courtesy of Char-Broil, with photography by Freeze Frame Studio, Glenn E. Teitell, and Glenn Moores, except as noted below.

iStock: bhofack2 (311, 314); dutchicon (21–23 food icons); LauriPatterson (326); mphillips007 (290, 301)

Shutterstock: 13Smile (233); Africa Studio (101, 303); al1962 (140); Alexandralaw1977 (148); alisafarov (325 bottom); Angorius (289 center); Anna81 (288 top); Anna Voloshyna (278 bottom); Antonova Ganna (78); apolonia (103); AS Food studio (223, 264 bottom); Barbara Dudzinska (59 top); bergamont (201); Best_photo_studio (57); Billion Photos (6); Brent Hofacker (86, 89 top, 98, 228, 240, 243 bottom, 245, 281 top, 299); Brian C. Weed (257); BW Folsom (135); Cameramannz (227); Catalin Petolea (285 top); Catherine Murray (136); chaechaebyv (49 top); Charles Brutlag (189); Dan Kosmayer (266 top); dbullock (114); designs by Jack (243 top); dragon_fang (259 top); Elena Shashkina (236); Elena Veselova (176, 181, 265 top); Elnur (306); Evgeny Tomeev (43); exOrzist (235); FamVeld (18); Foodio (283 bottom); from my point of view (60, 106); Gaus Alex (234); Gita Kulinitch Studio (171); gkrphoto (186); Glenn Price (266 bottom); Gregory Gerber (305); Happy Moments (229 top); Hekunechi (260 bottom); ILEISH ANNA (64); Ioomitz (149); istetiana (117, 147); Isuaneye (89 bottom); Jacek Chabraszewski (187, 271); Jan Danek jdm.foto (177); Jaroslav Francisko (17 left); JIB Liverpool (264 top); joannawnuk (231 top); Joe Gough (67, 237); Juraj Kovac (127); Juriah Mosin (340); Kaiskynet Studio (287 bottom center); kina8 (231 bottom); Kuzz (279 top); Maksim Toome (152); Maks Narodenko (273); margouillat photo (66); Mariontxa (242); Michelle Lee Photography (277 top, 338 top); Mikhail Valeev (217); Monkey Business Images (5); MSPhotographic (265 bottom); MWeen (280 top); My Lit'l Eye (232); nadianb (24); Nataliia K (279 bottom); Nataly Studio (280 bottom, 289 bottom left); Nattika (289 bottom right); New Africa (32 bottom); Nikolay Litov (179); Oleksandra Naumenko (59 bottom); Olesia Reshetnikova (259 bottom); Olga Miltsova (284); Oliver Hoffmann (49 bottom); Paul_Brighton (144); Peredniankina (239); Photographee.eu (45 top); Rasulov (258); Ruslan Mitin (139); sichkarenko.com (241); ssimone (325 top); stockcreations (105); Superheang168 (287 bottom left); Timolina (302); Tobik (229 bottom); T.TATSU (246); verchik (137); vm2002 (230); wavebreakmedia (2); xpixel (277 bottom left); Yaroslav Melnik (327 (bottom); Y Photo Studio (45 bottom); Yulia Davidovich (260 top); Zuzuan (95)

This book is dedicated to backyard cooks who celebrate everything from family reunions to alfresco dinner dates by firing up the grill. There's nothing like cooking outdoors to make fantastic food and wonderful memories with family and friends. **Grill on!**

Contents

1

The ability to feed yourself and a few others with proficiency should be taught to every young man and woman as a fundamental skill.

–Anthony Bourdain

Grill It!

Searing locks in the meat's juices and adds a delicious smoky taste.

ALWAYS TIME TO GRILL

There's one thing most people agree on—we love to fire up the grill. After all, outdoor cooking methods, such as grilling and barbecuing, are easy ways to prepare a meal—and the food tastes great, too. Besides, the cookout is a summertime tradition and a fun way to spend time outdoors—at home, at the game, at the beach, or at the campsite. But why stop when the weather turns cool? As year-round grillers will attest, you can enjoy the deliciousness of food cooked on the grill anytime. When the temperature dips, an outdoor heater or fire pit can keep you toasty while you're waiting for the cheese to melt on your burgers.

SEAR IT, GRILL IT, SMOKE IT

Because steaks, chicken parts, fish fillets, burgers, chops, and other foods eaten in individual portions can become dry quickly, it's important to lock in the juices by searing the meat first. Besides, searing is what produces that delicious crust that makes many people want to grill in the first place.

For the most satisfying grilled or barbecued meals, know your heat. You may have heard the terms *direct heat* and *indirect heat*. Understanding these two terms and employing their methods is the key to preparing mouth-wateringly moist and delicious outdoor-cooked dishes.

Grilling, or **direct-heat** cooking, refers to preparing food directly over the heat source (propane- or natural-gas-powered burners, hot coals, burning wood), usually at a high temperature. It's a popular technique for cooking burgers, steaks, chops, and fish. Rotisserie cooking is done by direct heat, too, as is frying a turkey.

Large, less-tender cuts of meat are best cooked by **indirect heat**. This process of slow roasting at a low temperature, or **barbecuing**, takes longer, but adds flavor and tenderness to meat. Using a smoker? Then you're cooking with indirect heat. Sometimes you might start cooking over direct heat, to brown or sear a piece of meat, for example, and then finish with indirect heat. You'll find references to direct and indirect heat in almost every outdoor cooking recipe.

Finally, don't forget to practice safe food-handling habits, and always start with a clean grill.

INFRARED COOKING

With an affordable line of *infrared* gas grills, Char-Broil has made the technology used by professional chefs for decades available to backyard grillers. You'll find it in Char-Broil's Tru-Infrared grills, as well as The Big Easy®, an infrared turkey fryer that cooks without using oil.

Infrared heat is a great way to cook because it can generate higher temperatures than conventional grills for faster cooking and searing. Infrared waves start to cook the food the instant they reach its surface, quickly creating a sear on the meat that locks in moisture and creates exceptional browning. Char-Broil's infrared cooking systems offer a wide temperature range, from high-heat searing to "slow and low" barbecuing and rotisserie grilling. Because most flare-ups are eliminated, you can simply drop unsoaked wood chips between the grill grates to create a slow-cooked smokehouse flavor in a fraction of the time, using one-third less fuel than standard convection gas grills.

Experience with your new infrared grill will help you determine what temperatures and cooking times deliver the best results. At first, you may want to adjust your regular cooking times. If you have cooked on a charcoal fire, this should be fairly easy to do. If you are more familiar with cooking on a regular convection gas grill, reduce the heat settings you normally use by at least 30 percent, and the cooking time by about 50 percent. Here are some other ideas that will help you master infrared cooking:

■ Coat each piece of meat, fish, or poultry with a light spritz of high-heat oil, such as canola.

■ Plan your cooking according to technique, required times, and the best use of the grill surface. For example, steaks can be seared over high heat and then finished over medium or low heat. Begin with steaks you intend to cook to medium doneness, and end with those you want rare.

TO SEAR ... OR MAYBE NOT TO SEAR

Not every cut of meat is right for searing. Cuts with a lot of connective tissue, such as beef brisket, pork shoulder, or ribs, are best slowly roasted, or barbecued, at a low temperature. This "low and slow" method of cooking literally melts the cartilage in the meat, making it juicy and tender.

Char-Broil's Commercial grills use Tru-Infrared technology that gives you juicier food and eliminates flare-ups and hot or cold spots.

THAT GREAT GRILLED TASTE

Many people make the mistake of overgrilling their food. To get tasty grill marks on your food, particularly meat, and still keep it moist and done to perfection, use the "sear and hold" technique that's practiced by professional chefs. Over direct heat, sear both sides. Then finish the food in a 350°F oven or place it on a tray loosely covered with foil, and set it on the grill away from direct heat until it reaches the desired internal temperature. That's it.

However, getting a yummy caramelized crust using a conventional gas grill can be challenging because you need very high heat (550°F to 650°F); gas flames simply don't get as hot as the hottest charcoal fire that can be banked up in a heap. So to get the grates as hot as possible, cover them with aluminum foil; turn up the heat to high; and close the lid.

Wet meat won't sear; it will steam, which isn't the way to grill a piece of meat. So while the grates are heating, blot off any moisture on the meat using a paper towel. Then spray one side of the food with a high-smoke-point oil, such as canola; open the grill lid; remove the foil; and place the meat directly on the hot grates, sprayed-side down. Check for sear marks by lifting one edge of the meat, using tongs. As soon as you see sear marks, spray the top side of the meat and then flip it over onto a clean section of the hot grates.

When searing is done, use tongs to remove the meat to a holding tray that you can cover. Lower the heat, and allow the meat to finish at about 200°F to 300°F. Use an instant-read thermometer to check for doneness. If you want to apply a glaze, do so when the meat is fully cooked and then place it once more directly on the hot grates *for just a few seconds* prior to serving.

1. Season meat with spices.

2. Sear both sides, using tongs to flip.

3. Remove to a holding tray and cover.

4. Check internal temperature for doneness.

Grill It!

CAPTURE THE FLAVOR

Whatever method you choose for smoking, keep that aromatic hot air trapped inside the grill. Resist the urge to keep "checking." Keep the grill closed until the food is cooked.

ADDING SMOKY FLAVORS TO GRILLED FOOD

Smoking is a low-and-slow cooking method that infuses food with flavor imparted by smoldering wood, charcoal, or aromatics. (Be sure to follow individual recipes for specific directions.) You can smoke food in several easy ways. The first uses a smoker box that sits under the grates, but on top of the grill burners, holding wood, such as mesquite, hickory, apple, cherry, or alder. The chips will not burn; instead, they'll produce smoke, which penetrates the food and flavors it. Just remember: the more smoke you create, the stronger the flavor.

You can also wrap wood chips in a couple of layers of aluminum foil shaped into something that looks like a large snowball. Puncture the foil in several places to create small holes. Then place your "smoke bomb" on the grill above the heat. The holes you've made in the foil will release the smoke of the smoldering wood, which will flavor your food.

If you prefer, you can use chunks of your favorite wood or aromatic branches or herbs directly on the grill and let them smoke. Another method, called "wet smoking," is done with a pan of water—or fruit juice or wine for extra flavor—placed inside the grill or smoker away from the direct heat. As the liquid evaporates in the dry air of the cooker, it adds flavor to the meat.

ADDING FLAVOR BEFORE COOKING

Many recipes call for marinating before cooking. But be careful: the container you use to marinate should not react with the food. For example, acids in a marinade can react with copper or aluminum, giving the food a metallic taste. To prevent this, marinate only in nonreactive cookware, such as stainless steel, glass, and ceramic.

Smoker box (shown on top of grates for clarity)

"Smoke bomb"

Wood chips

HOT OFF
THE SPIT

Rotisserie cooking is yet another way to roast large pieces of meat or poultry. A rotating spit driven by an electric or battery-powered motor is set directly over the heat source and turns at a constant, consistent speed to allow for even cooking. Use an instant-read thermometer inserted into the deepest part of the food to check for doneness—just be sure to stop the rotisserie motor first. It's also a good idea to wear heat-resistant gloves when you're removing the spit rod from the grill.

A rotisserie cooks large roasts and whole poultry over direct heat.

WHAT TO LOOK FOR
WHEN BUYING A GRILL

According to a national survey, Americans grill twice a week or more. With all of that use, it's no wonder that the average grill is replaced about every five years. If the last time you updated your grill was before beer-can chicken became popular, then prepare to be pleasantly surprised. Grills today come with accessories and innovations that help you make the most of your multi-year investment. Whether you're shopping based on budget, brand, or the goal of simply cooking better food, here are some tips straight from industry experts.

A NEW SET OF STANDARDS

Charcoal grills still have a big following, but the convenience of gas grills has made them the most popular choice in America. Small electric grills are great for high-rises and other restricted spaces. The first thing you'll find as you shop is that the traditional gas grill, which heats the air and tends to dry out food, is becoming obsolete.

Char-Broil Tru-Infrared Grill

**Char-Broil Cool
Clean Brush**

**Char-Broil
Instant-Read
Digital Thermometer**

Today, new infrared grills are the latest innovation
on the market for many reasons:
- Preventing flare-ups
- Delivering even heat across the grill grates, with
  no hot or cold spots
- Promising much juicier foods
- Delivering greater fuel efficiency
- Providing the widest infrared temperature range

No matter what type of grill you choose, features like
the following can make your grilling experience easy
and more enjoyable:
- Electronic ignition system, for easy starting
- Porcelain-coated cast-iron cooking grates, for easy
  cleanup and great results
- The option to cook with propane or natural gas
- Warming racks

And don't forget the huge array of accessories
available today. Spatulas, digital thermometers, and
brushes make grilling easy. Griddles, baskets, steamers,
or skewer sets can help you prepare a greater variety of
foods, even eggs and bacon for breakfast.

As you shop all the options, one thing is for sure:
there's a whole lot to love about grilling today, especially
the good times together with family and friends.

**Char-Broil
Comfort-Grip
Tongs and Sputula**

PLAY IT SAFE AND **HANDLE WITH CARE**

The importance of good grilling hygiene can't be overemphasized. The food you serve to your family and friends must be wholesome as well as tasty. By adopting safe food-handling practices in your kitchen—and outside at your grill—you can significantly decrease your risk of food-borne illness.

KEEP IT CLEAN

Wash your hands thoroughly with hot water and antibacterial soap, especially after handling raw meat. Better yet, consider using food-safe disposable gloves—they're great for handling hot chili peppers, too. Be sure to toss them before moving on to other tasks.

If you're using a paper towel to wipe up excess moisture from uncooked meat, seafood, or poultry, dispose of it immediately when you're done. Sterilize a damp sponge in the microwave, set on high, for about 60 seconds or more until it becomes hot. Then let it cool before you grab it, or use tongs to remove it. Launder dish towels and rags in hot water.

Plastic cutting boards can be thrown in the dishwasher. Use several color-coded boards—one for raw poultry, one for vegetables, one for cooked food, and so forth—to prevent cross-contamination. And don't forget to sanitize the sink. Pour diluted bleach down the drain or waste-disposal unit to kill any lingering bacteria, especially after preparing raw meat.

THAT GOES FOR YOUR GRILL, TOO

Burned gunk on the grates is not "seasoning." It's just old, dirty food and will add bad flavors to your next grilled meal. Take care of your grill's grates as you would a favorite cast-iron pan by preseasoning them before the first use. (Refer to your product manual for complete instructions.)

If you don't own one of Char-Broil's infrared gas grills with a built-in self-cleaning feature, here's a secret: fold a large piece of heavy-duty aluminum foil into three layers, forming a sheet that measures about 11 x 24 inches. (A disposable foil tray works well.) Place the sheet on the grates immediately after grilling. Keep the heat turned on high on a gas grill, or lower the grates on a charcoal grill until they are just about touching the coals. The foil concentrates the heat on the grates, which helps to burn off any cooking residue. The stuff usually turns to a white ash that is easy to brush off once the grates are cool again. Follow this by spritzing the grates with a little canola oil spray to season.

Clean your cutting boards and countertops before and after preparing food.

Food will taste better when cooked on a clean grill.

GRILL **SAFETY**

Have you ever noticed grills on apartment terraces and backyard decks, and shook your head in disbelief? Many of these devices are way too close to wooden railings, siding, and fences. Regardless of the type of cooker you own, keep it at least 3 feet from any wall or surface, and 10 feet from other flammable objects. Here are some other tips for safe outdoor cooking from the Hearth, Patio & Barbecue Association (*www.hpba.org*):

■ **Read the owner's manual.** Follow its specific recommendations for assembly, usage, and safety procedures. Contact the manufacturer if you have questions. For quick reference, write down the model number and customer service phone number on the cover of your manual.

■ **Keep outdoor grills outdoors.** Never use them to cook in your trailer, tent, house, garage, or any enclosed area because toxic carbon monoxide may accumulate.

■ **Grill in a well-ventilated area.** Set up your grill in a well-ventilated, open area that is away from buildings, overhead combustible surfaces, dry leaves, or brush. Avoid high-traffic areas, and be aware of windblown sparks.

■ **Keep it stable.** Always check to be sure that all parts of the unit are firmly in place and that the grill can't tip.

■ **Follow electrical codes.** Electric accessories, such as some rotisseries, must be properly grounded in accordance with local codes. Keep electric cords away from walkways or anywhere people can trip over them.

■ **Use long-handled utensils.** Long-handled forks, tongs, spatulas, and such are designed to help you avoid burns and splatters when you're grilling food.

■ **Wear safe clothing.** That means no hanging shirttails, frills, or apron strings that can catch fire, and use heat-resistant mitts when adjusting hot vents.

■ **Keep fire under control.** To put out flare-ups, lower the burners to a cooler temperature (or either raise the grid that is supporting the food or spread coals out evenly, or both, for charcoal). If you must douse flames, do it with a light spritz

of water after removing the food from the grill. Keep a fire extinguisher handy in case there is a grease fire. If you don't have one, keep a bucket of sand nearby.

■ **Install a grill pad or splatter mat under your grill.** These naturally heat-resistant pads are usually made of lightweight fiber cement or plastic and will protect your deck or patio from any grease that misses the drip pan.

■ **Never leave a lit grill unattended.** Furthermore, don't attempt to move a hot grill, and always keep kids and pets away when the grill is in use and for up to an hour afterward.

KID SAFETY

Never tire of saying "stay back!" to children wanting to be near the grilling action. Keep kids and pets at least 3 feet away from the grill. If you own a charcoal grill, keep the lighter fluid and matches or lighters out of children's reach and away from heat sources. More than 16,500 people go to the emergency room each year due to injuries involving grills, according to the National Fire Protection Association. Don't let your kids be part of that statistic.

You Won't Know It's Not
Potato Salad, page 252.
Chill this salad for at least
1 hour before serving.

THE BIG THAW

There are three safe ways to defrost food: in the refrigerator, in cold water, and in the microwave.

Refrigerator Thawing

Planning ahead is the key. A large frozen turkey requires at least a day (24 hours) for every 5 pounds of weight. Even a pound of ground meat or boneless chicken breasts needs a full day to thaw. Remember, there may be different temperature zones in your refrigerator, and food left in the coldest one will take longer to defrost.

After thawing in the refrigerator, ground meat and poultry can be chilled for an additional day or two before cooking; you can store defrosted red meat in the refrigerator for 3 to 5 days. You can also refreeze uncooked foods that have been defrosted in the refrigerator, but there may be some loss of flavor and texture.

Cold-Water Thawing

This method is faster than refrigerator thawing but requires more attention. Place the food in a leakproof plastic bag and submerge it in cold tap water. Change the water every 30 minutes until the food is defrosted. Small packages of meat or poultry—about 1 pound—may defrost in an hour or less. A 3- to 4-pound roast may take 2 to 3 hours. For whole turkeys, estimate about 30 minutes per pound. Cook the food immediately after it defrosts. You can refreeze the cooked food.

Microwave Thawing

This is the speediest method, but it can be uneven, leaving some areas of the food still frozen and others partially cooked. The latter can reach unsafe temperatures if you do not completely cook the food immediately. Foods thawed in the microwave should be cooked before refreezing.

KEEP COLD FOODS COLD AND HOT FOODS HOT

The in-laws will be here soon, and you forgot to defrost that package of chicken thighs you were going to grill for dinner! Should you run hot water over it to thaw it quickly? What if you remembered to take the chicken out of the freezer but left the package on the counter all day while you were at work?

Both of these scenarios are bad news. As soon as food begins to defrost and become warmer than 40°F, any bacteria that may have been present before freezing can begin to multiply. So, even though the center of those chicken thighs may still be frozen as they thaw on the counter, the outer layer of the food is in the danger zone. Maintain the temperature of frozen foods at under 0°F, and raw, unfrozen foods at under 40°F.

For hot foods, the minimum safe-holding temperature is above 140°F. Food can certainly pass through this temperature zone during cooking, but if it does not rise above 140°F, you are flirting with bacteria growth that will make you sick. Use an accurate meat thermometer.

As a rule of thumb, veal, beef, pork, and most seafood should be cooked to at least 145°F; ground beef, pork, lamb, and veal should be cooked to at least 160°F; chicken and turkey breasts, as well as ground poultry, should be cooked to at least 165°F.

See the cooking temperature charts and guidelines on pages 21–23 for more specific information.

A WORD ABOUT KNIVES

By Karl Guggenmos, WACS Global Master Chef
University Dean of Culinary Education for Johnson & Wales University

The knife is one tool that gets chefs and home cooks equally excited and divided. You can spend a fortune on knives of all sorts, but really there are only a few that we use all of the time. Here are my recommendations for knives that you must have; all others are just nice to own (and show off):

- A French, or chef's, knife comes in lengths of anywhere from 8–14 inches. I recommend 10 inches. Use it for major cutting, chopping, and dicing.
- A utility knife is smaller and lighter, 5–7 inches at the blade. It is ideal for smaller hands and versatile enough for a majority of cutting techniques.
- A Santoku knife is a very popular knife. Japanese by origin, it is used just for chopping, dicing, and mincing. Some chefs use a Santoku knife exclusively. It typically has a 5–7-inch blade and is known for its sharpness; beveled, or hollow, ground; and scalloped edge, which helps release sticky food and slices after cutting.

- A slicer is a serrated, long, narrow knife, with its blade 12 inches or longer. Use it for slicing crusty foods, breads, and roasts.
- A paring knife is a short, pointed knife, about 2–4 inches in length. Use it for peeling, trimming, and paring vegetables and fruits.

(Note: For the grill cook, a braising fork, tongs, and spatula will also be helpful.)

Using knives the right way:
- Hold the knife firmly by the handle only.
- Use the right knife for the right task.
- Always hold the blade down while walking with a knife.
- Always use a cutting board.
- Always use a sharp knife.
- Never try to catch a falling knife.
- Always wash and sanitize the knife after each use.
- Sharpen the blade with appropriate tools. (Note: You need a rotating stone sharpener to actually keep the blade sharp.)
- Do not leave knives in standing water.
- Do not clean knives in the dishwasher. The chemicals are just too strong.

BEEF AND LAMB COOKING-TEMPERATURE TABLE

CUT OF MEAT	INTERNAL TEMPERATURE	VISUAL DESCRIPTION
Roasts, steaks, and chops: beef, lamb, veal	USDA guidelines	Depending upon how the meat is being prepared and which cut, different temperatures may be used
medium rare	145°F	Center is very pink, slightly brown or gray toward the exterior portion
medium	155°F	Center is light pink, outer portion is brown or gray
medium well	Above 155°F	No pink
well done	Above 165°F	Steak is uniformly brown or gray throughout
Ground meat: beef, pork, lamb, veal	160°F to 165°F	No longer pink but uniformly brown or gray throughout

POULTRY COOKING-TEMPERATURE TABLE

MEAT	TEMPERATURE	VISUAL DESCRIPTION
	USDA guidelines	
General poultry	165°F	Cook until juices run clear
Whole chicken, duck, turkey, goose	165°F	Cook until juices run clear and leg moves easily
Parts of chicken, duck, turkey, goose	165°F	Cook until juices run clear

NOTE: Always cook meat, poultry, and fish to at least the temperatures recommended by the United States Department of Agriculture to prevent food-borne illness. However, some parts of poultry, such as legs and thighs, cooked to 165°F, while safe, would be considered undercooked by many people. Consult individual recipes for finish cooking temperatures. ALSO NOTE: A 12-pound turkey can easily require up to 60 minutes of resting. During that time, the internal temperature can rise 30 degrees if not exposed to drafts.

PORK COOKING-TEMPERATURE TABLE

CUT OF MEAT	INTERNAL TEMPERATURE	VISUAL DESCRIPTION
Roasts, steaks, chops	**USDA guidelines**	
	145°F	Medium-rare, pale pink center
	160°F	Medium, no pink
	160°F and above	Well done, meat is uniform color throughout
Pork ribs, pork shoulders, beef brisket	160°F and above	Depending upon how the meat is being prepared and which cut, different temperatures may be used. A pork shoulder may be prepared as a roast and would be done at 160°F, whereas the same cut when barbecued "low and slow" for pulled pork may be cooked to an internal temperature of 195°F to 200°F
Sausage, raw	160°F	No longer pink
Ham, raw	160°F	Dark pink color throughout
Ham, precooked	Follow printed instructions	Dark pink color throughout

STANDARD TERMINOLOGY AND TEMPERATURE GUIDELINES

HEAT SETTING	GRATE TEMPERATURE RANGE	PULL YOUR HAND AWAY (5 IN. ABOVE GRATE)
High	Approx. 450°F to 550°F	Approximately 2 to 4 seconds
Medium	Approx. 350°F to 450°F	Approximately 5 to 7 seconds
Low	Approx. 250°F to 350°F	Approximately 8 to 10 seconds

GRILLING TEMPERATURE GUIDELINES

METHOD OF HEAT	GRATE TEMPERATURE RANGE	DESCRIPTIVE LANGUAGE MOST OFTEN USED
Direct	Approx. 450°F to 650°F and higher	Sear, searing, or grilling on high
Direct	Approx. 350°F to 450°F	Grilling on medium
Direct	Approx. 250°F to 350°F	Grilling on low

ROTISSERIE TEMPERATURE GUIDELINES

METHOD OF HEAT	BURNER TEMPERATURE RANGE	DESCRIPTIVE LANGUAGE MOST OFTEN USED
Direct	Approx. 350°F to 450°F	Rotisserie or "spit" roasting

FISH AND SEAFOOD COOKING TEMPERATURES AND TIMES

FRESH OR THAWED FISH	INTERNAL TEMPERATURE	VISUAL DESCRIPTION
Salmon, halibut, cod, snapper (steaks, filleted, or whole)	145°F	Fish is opaque, flakes easily
Tuna, swordfish, marlin	145°F	Cook until medium-rare. (Do not overcook, or the meat will become dry and lose flavor.)
Shrimp	**Time Cooked**	
medium-size, boiling	3 to 4 min.	Meat is opaque in center
large-size, boiling	5 to 7 min.	Meat is opaque in center
jumbo-size, boiling	7 to 8 min.	Meat is opaque in center
Lobster		
boiled, whole in shell, 1 pound	12 to 15 min.	Shell turns red, meat is opaque in center
grilled, whole in shell, 1½ pounds	3 to 4 min.	Shell turns red, meat is opaque in center
steamed, whole in shell, 1½ pounds	15 to 20 min.	Shell turns red, meat is opaque in center
baked, tails in shell	15 min.	Shell turns red, meat is opaque in center
grilled, tails in shell	9 to 10 min.	Shell turns red, meat is opaque in center
Scallops		
baked	12 to 15 min.	Milky white or opaque, and firm
seared	varies	Brown crust on surface, milky white or opaque, and firm
Clams, mussels, oysters	varies	Point at which the shell opens, throw out any that do not open

ROASTING TEMPERATURE GUIDELINES

METHOD OF HEAT	COOKING CHAMBER TEMPERATURE RANGE	DESCRIPTIVE LANGUAGE MOST OFTEN USED
Indirect	Approx. 350°F to 450°F	Indirect grilling or indirect cooking
Indirect	Approx. 250°F to 350°F	Indirect grilling or indirect cooking, "low and slow"

SMOKING TEMPERATURE GUIDELINES

METHOD OF HEAT	COOKING CHAMBER TEMPERATURE RANGE	DESCRIPTIVE LANGUAGE MOST OFTEN USED
Indirect, with wood smoke	Approx. 250°F to 350°F	Hot smoking "low and slow" wood smoke
Indirect, with wood smoke	Approx. 150°F to 250°F	Smoking "low and slow" wood smoke

2

Careful cooking is love.
–Julia Child

Flavor & Nutrition for the Whole Family

Nut-Crusted Ribs with Bourbon Mop Sauce, page 178

Basic "Wet" Rub, page 285

MARINADES, RUBS—RULES OF THUMB

By Karl Guggenmos, WACS Global Master Chef
University Dean of Culinary Education for Johnson & Wales University

For centuries, cooks have used a variety of techniques to enhance the flavor and texture of foods that they prepare. Marinades and early forms of rubs, primarily salt, were originally used for preservation. Fish and meat were air-dried and then heavily salted, and thereby preserved. Marinades, especially pickling techniques, were used to preserve vegetables and fruits. Over the years, cooks discovered that applying acidic marinades to certain tough cuts of meat had a tenderizing effect. In recent times, the application of rubs and marinades has become very popular, primarily because it adds exciting flavors.

During my career I have used—and still use—dry rubs, wet rubs, marinades, and brines to add great flavors—and in some cases to reduce undesirable ones. Red-wine-based marinades, for example, reduce the "gamey flavor" of game meat. Another good reason for rubs is the health benefit derived from the various herbs and spices used in them. (See "Health Benefits of Spices," on page 28.)

- **Dry rubs** can contain a variety of seasoning herbs and spices, applied (rubbed) onto meats and seafood prior to grilling. They enhance or bring out the flavor of the item to be cooked.
- **Wet rubs** are created by adding oil or another wet substance (paste) to a dry rub.
- **Marinades** consist of spices, herbs, and flavor-enhancing liquids such as fruit juices, sauces, oils, wines, vinegars, and even dairy. I also use marinating liquid to make sauce when roasting or grilling. Adding sweet ingredients to a marinade will help caramelize and crisp grilled meats.
- **Brines** are salt-based solutions that help meats keep their moisture so that they stay juicy during grilling. They are popular for poultry and lean meats. Herbs, spices, and sweets like honey can be added for additional flavor. When using brines, make sure the food is completely immersed. (Some prefer to inject brines into whole poultry.) Make sure that you rinse the food before grilling.

Adobo Marinade,
page 272

Basic Brine Recipe,
page 335

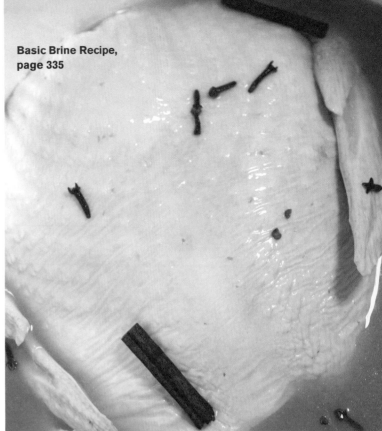

MARINADE & RUB DOs AND DON'Ts

DO blanch vegetables before rubbing or marinating.

DO choose mild herbs and spices.

DO spread rubs evenly over the whole product.

DO taste your rub or marinade before applying it. If it's too strong or weak, you can correct it before finishing the process.

DO use the right temperature: high for meats; medium to low for seafood and vegetables

DON'T overpower your food: cooks often add too much or too strong a flavor to the food they are cooking, especially seafood.

DON'T marinate or rub too early before cooking, especially when cooking seafood and vegetables. Prolonged marinating or resting food after applying a rub results in loss of moisture and a dried texture after cooking. For best results, marinate single portions of seafood and vegetables no more than 30 minutes before grilling; marinate single portions of steaks no more than 1 hour beforehand. The exceptions to this are large cuts of meats, whole poultry, and whole fish. The best time for large meat cuts and whole poultry, for example, is 24–36 hours.

In addition to using herbs and spices as parts of rubs and marinades, check out their benefits and some other ways that you can use them.

	SPICE	SERVING SIZE	ORAC*	TRY IT OUT!
	Cinnamon	1 tsp	3417	Sprinkle cinnamon in your oatmeal or dip berries into yogurt sweetened with cinnamon.
	Turmeric	½ tsp	1398	Add turmeric to water when cooking brown rice or add to egg or tuna salad.
	Cayenne	1 tsp	638	Try adding cayenne to spice up your tomato sauces, soups, hummus, fish, or marinades.
	Oregano	½ tsp	1598	Add oregano to pasta sauce or sprinkle onto a grilled cheese sandwich.
	Ginger	1 tsp	703	Try adding ground ginger to vegetables or using fresh ginger root in tea.
	Paprika	1 tsp	504	Try adding paprika with thyme and red pepper to spice up your popcorn or adding paprika to lean meat.
	Rosemary	1 tsp	1983	Add rosemary to whole- grain rolls and bread, tomato sauces, and grilled potatoes.
	Saffron			Try seeping saffron into tea or in water to prepare brown rice.
	Garlic	1 tsp (powder)	207	Add to sauces or marinades.

*Oxygen radical absorbance capacity (ORAC) is a method developed by the National Institute on Aging in the National Institutes of Health (NIH) of measuring antioxidant capabilities in a food. A high ORAC value indicates a high amount of antioxidants in the food. Antioxidants are the helpful vitamins, minerals, and enzymes in your body that minimize damage caused by free radicals, which are created during oxidation, when molecules in your body become damaged and lose an electron. Antioxidants help heal that damage.

WHAT'S IN A **PORTION?**

Learn healthier portion sizes to help you serve up the right amount for you and your family at home. It seems a bit much to weigh and measure everything we eat; however, it can be a great exercise to try at least once to see whether, when you are "eyeballing" ½ cup of rice, for example, you are even close or not. One research study asked trained nutrition professionals (dietitians) to guess at the calories and fat in a number of meals, and even they underestimated the number of calories by 37 percent and amount of fat by 49 percent. Look at the Serving Sizes table for a handy reference of portion sizes.

However, we also know that not everyone has the same food preferences or style of eating. The American Academy of Sciences (AAS) recognizes that there is a range of values for macronutrients that you can consume as part of a healthy diet (see the table on page 30). For weight loss, for example, you may do better with a slightly higher protein intake and a slightly smaller starch intake. Or if a Mediterranean

SERVING SIZES

FOOD	VISUAL CUE
1 cup broccoli	1 baseball
½ cup sliced fruit; 1 small apple or orange	1 tennis ball
½ cup pasta, rice, or cereal; ½ bagel	1 hockey puck
1 slice whole grain bread; 1 pancake	1 CD case
3 oz. meat	1 deck of cards
4 oz. fish	1 checkbook
1 tsp. butter or margarine	1 postage stamp
1 oz. cheese	2–4 dice
2 tbs. peanut butter	1 golf ball

PORTION CONTROL: PLATE METHOD
Use 8–9-in. plate as main plate.

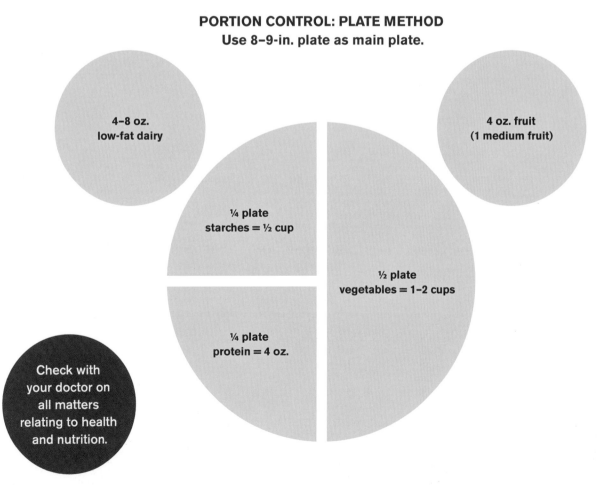

4–8 oz. low-fat dairy

4 oz. fruit (1 medium fruit)

¼ plate starches = ½ cup

½ plate vegetables = 1–2 cups

¼ plate protein = 4 oz.

Check with your doctor on all matters relating to health and nutrition.

AAS GUIDE TO MACRONUTRIENT INTAKE

TOTAL CALORIES IN DIET	PERCENT TOTAL CALORIES		
	45%–65% CARB (G)	10%–35% PROTEIN (G)	20%–35% FAT(G)
1,200	135–195	30–105	27–47
1,400	158–228	35–123	31–54
1,500	169–244	38–131	33–58
1,800	203–293	45–158	40–70
2,000	225–325	50–175	44–78
2,200	248–358	55–193	49–86
2,500	281–406	63–219	56–97

style of eating suits you and your health goals, your fat intake may be as high as 40 percent (but from healthy fats like olive oil, avocado, nuts, and fatty fish). Mediterranean-style eating is extremely healthy for everything from maintaining healthy blood pressure to a reduced risk of heart disease and diabetes.

The goal in healthy eating is not necessarily to eat the fewest calories or fats or proteins or carbohydrates, per se, but to put together balanced, satisfying meals. Balance appetizers with entrées and sides. Perhaps leave off a side starch if you choose an appetizer that is higher in carbohydrates or choose a higher protein appetizer if your entrée is higher in carbohydrates or low in protein. Skip the appetizer if you are going to have a drink, or skip the drink if you are going to have dessert. In the end, it will come down to selecting the overall appropriate portion size for your weight goal, taking into account how much activity you do, your weight and appetite histories, genetics, and all the factors that drive us to eat.

Sea Bass with Tropical Salsa, page 222

Champagne: 4 oz., 105 calories

Merlot: 5 oz., 119 calories

Light Beer: 12 oz., 96 calories

BEVERAGES & **HEALTHY LIVING**

ALCOHOLIC DRINKS

Thinking about a party on the deck? What is the harm of two cool, refreshing piña coladas to go with the fun, family, and food at your backyard grilling bash? Let's say you need 1,800 calories to maintain your weight and 1,500 calories to lose weight. Before you even begin eating, your alcoholic beverage of choice racks up 874 calories, or 58 percent of your total caloric needs for the day!

If weight loss is your aim, skip the frozen umbrella drink and go with a simple red or white wine, sipped leisurely with your deliciously grilled meal.

Here are some other ways consuming too many alcoholic drinks can sabotage weight loss efforts:

- Less inhibited about what and how much you eat
- Interferes with sleep—and being tired can interfere with appetite-regulating hormones, increasing the risk of confusing being tired with being hungry and increasing the risk of overeating the next day
- Interferes with sleep and, therefore, recovery (and muscle building) from exercise
- Can throw off your blood sugar the following day, thereby increasing cravings

Sip away if you'd like, enjoying the food and conversation. Just remember that if you drink, do so mindfully and within the parameters that match your goals.

Piña Colada: 8 oz., 437 calories

Cola: 20 oz., 240 calories

Pink lemonade, 16 oz., 190 calories

Vitamin Water™: 20 oz., 120 calories

NONALCOHOLIC DRINKS

When trying to lose weight, or simply maintaining a healthy diet, do not drink your calories in the form of sugar-laden, nutrient-empty drinks. They may keep your sweet cravings going. They will not fill you up as food does because beverages do not register the same as solid foods or even soup.

It is not just the colas; sweetened iced teas, lemonades, and vitamin-infused waters can all add up. Check the ingredients on the label!

The first two ingredients in certain popular beverages are as follows:

- Cola: water, cane sugar (or corn syrup)
- Iced tea: tea, cane sugar (or corn syrup)
- Lemonade: water, sugar
- Vitamin Water™: crystalline fructose, cane sugar

HEALTHY ALTERNATIVES

So what can you drink when water seems boring?

- Fresh mint leaf and lemon added to a pitcher of water
- Herbal teas—hot or cold
- Unsweetened teas with fresh lemon
- Flavored seltzers
- 1 part real fruit juice mixed with 3 parts seltzer for a carbonated delight

And if you really want to add sugar, go ahead, but taste along the way. You may be surprised that you can add much *less* than that which is in the presweetened beverages that you buy.

Water with lemon and mint: 8 oz., less than 1 calorie

Flavor & Nutrition for the Whole Family

HEALTHY GRILLED MEALS **ALL DAY LONG**

BREAKFAST

You'll find some heartier options, some more traditional options, and some lighter fare offered in this book. Experiment. See how you feel later in the day when you eat a substantial breakfast or one a bit more well rounded than you may usually eat. See what happens if you eat a higher-protein breakfast. As you will discover, breakfast eaters win out over breakfast skippers in so many ways.

Why Bother with Breakfast?

Breakfast may not be the first meal you think of when you think of grilling . . . but it's a great option for healthy eating for the whole family. The science is clear: breakfast eaters typically have a lower body-mass index (BMI) than breakfast skippers. Overweight and obese individuals are more likely to skip breakfast or eat fewer calories at breakfast than trimmer counterparts. Even in those with relatively stable body weight, body composition is better when they consume food at more regular intervals throughout the day.

More frequent eating (smaller amounts) is associated with lower fasting serum lipid levels, lower fasting serum concentrations of total cholesterol levels, low-density lipoprotein, decreased mean serum insulin level, and lower mean 24-hour urinary cortical levels. Skipping breakfast is associated with an increased risk of developing metabolic syndrome in adults.

Studies that look at selected indicator nutrients found that breakfast eaters have a better overall intake of nutrients than those who rarely eat breakfast. Women who eat a more energy-dense breakfast (more calories, within reason of course) tend to eat less overall for the entire day. Men, on the other hand, may need to be more mindful about their breakfast choices and eat a more moderate amount of calories at breakfast to keep in line with total caloric needs. Eating breakfast may help with problem-solving skills, mood, and concentration in school or at work.

What Makes a Good Breakfast?

When you eat one plain bagel, you have consumed 320 calories and 63 grams of carbohydrate, the equivalent of eating four slices of white bread, with no other nutrients to nourish you. No protein, no

NUTRITION 4-1-1: EGG SENSE

When choosing egg whites for a meal, throw in a whole egg; the yolk contains lutein, which is beneficial for eye health, and lecithin, a natural cholesterol buster. The choline in egg yolk may reduce inflammation markers such as C-reactive protein (CRP) and homocysteine.

Grilled Breakfast Pizza, page 53

TOP 10 BENEFITS OF EATING BREAKFAST

- Lower BMI
- Better body composition
- Better blood sugar control
- Less cortisol production
- Better ability to concentrate
- Better ability to problem-solve
- Better mood
- Lower calorie intake overall for the day
- Better nutrient intake
- Better appetite management

vitamin C, no calcium . . . . Grab a granola bar, and it may have many fewer calories (80), but there are still too few nutrients because only one food group, starch, is represented. The ideal breakfast will include some starch but also dairy and/or protein and some fruit for healthy phytonutrients, vitamins, and minerals. Add some healthy fat, too. That breakfast will help your feeling of satiety; you will eat more moderately at every other meal, and it will even help keep your immune system humming along.

How many calories should you shoot for? That is variable. Do you exercise in the morning? Do you

wake up hungry? Do you have an appetite first thing in the morning? Even on a low-calorie diet, a 300- to 500-calorie start to the day is the right start to the day.

APPETIZERS

Appetizers began in ancient Greece as tiny pre-dinner portions of food to stimulate the appetite for the coming meal. Emphasis: *tiny*. The popularity of chain-restaurant appetizers, which can contain more calories than entrées, easily alters the way one views appropriate meal size. Most people who eat those appetizers are full before their entrée arrives but feel cheated if they only eat appetizers, so they may go on to overeat. Additionally, the most popular appetizers are often fried or laden with excessive cheese or meat—or all three.

Appetizers are great to share or to eat as the main dish (like tapas, compliments of Spanish-style eating) for your entire meal. If you like to eat more than just a small amount of appetizer, have a smaller portion of main course. Or select the main course based on appetizer selection by balancing calories and macronutrients like carbohydrates and proteins. Want a pasta dish for your entrée? Go with a protein appetizer like a satay or a simple shrimp cocktail. Want steak, fish, or poultry for your

Guacamole-Style Edamame, page 65

Grilled Salmon Salad
with Vinaigrette,
page 253

meal? Choose a grain-based or vegetable-based appetizer. When dipping, use vegetables instead of chips or bread, which add calories quickly. Choose lean meats in simple sauces.

It is not just about calories or fat grams; it's about the quality of those calories. Is the fat coming from olives, nuts, avocado, or fish rich in omega-3s rather than land-animal sources? Are the calories from whole grains, which carry nutrient-rich vitamins, minerals, and phytonutrients, or just processed starch?

You don't have to be afraid of appetizers. Just be smart. Enjoy the variety of appetizers that appears in this book. Just remember: appetizers are best shared and in small portions, even in your own home.

Salads

Salad . . . you just feel healthier eating one, and for good reason! Consuming a plant-based (not necessarily plant-only) diet has been shown time and again to reduce the risk for heart disease and heart attacks, stroke, and diabetes. Certain vegetables may offer protection against some types of cancers. The array of vitamins, minerals, and phytonutrients in all plant-based foods helps keep

> The U.S. Department of Agriculture's *MyPlate.gov* recommends that one-half of your meal plate be fruits and vegetables.

our eyes healthy, our skin supple, and our arteries pumping blood at just the right rate. The fiber and water content of vegetables certainly helps anyone trying to lose weight. But when we dress them up, salads can do more harm than good.

HOW TO BUILD A HEALTHY SALAD

Loading high-fat meats, cheeses, croutons, and mayonnaise-laden toppings of low nutritional value on lettuce will not make for a healthy meal. Instead, start with a base of colorful lettuce or chopped vegetables, and then (depending on whether it's your main entrée or a side dish) add lean meats, more nutrient-rich vegetables, some beans, grains, nuts, or even fruit. Lastly, toss with a delicious yet healthy olive-oil-based dressing—in fact, the oil may help you absorb some of the fat-soluble nutrients in the vegetables.

Not all salads start with a green leafy foundation. Some are protein based (grilled flank steak),

Grilled Honey &
Lime Gulf Prawns,
page 207

predominately starch based (potato or corn salad), or vegetable based (beet salad) and are meant to be a starter or side dish or rounded out as part of a complete meal.

Because there is no fat in vegetables, most of the fat in salads comes from healthful sources like olive or olive oils, nuts, or avocado. Still, you must choose your portions wisely, depending whether the salad is intended as a main course or as a side dish. If the salad is your entrée, for example, ensure that it has adequate protein (15 to 21 grams). If it doesn't, add some grilled chicken, fish, beef, or tofu on top—or choose a protein-rich appetizer as a pairing.

SEAFOOD

You may have heard the old joke "I am on a seafood diet: whenever I see food, I eat it!" This is not the best strategy when it comes to healthy living, but eating more fish is a great strategy when it comes to weight and well-being.

The omega-3 fatty acids found in fish are the healthiest of fats that can be consumed and have been linked to keeping our hearts and brains healthy. Fish highest in omega-3s are the fattier species such as salmon, trout, sardine, herring, mackerel, and oyster.

Science continues to discover ways in which these essential fatty acids function during fetal brain, nerve, and vision development. Fish provides other nutrients, too, such as vitamin D, B2 (riboflavin), calcium, zinc, magnesium, and potassium.

The simplest way to prepare fish is to sprinkle on a little salt and pepper. Try using lots of different spices—plus olive oil instead of butter—to keep the fish as healthy and delicious as can be. The general guideline for grilling fresh fish is to allow 10 minutes for each inch of thickness; grill until the fish separates easily with a fork.

Butter as an accompaniment is what first may come to mind for the uninspired when thinking lobster. Unfortunately for the health and weight conscious, one 1.5-ounce serving of melted butter is 350 calories and 38 grams of fat. And that's before you add any food!

Rainbow Trout Stuffed with Lemon, Shallots & Herbs, page 214

BBQ Turkey Drumsticks, page 123

Ostrich with Jicama Slaw, page 131

POULTRY

Does chicken come to mind first when someone says "poultry"? Chicken has become many people's alternative to red meat—leaner and protein packed. But, of course, there is more to poultry than chicken. You'll find recipes for chicken, turkey, duck, and ostrich. Skinless chicken and turkey are lean proteins. So is duck—again, as long as you don't eat the skin.

But ostrich? Give it a try. Ostrich is a bird, but it is actually not considered poultry. Rather, it is part of a species that includes the rhea, cassowary, and emu. Its flesh is more like a red meat, yet it's even leaner than chicken. Ostrich is rich in iron— the oxygen-carrying component of blood and an important nutrient that helps your immune system work. Women, in particular, tend to need more iron from their diet.

Aim for Variety

Most people tend to fall back on chicken, and eating the same food all of the time can get old. If you are eating chicken at almost every meal, change it up! Try to rethink menu planning. If you eat three meals plus snacks each day, that gives you 21 meals to create. Try planning so that you eat your protein from a variety of sources:

- Chicken four times a week
- Turkey a few times a week
- Fish three times a week
- Red meat once or twice a week
- Ostrich and duck once in a while
- Eggs a few times a week
- Soy- or bean-based dishes a few times a week
- Dairy most days

Also, keep vegetables abundant. Your meal plan will be complete, varied, and satisfying. You'll feel better and healthier!

BETTER BURGERS, SMARTER SLIDERS

You can make the recipes smaller or larger, based on your mood, taste preference, and caloric needs. Sometimes you just want to eat a good old burger, complete with bun. If you are eating several side dishes, you may want to skip the bun altogether or try an open-faced burger.

Mustard-and-Mint Ground Lamb with Feta-Yogurt Sauce, page 160

Grilled Fruit Parfait, page 263

MEAT

The benefits of red meat include providing a rich source of zinc and iron, absorbed easily by the body and particularly important for growing children and active women during childbearing years, who are more prone to iron deficiency. As we age, and sarcopenia (a loss of muscle mass) occurs, consuming nutrient-rich foods and adequate protein is that much more essential. Red meat also provides vitamins B12, B6, B1, chromium, and vitamin K.

Red meat three times a day? No way. Small portions of lean red meat twice a week? Yes, that can work. Additionally, try some foods outside your comfort zone and popular fare. Cervena is farm-raised venison from New Zealand. Because the venison is farm raised, there is no gamey taste. Instead, these grass-fed, open-range animals produce very lean red meat—providing all of the benefits of vitamins and minerals but with a much healthier fat profile. Cervena is a bit more expensive, so may not be your everyday choice, but for a special family meal or event, it is a great way to go. Bison is another game meat that comes in extremely lean with a healthier nutrient profile than many beef cuts. If you have yet to try it, this is your time.

DESSERT

Some people are dessert eaters; others, not so much. There's no reason to eat dessert. Clearly, all of the nutrients we need can be consumed from the meals and healthy snacks we eat. Yet, the call of a sweet treat is hard to resist!

If you are someone who has a hankering for something sweet after you eat, then enjoy it but try to share a dessert. Focus on the taste, texture, and sensation of what you are eating, and savor each bite to make it count. Try lower-calorie alternatives, like sweet berries with a chocolate drizzle on top or some grilled fruit.

Balance your choices. If you know you are going to eat dessert, skip the alcohol or sweet drink, extra bread, or heavy appetizer, and save some calories for dessert. A general rule of thumb is that 10–15 percent of our daily calories can come from "discretionary," or nonnutritive, calories. This allows for approximately 200 calories for someone on a 2,000-calorie regimen.

3

All happiness depends on a leisurely breakfast.
–John Gunther

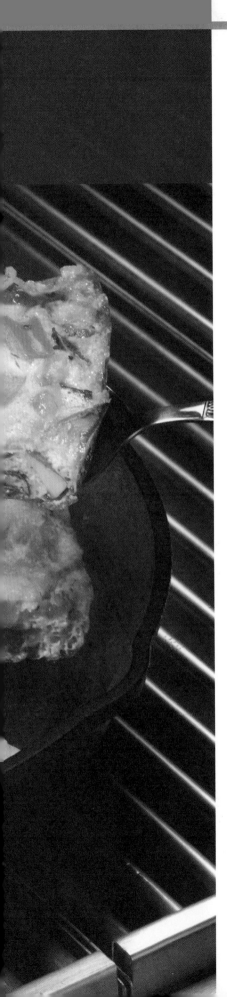

Breakfast from the Grill

ALL HANDS ON DECK!

START YOUR DAY OFF RIGHT

with a special breakfast prepared by the whole crew. From the youngest to the oldest, there's a prepping or cooking job available for every family member. Here's a delicious recipe with tips on how to make sure each person has the best task for his or her skill level. But don't stop with this recipe! Look for ways to include everyone in the family when making a grilled feast for any occasion. The more, the merrier!

GRILLED FRUIT OVER YOGURT

4 SERVINGS • PREP: 15 MIN. • GRILL: 4–6 MIN.

2 bananas, peeled and left whole
¼ pineapple, cut into 1-inch cubes
2 plums, pitted and cut in half lengthwise
8 strawberries, tops cut off, left whole
1 peach, pitted and cut in half lengthwise
4 cups vanilla nonfat Greek yogurt
(or your favorite flavor)

Preheat grill to medium-high. Grill all of the fruit. (Use skewers if that's easier; remember to soak the skewers in water first to prevent burning.) Take the fruit off of the grill. Cut the bananas and the peaches into four equal pieces. Mix all of the fruit together and serve over the yogurt.

This is a perfect breakfast just as it is, but you may want to add nuts for some crunch and "sticking" power to tide you over until lunch.

CHEF TASKS

COOKING RULES FOR ROOKIES & PROS!

- Wash your hands.
- Tie back long hair.
- Clean up any messes right away.
- Ask before you taste test.
- Always listen to the Head Chef!

KIDDO CHEF

- Peel the bananas.
- Rinse the plums, strawberries, and peach before they're cut by the Sous Chef.
- Stir all of the grilled fruit together in a large bowl.
- Scoop the yogurt into each person's bowl.
- Add fruit to each person's bowl.
- Sprinkle nuts on top, if desired.

TEENAGE SOUS CHEF

- Cut the pineapple into 1-inch cubes.
- Cut the pitted plums in half lengthwise.
- Cut the tops off the strawberries.
- Cut the pitted peach in half lengthwise.
- Stick the fruit pieces on skewers.
- Cut the grilled bananas and peaches into four equal pieces.

HEAD CHEF (AKA THE GROWN-UP)

- Keep an eye on your helpers!
- Preheat the grill to medium-high.
- Make sure the skewers have been soaked in water to prevent burning.
- Grill all of the fruit for about 4–6 minutes.

GRILLED APPLE STUFFED WITH OATMEAL

4 SERVINGS • PREP: 10 MIN. • GRILL: 20–25 MIN.

4 apples (McIntosh, Fuji, or
  Golden Delicious)
½ cup oatmeal, plain (instant)
1½ cups water
½ banana (very ripe, puréed)
1 teaspoon ground cinnamon
⅛ teaspoon ground nutmeg
⅛ teaspoon ground cloves
1 teaspoon vanilla extract
8 walnuts, coarsely ground
1 tablespoon light brown sugar
1–2 lemon slices

Begin by cooking the oatmeal on your stove (medium-high heat). Bring the water to a boil; stir in the oatmeal; add the banana, cinnamon, nutmeg, cloves, vanilla, light brown sugar, and walnuts. Cook for 1 minute, stirring regularly. Cover and remove from heat.

Trim a thin slice off of the bottom of each apple (keeping it level). Cut off the top of the apple and, using a small paring knife, hollow out the apple to create a cavity for the oatmeal filling.

Preheat one side of grill to medium. Rub the cut parts of the apples with a lemon slice (to keep from browning). Stuff the apples with oatmeal filling; place them on the grill over indirect heat; and close the grill. (The apples will cook more evenly.) Cook for 20–25 minutes.

Add some yogurt to round out this breakfast and help you feel satisfied until lunch.

FRUIT KEBABS

6 SERVINGS

5 firm bananas, peeled
1 small cantaloupe, seeded
    and rind removed (or
    3 kiwis, peeled)
12 large, firm strawberries,
    stemmed
¼ cup butter, melted
2 tablespoons fresh lime juice
1 tablespoon honey

Preheat grill to medium heat. Cut bananas and cantaloupe (or kiwi) into 1½-inch chunks. Thread on skewers* alternately with strawberries. Combine butter, lime juice, and honey; brush kebabs with mixture and place on grill. Cook about 5 minutes on each side, brushing occasionally with butter mixture. Serve immediately.

If using wooden skewers, be sure to soak in water for at least 30 minutes before using to prevent burning.

GRILLED FRUIT 'N' BLUEBERRIES

6 SERVINGS

6 medium apricots, nectarines, or peaches, halved and pitted
2 cups fresh blueberries
¼ cup brown sugar
¼ cup butter
2 tablespoons lemon juice

Preheat grill to medium-low heat. Place fruit halves cut side up on 12 x 12-inch pieces of heavy-duty aluminum foil. Sprinkle each fruit half with some of the blueberries, brown sugar, butter, and lemon juice. Fold foil around fruit and seal tightly. Close lid and grill 18 to 20 minutes or until tender.

GRILL-TOP VEGETABLE FRITTATA

4 SERVINGS • PREP: 20 MIN. • GRILL: 8–10 MIN. • REST: 3–5 MIN.

1 pint egg whites or yokeless
    egg substitute
2 tablespoons olive or canola oil
½ cup parboiled and diced
    new potato
1 cup julienned red onion
1 cup julienned red bell pepper
1 cup chopped fresh baby
    spinach (or frozen
    if unavailable)
½ cup shredded sharp
    cheddar cheese
Salt and pepper to taste

Preheat grill to high. Place a seasoned 9- to 12-inch cast-iron pan atop the heat. Once the pan is heated, add the oil and potatoes and cook until crisp, about 3–5 minutes. Add onions and peppers and soften while stirring.

Reduce heat to low, and add eggs, spinach, cheese, salt, and pepper. Cover the grill and bake until the egg firms. Let cool for 3–5 minutes; slice into four wedges; and serve straight from the pan.

EGGS-CELLENT EGGS

Eat your yolks! The lutein and zeaxanthin responsible for the yolk's yellow pigment have been shown to help prevent macular degeneration. Additionally, eggs are one of the only foods that contains naturally occurring vitamin D.

There are some nutrient-packed vegetables in this breakfast. If you want, add a slice of whole-grain bread.

Serve with a 6-ounce glass of orange juice for a vitamin C punch!

SALMON "EGGS BENEDICT" OVER SWEET POTATO LATKES

4 SERVINGS • PREP: 20 MIN. • BAKE: 20 MIN. • GRILL: 8–10 MIN.

1 8-ounce salmon fillet, seasoned with salt and pepper (leave skin on; take off before serving)

1 sweet potato, grated

¼ onion, grated

4 eggs

2 egg whites

¼ cup flour

2 scallions

¼ tablespoon salt

¼ tablespoon pepper

2 cups water

1 tablespoon vinegar

HOLLANDAISE SAUCE

⅔ cup plain nonfat Greek yogurt

2 egg yolks

1 tablespoon orange Juice (fresh)

¼ teaspoon orange zest

1 teaspoon dill (fresh)

¼ teaspoon Dijon mustard

¼ teaspoon salt

¼ teaspoon pepper

Begin by making the hollandaise sauce. In a double boiler on your stove, whisk the egg yolks; add the orange juice; and continue whisking. (Egg yolks will become a light pale color when they are cooked; make sure not to let them curdle.) Take the bowl with egg yolks off the stove, and mix in yogurt and remaining ingredients for the hollandaise. Set the mixture aside and begin making potato pancakes.

Place the grated sweet potato and grated onion in a bowl. Add the egg whites (beaten), flour, salt, and pepper. Mix well to combine. Form four pancakes (latkes) with the potato mixture. Place them on a baking sheet and bake them in an oven at 375°F for 20 minutes.

Preheat grill to medium-high. While the latkes are baking, place the seasoned salmon fillets on the grill and cook until fully done. Right before the salmon is cooked, begin making the poached eggs.

Boil the water in a pot and add the vinegar. Crack the eggs in a small bowl (individually); add one egg at a time to the boiling water. When the eggs are cooked, take them out of the boiling water using a slotted spoon.

Place a latke on a plate; put a 2-ounce piece of salmon on top of the pancake; top with one poached egg; and drizzle about 1–2 tablespoonfuls of hollandaise sauce over the top. Garnish the dish with dill and enjoy!

GRILLED STEAK & EGGS

4 SERVINGS • PREP: 15 MIN. • GRILL: 10–15 MIN.

4 3- to 4-ounce beef
    tenderloin steaks
4 slices turkey bacon
4 shelled eggs
1 bunch asparagus
½ cup diced fresh tomatoes
½ cup julienned red onion,
Spice mixture of salt, pepper, and
    ground fennel seed (for steak)
    to taste
Salt and pepper to taste

Preheat grill to high. Wrap each steak with a slice of turkey bacon; secure it using a toothpick or two; season with spice mixture; and sear on both sides. Move steaks to a cooler section of the grill to finish.

As the steak cooks, grill the asparagus. Split the grilled asparagus into four portions and transfer to the four sheets of oiled aluminum foil, already on the grill. Top the asparagus with tomatoes, onions, and one egg per batch, and season to taste. When the eggs and steak are cooked to desired doneness, transfer to a plate and serve.

CINNAMON FLAT ROLLS

---

6 SERVINGS

¼ cup sugar
1 ½ teaspoons ground cinnamon
6 frozen white dinner rolls, thawed
2 tablespoons olive oil, divided

Preheat the grill to medium heat. In a small bowl, combine sugar and cinnamon; set aside. On a floured surface, flatten each dinner roll into a 5-inch round. Brush one side with oil. Grill, oil side down, uncovered, 1 minute or until golden brown, bursting any large bubbles with a fork. Turn roll over, brush with oil, and sprinkle with cinnamon-sugar mixture. Grill until golden brown.

Add a tall glass of cold milk for added protein (8 more grams) and calcium, and to help wash down this delicious twist on an old-fashioned classic.

GRILLED PEANUT-BUTTER-AND-BANANA SANDWICHES

4 SERVINGS • PREP: 5 MIN. • GRILL: 5 MIN.

8 slices multigrain bread of
   your choice
½ cup natural peanut butter
2 large bananas
2 tablespoons clover honey
4 pinches salt
Cooking spray as needed

Preheat one side of grill to low. Make four peanut-butter-and-banana sandwiches by adding 1 tablespoon of peanut butter to each slice of bread. To that, add a half banana per sandwich, sliced lengthwise. Drizzle each sandwich with ½ tablespoon of honey and a pinch of salt.

Apply cooking spray as needed to the grill, and place each sandwich at a 45-degree angle to the grates. After 1 or 2 minutes, rotate the sandwich 90 degrees. When browned, flip each sandwich and repeat. Serve sliced into triangles.

People who love to eat are always the best people.
–Julia Child

GRILL-TOP BAKED EGGS WITH SALSA

4 SERVINGS • PREP: 20–30 MIN. • GRILL: 5–10 MIN.

4 zucchini, cut into thin strips
  and grilled
2 tablespoons olive oil
8 shelled eggs (or 1 pint
  egg substitute)
½ cup shredded Gruyère cheese
Salt and pepper to taste

SALSA
1 cup diced heirloom tomatoes
¼ cup diced red onion
1 tablespoon seeded and diced
  jalapeño pepper
1 lime, juiced
2 tablespoons chopped cilantro
Salt and pepper to taste

Preheat grill to high. Vertically line the walls of four 8-ounce round casserole dishes with the pregrilled zucchini slices, and place them on the grill to preheat. Add ½ tablespoon of oil to the bottom of each dish and then add two eggs or ½ cup of egg substitute. Top with cheese; season with salt and pepper; and cover the grill to bake the eggs.

In a bowl, mix all of the salsa ingredients, and season to taste. When the eggs are mostly firm, remove the dishes from the heat; top with salsa; and serve.

Pair with a cup of berries or melon.

SCRAMBLED TOFU WITH POTATO, LENTIL & SWEET ONION HASH

4 SERVINGS • PREP: 15–20 MIN. • GRILL: 20 MIN

POTATO, LENTIL & SWEET ONION HASH

½ cup red lentils, cooked
1 tablespoon olive oil
2 cups small-diced onion
¾ cup quartered small red bliss potatoes, cooked
Salt and pepper to taste
1 teaspoon finely chopped fresh thyme
2 tablespoons finely chopped chives

SCRAMBLED TOFU

2 tablespoons olive oil
1 cup small-diced onions
1 cup seeded and small-diced red bell peppers
1 clove garlic, peeled and minced
1 cup medium-diced plum tomatoes
1 pound/pack tofu, firm, diced into ½-inch cubes
2 tablespoons tamari, low-sodium
1 teaspoon turmeric
Salt and pepper to taste

Gather all of the hash ingredients and a large, nonstick sauté pan. Preheat grill to medium-high; heat the olive oil in the pan; add the onions; and stir until they begin to brown. Add the potatoes and, without stirring, cook until crispy. Add the lentils; season with salt, pepper, and thyme; and stir. Allow the hash to form a crust on the bottom of the pan.

Now gather all of the scrambled tofu ingredients and a cast-iron pan. Pour the oil into the pan, and sauté the onions, bell peppers, and garlic until tender. Add the tomatoes, tofu, tamari, and turmeric, and bring to a simmer. Season with salt and pepper. Serve the scrambled tofu over the hash.

In this healthy pizza, you are getting more than 100 percent of your vitamin C for the day. Serve with fruit.

GRILLED BREAKFAST PIZZA

4 SERVINGS • PREP: 20–25 MIN. • REST (DOUGH): 45–60 MIN. • GRILL: 8–10 MIN.

DOUGH (MAKES 2 PIZZAS)

1 teaspoon real maple syrup

1¼ cups warm water

2¼ teaspoons active dry yeast (1 packet/envelope)

1 cup bread flour (or all-purpose flour if bread is unavailable)

1½ cups whole-wheat flour

⅔ cup fine-ground cornmeal

1 teaspoon salt

1 tablespoon dry "rubbed" sage

FIXINGS

¼ pound lean breakfast sausage (Canadian or turkey bacon optional)

2 tablespoons olive oil (optional)

½ bunch green onion (scallion)

1 cup julienned red bell pepper

2–3 eggs (or 1 cup egg substitute)

½ cup diced tomatoes

½ cup broccoli, steamed soft

2 slices sharp cheddar cheese (about 2 ounces)

For the pizza dough, add all dry ingredients together in a mixer. Add syrup and water, and mix on low speed for 10–12 minutes. Set aside and allow to double in size (30 minutes at room temperature). Punch the air out of the dough; split the batch into two; reshape each portion into a ball; and let it rest, undisturbed, for 15–30 minutes.

Preheat grill to high. Using your hands or a rolling pin, shape the dough on a pan, plate, or peel board, which will allow you to easily transfer the dough to the grill. Carefully place the dough on the grill and reduce heat to medium-low.

Make grill marks on one side of the dough; flip it as soon as marks appear; and top the pizza with the fixings, leaving the egg and cheese for last. Once all of the meat and vegetables are on the pizza, crack the raw eggs on top and cover with the cheese.

Cover the grill and bake until the eggs are a desired doneness. (If the pizza dough starts to burn, move it to a section of the grill that has been turned off or place it on top of a pizza stone or aluminum foil.) Remove the pizza from the grill; cut it into quarters; and serve.

Note: This recipe will make more dough than intended to be used; only use only 6 ounces of dough per recipe. You can always freeze the remaining dough for another time or keep it in the refrigerator for 3 days.

4

Food is maybe the only universal thing that really has the power to bring everyone together.
–Guy Fieri

Appetizers & Snacks

IT'S TIME TO GET THE PARTY

started with some great appetizers. Everyone, from youngest to oldest, can help prep and cook these yummy recipes. Match each person's age and skill level with each cooking task, and you'll be making family memories before the meal even begins! Here's an appetizer recipe the whole gang will enjoy.

BACON-BRIE APPETIZER

8 SERVINGS • PREP: 15 MIN. • GRILL: 15–20 MIN.

Recipe courtesy of Ray Lampe, who writes the food blog drbbq.com.

1 pound bacon
1 16-ounce Brie wheel
½ cup barbecue sauce

Cook the bacon in a large skillet over medium heat until just crispy. Meanwhile, prepare the grill for indirect cooking, heated to medium.

Unwrap the Brie and place it in a disposable pie pan. Top with the barbecue sauce. When the bacon is cooked, drain on a paper towel and then chop the bacon medium-fine. Top the cheese with the bacon.

Place the pan with the Brie on the unheated side of the grill and cook until the cheese is soft, about 15 to 20 minutes.

Add crackers around the Brie and serve warm.

CHEF TASKS

KIDDO CHEF

- Unwrap the cheese and place it in the pie pan.
- Pour and measure the barbecue sauce.
- Spread the barbecue sauce over the cheese.
- Sprinkle the chopped bacon on top of the cheese.
- Add crackers around the cheese before serving.

TEENAGE SOUS CHEF

- Cook the bacon in a skillet. Use a lid to control grease splatter.
- Drain the bacon and carefully chop it medium-fine on a cutting board.

HEAD CHEF (AKA THE GROWN-UP)

- Keep an eye on your helpers!
- Prepare the grill for indirect cooking, heated to medium.
- Place the pan with the Brie on the unheated side of the grill.
- Cook for about 15–20 minutes until the cheese is soft.

GRILLED BREAD & TOMATOES

4 SERVINGS • PREP: 15 MIN. • MARINATE: 30 MIN. • GRILL: 6–8 MIN.

¼ cup butter, melted

1 tablespoon chopped garlic

½ loaf day-old French bread, cut into 1-inch slices

5 tomatoes, seeded and cut into chunks

½ red onion, finely chopped

¼ cup extra-virgin olive oil

¼ cup balsamic vinegar

Salt and pepper to taste

1 tablespoon coarsely chopped Italian parsley

1 tablespoon coarsely chopped fresh basil leaves

Preheat the grill to medium-high. Melt the butter in a small saucepan and then add chopped garlic. Brush the garlic butter on both sides of the bread slices. Grill the bread over medium-high heat until lightly browned, 3 to 4 minutes for each side.

Cut the grilled bread slices into quarters and place them on a plate. Top with the chopped tomato and red onion. Drizzle the olive oil and balsamic vinegar over the top. Sprinkle with salt, pepper, parsley, and basil. Let stand about 30 minutes to allow the bread slices to absorb the liquids. Serve at room temperature.

HOT GARLIC BREAD

16 SERVINGS

1 cup butter
5½ tablespoons minced garlic
2½ tablespoons crumbled
    blue cheese
3½ tablespoons mixed herbs
1 tablespoon crushed red
    pepper flakes
Sea salt and pepper to taste
Dash of Worcestershire sauce
1 thin baguette, cut into
    thick slices

Preheat grill to high heat. Place a medium saucepan over grill. Place butter in saucepan until melted and stir in minced garlic, crumbled blue cheese, mixed herbs, red pepper flakes, sea salt, pepper and Worcestershire sauce. Mix well until thoroughly heated through. Dunk baguette slices in melted butter mixture to coat both sides. Place coated baguette slices over grill and toast for 1 minute on each side, brushing with any remaining butter mixture.

CHEESY PESTO BREAD

MAKES ENOUGH FOR ONE 1-POUND LOAF

1 (1-pound) loaf French bread, unsliced
⅔ cup sun-dried tomato pesto or basil pesto
2 cups shredded mozzarella cheese

Cut bread diagonally into 24 slices, leaving ½ inch of bottom of loaf intact. In a medium bowl, combine pesto and cheese. Spread pesto mixture on both sides of cut bread. Wrap in foil and grill.

BERRY-PEACH BRUSCHETTA

MAKES APPROXIMATELY 24 SLICES • GRILL: 2–3 MIN.

1½ cups chopped fresh
    strawberries (or
    whole raspberries)
¾ cup chopped, peeled
    fresh peaches
1½ teaspoons minced fresh mint
1 lb. loaf French bread, cut into
    ½-inch slices
2 tablespoons olive oil
½ cup mascarpone cheese

In a medium bowl, combine strawberries, peaches, and mint. Preheat grill to medium heat. Spread bread slices with olive oil and grill on one side for about 1 minute. Remove from grill and spread grilled sides with cheese. Top cheese with fruit mixture and grill 1 to 2 minutes more until cheese is slightly melted. Carefully remove from grill.

EASY GRILLED "TAPAS" SANDWICHES

3–4 SERVINGS • PREP: 20 MIN. • GRILL: 10–15 MIN.

Courtesy of Barry "CB" Martin, on Twitter: @BarryCBMartin.

1 loaf crusty country-style bread
4 tablespoons butter, melted
Assorted vegetables (such
    as eggplant, zucchini,
    onions, peppers, and lettuce)
Sliced cheeses
Thinly sliced cold cuts

Preheat grill to high. Cut bread into medium-thick slices. Cut vegetables into thin slices, making sure slices are large enough not to fall through the grill grates. Slice cheeses and meats into appropriate size for bread.

Brush vegetables with olive oil; grill about 3 minutes per side and remove. Cover and keep warm.

Place bread slices on grill and lightly brown one side, and then turn and brush browned side with butter. Brown other side. Remove bread and cover to keep warm.

Cover grill with aluminum foil. Turn heat to medium. After foil is warm, place meat slices directly on sheet to warm. Remove and keep warm. Add cheese slices to toasted bread. Place on sheet and then close lid for 2 to 3 minutes. This will warm bread and slightly melt cheese.

Open grill and layer bread with warmed meat and grilled vegetables. Serve on warmed plates with condiments.

SPICY GRILLED VEGETABLE QUESADILLAS

4–6 SERVINGS • PREP: 10 MIN. • GRILL: UNTIL DONE

1 each red, yellow, and green bell pepper, seeded and halved

1 red onion, cut into ½-inch slices

¾ cup olive oil

¾ cup fresh cilantro, chopped

2 tablespoons fresh lemon juice

Salt and black pepper

¾ cup Colby or Monterey Jack cheese, shredded

¾ cup sharp cheddar cheese, shredded

1 tablespoon cayenne pepper

1 tablespoon oregano

1 tablespoon garlic powder

8 flour tortillas (8- to 10-inch)

Preheat grill to medium. Brush pepper halves and onions with olive oil; grill over medium heat until tender. Cool and then coarsely chop. In bowl, combine chopped pepper and onions, cilantro, lemon juice, and salt and pepper to taste. Combine cheeses, cayenne pepper, oregano, and garlic powder. Brush tortillas with olive oil. Place four tortillas on grill surface over low heat. Spread pepper/onion mixture to cover tortilla and then sprinkle liberally with cheese mixture. When bottom of tortilla is brown, place another tortilla over top of each. With wide spatula, carefully turn quesadilla and continue to grill until golden brown. Slice into wedges and serve with tomato salsa.

GRILLED CHILI-CHEESE BREAD

3–4 SERVINGS • PREP: 10 MIN. • GRILL: 15–20 MIN.

1 loaf French bread
½ cup mayonnaise
2 cups cheddar or Monterey Jack
   cheese, shredded
1 teaspoon chili powder
¼ cup green chiles, chopped
½ teaspoon ground cumin

Preheat grill to medium-low. Slice bread diagonally but don't cut through bottom. Combine mayonnaise, cheese, chili powder, chiles, and cumin in a bowl. Spread mixture over cut surfaces of bread. Wrap in foil. Grill over medium-low heat (350°F) for 15 to 20 minutes, turning occasionally until heated through.

Good food and a warm kitchen are what make a house a home.
–Rachael Ray

MOZZARELLA & TOMATO SKEWERS

6–8 SERVINGS • GRILL: 2–4 MIN.

1 loaf crusty bread
12 ounces grape tomatoes
8 ounces fresh mozzarella
    cheese, cut into 1-inch chunks
¼ cup olive oil
2 teaspoons chopped fresh basil
1 teaspoon garlic powder
Salt to taste
Black pepper to taste

Preheat grill to high heat. Slice bread into bite-size pieces. Thread bread, tomatoes, and cheese on skewers*. In a small bowl, combine oil, basil, and garlic. Brush over both sides of skewers. Sprinkle with salt and black pepper. Grill 1 to 2 minutes on each side until bread is toasted.

If using wooden skewers, be sure to soak in water at least 30 minutes to prevent burning.

GUACAMOLE-STYLE EDAMAME

4 SERVINGS • PREP: 10 MIN. • GRILL: 3–5 MIN.

2 limes, quartered
1 cup shelled and defrosted
   frozen edamame
½ cup roughly chopped cilantro
½ teaspoon freshly
   ground cumin
2 cloves garlic, minced
¼ red onion, roughly chopped
¼ cup finely chopped red
   bell pepper
1 pinch cayenne pepper (optional)
Water as needed
Salt and pepper to taste

Preheat grill to high. Place limes on the grill until lightly charred; remove them; and let them cool. In a food processor, add edamame, cilantro, cumin, garlic, onions, peppers, and cayenne (if desired); squeeze juice from grilled limes into the mixture; and pulse until you achieve desired texture. If needed, add small amounts of water to smooth out texture. Season with salt and pepper, and serve with your favorite vegetables as a dip.

Try using crudités (raw vegetables) instead of pita or bread with this dip to enhance the nutrient punch and save calories for other meal options.

POTATO WEDGES

3–4 SERVINGS

2 to 3 large potatoes, washed
   and scrubbed
1 tablespoon olive oil
½ teaspoon dried thyme
½ teaspoon dried oregano
Salt and pepper to taste

Cover grill grate with aluminum foil. Preheat grill. Cut potatoes into ⅓- to ½-inch wedges. Brush potato slices with olive oil and sprinkle with dried thyme and dried oregano. Lay potato wedges over aluminum foil on grill. Sprinkle with salt and pepper to taste. Grill wedges to desired tenderness, turning occasionally.

My idea of Heaven is a great big baked potato and someone to share it with.

–Oprah Winfrey

CAJUN GRILLED POTATO WEDGES

4-6 SERVINGS • GRILL: 40 MIN. (IN PACKETS), 15–20 MIN. (DIRECTLY ON GRILL)

3 large russet potatoes with peel, washed and scrubbed
¼ cup olive oil
2 cloves garlic, minced
1 teaspoon salt
1 teaspoon paprika
½ teaspoon dried thyme
½ teaspoon dried oregano
¼ teaspoon pepper
⅛ to ¼ teaspoon cayenne pepper

Preheat grill to medium-high heat. Cut potatoes into wedges. Place potato wedges in a large bowl and add olive oil, tossing until coated. Add minced garlic, salt, paprika, dried thyme, dried oregano, pepper, and cayenne pepper. Mix together until potato wedges are completely covered. Divide potato wedges on two or three large sheets of aluminum foil. Fold foil to enclose potatoes in packets and place packets on grill. Grill for 40 minutes or until potatoes have softened slightly. Remove packets from grill. Carefully open packets and remove potatoes from aluminum foil. Place potatoes cut side down on grill. Cover grill and cook for 15 to 20 minutes, until potatoes are browned and tender.

You can use the scooped-out potato left over from this recipe for mashed potatoes.

SMOKIN' SOON'S POTATO SKINS

4 SERVINGS • PREP: 10 MIN. • GRILL: 10–15 MIN.

Smokin' Soon is a frequent contributor to Char-Broil's "Sizzle on the Grill" users' forums.

4 baked Russet potatoes, halved and scooped out, ¼ inch of flesh remaining
¼ cup olive oil or melted butter
Hot sauce to taste
Coarse salt and black pepper to taste
4 tablespoons finely grated Parmesan cheese (about 1½ teaspoons per potato skin)

After slicing and scooping baked potatoes, mix oil or butter with hot sauce in a plastic bag. Add potato skins to bag and massage to coat them, about 1 minute.

Preheat grill to medium-high. Remove skins from bag; place flesh side down on grill to brown; turn with tongs; remove; and season with salt, pepper, and Parmesan. Serve immediately.

GRILLED CRAB CAKES

4 SERVINGS • PREP: 15–20 MIN. • GRILL: 10–15 MIN.

½ pound lump crab meat, picked through for shells

1 red bell pepper, finely diced

4 shallots (or ½ red onion), finely diced

½ cup chopped fresh parsley

¼ cup chopped fresh spearmint

2 garlic cloves

2 tablespoons low-fat mayonnaise

1 tablespoon Dijon mustard

½ teaspoon paprika

Salt and pepper to taste

Instant whole-wheat couscous, ground in a food processor, as needed

Cooking spray as needed

Preheat grill to medium. In a large bowl, mix all ingredients except for the couscous and cooking spray. Adjust seasoning. (Remember that the crab is cooked, so it should be safe to eat.) If you are unable to make sturdy crab cakes from the mixture, add small amounts of the ground couscous until the mixture comes together.

Place a piece of aluminum foil on the grill and spray with the cooking spray. Place the crab cakes on the aluminum foil and cook until browned. Flip, and brown the other side. Serve the cakes by themselves or on top of your favorite salad greens.

Though this recipe is an appetizer, you really could have two with a salad or vegetable and call it a meal.

WATERMELON & FETA SKEWERS

4 SERVINGS • PREP: 10–15 MIN. • GRILL: 5–10 MIN.

½ fresh watermelon, cut into
   1½- x 1½- x 5-inch blocks
1 lime, juiced
Salt and pepper to taste
Cooking spray as needed
4 bamboo skewers, soaked
   in water

FETA CHEESE MIX
½ cup feta cheese
½ cup peeled and finely
   diced cucumber
¼ cup thinly sliced fresh
   spearmint leaves
1 tablespoon rice or
   champagne vinegar
Salt and pepper to taste

Preheat grill to medium. Place a presoaked skewer into the end of the watermelon; drizzle with lime, salt, and pepper; and spray with cooking spray. Grill to desired doneness.

In a bowl, mix the cheese, cucumber, mint, and vinegar, and then season. To serve, place one piece of watermelon on a plate and top with a spoonful of the cheese mix.

KOREAN-STYLE CHICKEN LETTUCE WRAPS

4 SERVINGS • PREP: 15–20 MIN. • MARINATE: 1 HOUR
GRILL: 20–25 MIN., INCLUDING PINEAPPLE
(UNTIL INTERNAL TEMP. OF CHICKEN IS 165°F) • REST: 5 MIN.

4 chicken thighs without skin (can also use breast)
2 scallions
½ bag shredded cabbage (coleslaw mix)
12 Boston Bibb lettuce leaves
1 small can sliced pineapples

MARINADE FOR CHICKEN

2 tablespoons low-sodium soy sauce
½ cup pineapple juice reserved from canned pineapples
1 tablespoon toasted sesame oil

SAUCE FOR KIMCHI-STYLE CABBAGE

½ teaspoon sriracha hot sauce
2 teaspoons chili garlic sauce
2 tablespoons mirin rice-wine vinegar
1 teaspoon fresh ginger
1 teaspoon finely chopped garlic
1 tablespoon fish sauce

Mix the marinade ingredients in a bowl; place the chicken in the marinade; and marinate tor at least 1 hour. Preheat grill to high. Take the chicken out of the marinade and grill it to at least 165°F internal temperature (about 15–20 minutes).

While the chicken is cooking, mix all of the ingredients for the kimchi sauce together. Toss in the cabbage, making sure to coat well.

Once the chicken is cooked, take it off the grill and let it rest for 5 minutes. Grill the pineapple slices to use as a garnish. Slice the chicken into strips; arrange the lettuce on a plate; and place chicken in each leaf (about one chicken thigh sliced for 3 lettuce leaves).

Top chicken with kimchi cabbage. Cut the grilled pineapple slices in half and garnish each wrap with ½ slice.

LETTUCE WRAPS OF GRILLED TOFU & MOROCCAN COUSCOUS WITH SPICY TOMATO CHUTNEY

4 SERVINGS • PREP: 20 MIN. • GRILL: 5 MIN.

½ package or 8 ounces
    extra-firm tofu, sliced into 1-inch-
    thick slices
12 Boston Bibb lettuce leaves
Salt and pepper to taste

COUSCOUS
¼ cup whole-wheat couscous
¼ cup 100-percent apple juice
Pinch salt
⅛ teaspoon cinnamon
⅛ teaspoon cumin
Pinch coriander
1 tablespoon fresh orange juice
2 fresh apricots, cut in half
    and grilled
1 tablespoon raisins

SPICY TOMATO CHUTNEY
½ pint grape tomatoes
3 cloves garlic
⅛ habanero pepper (very spicy
    pepper, be sure to keep wear
    gloves when chopping, and only
    use a very little)
½ onion
1 teaspoon chili powder
½ teaspoon curry powder
½ teaspoon ginger powder

Preheat grill to medium-high. Before putting tofu on grill, make sure to squeeze out excess water, and pat dry with a paper towel. Season tofu with salt and pepper, and grill it and the apricots on both sides. Take the tofu and apricots off of the grill, and set them aside.

Cook the couscous in apple juice. Dice the grilled apricots, and add them and all other ingredients to the couscous. When the couscous is done, fluff it with a fork.

To make the tomato chutney, place a pot on the grill. Sauté the tomatoes and onions until they're very soft. Add in remaining ingredients for chutney, and cook for 20 minutes until a chutney consistency is formed.

Arrange lettuce on a plate; add 2 tablespoons of couscous into lettuce, and then top with tofu. Add tomato chutney last.

BACON-WRAPPED MUSHROOMS

12 SERVINGS • PREP: 15 MIN. • GRILL: 20–30 MIN.

This recipe is from Ka Honu, an active contributor to the "Sizzle on the Grill" users' forums.

12 medium-sized cremini or
    white mushrooms
Olive oil
12 garlic cloves, peeled
    and crushed (1 per
    mushroom cap)
Sliced jalapeño peppers,
    sausage, shredded cheese, or
    other ingredients for stuffing
12 slices thin, center-cut bacon
Salt and pepper to taste
Hot sauce, if desired

Wipe the mushrooms with a paper towel to clean them; pull the stems to remove them. Set the stems aside for future use.

Brush each mushroom with olive oil to prevent sticking to the grill. Insert a crushed garlic clove into each mushroom cap and then add a jalapeño slice and any other stuffing you desire.

Wrap each mushroom with a strip of bacon. (Take one turn around the top and twist to go around the sides, ending inside the cap.) Preheat the grill to medium. Place bacon-wrapped stuffed mushrooms, filling side up, on a rack or pan over the heat. Roast, hood closed, for 25 to 30 minutes or until the bacon is crisp. Remove and let mushrooms cool for a bit before serving.

MOINK BALLS

6 SERVINGS • PREP: 10 MIN. • GRILL: 50 MIN.

6 slices bacon
12 precooked beef meatballs
Favorite dry rub
Favorite barbecue sauce

Cut each bacon slice in half lengthwise to make 12 thin strips. Place one meatball in the center of each strip. Wrap bacon around meatball and secure with a toothpick. Dust with your favorite rub, if desired.

Preheat one side of grill to low, and add smoker chips if desired. Place the moink balls in an aluminum pan. Set the pan over indirect heat, and cook about 30 minutes, checking and turning moink balls as necessary. Brush with barbecue sauce, and continue cooking for additional 20 minutes or until bacon is crisp and sauce has set. Serve hot.

"MOO (beef) + OINK (pork) = MOINK" is the way barbecue chef Larry Gaian explains how he came up with the name for these bacon-wrapped meatballs.

FRITTATA ON THE GRILL

2 SERVINGS • PREP: 15 MIN. • GRILL: 15 MIN. (UNTIL INTERNAL TEMP. IS 160°F)

This recipe is presented courtesy of Gary House, "The Outdoor Cook" at Cooking-Outdoors.com.

4 eggs
2 green onions, sliced
4 large crimini mushrooms,
    stemmed and sliced
½ red bell pepper, diced
1 teaspoon capers (no juice)
½ cup sharp cheese
2 tablespoons grated
    Parmesan cheese
½ cup frozen shredded
    hash browns
1 teaspoon dried parsley flakes
2 cloves garlic, minced
Salt and pepper to taste
½ cup milk or more as needed

Preheat the grill to medium-high. Grease the inside of a cast-iron pan or heavy skillet.

Scramble eggs and milk together in a bowl; add all the other ingredients and mix. Pour mixture into the pan, and place on grill over indirect heat. Close hood and cook for about 15 minutes. You may want to move the skillet around on the grates to ensure even cooking. Frittata is done when eggs are set and an instant-read thermometer inserted in center registers 160°F. Slice into wedges, and serve hot or warm.

This recipe provides savory sustenance as a light lunch or while you await the dinner bell—all with some very simple preparation.

Use leftover grilled pork, chicken, fish, or beef to make these tasty appetizers.

PATIO DADDIO BBQ'S PULLED-PORK PASTIES

8 SERVINGS • PREP: 10 MIN. • GRILL: 20–25 MIN.

John Dawson, aka Patio Daddio BBQ, is a regular contributor to "Sizzle on the Grill."

1 cup pulled pork or other grilled meat, shredded

1 package refrigerated roll-up or extra-large biscuits

If filling is too dry, mix in a few drops of water, chicken stock, or barbecue sauce.

Roll out the biscuit dough and separate into precut triangles, squares, or rounds. Place about 1 teaspoon of the meat mixture in the center of each. Roll up dough to cover the meat and then pinch the sides. You can also use a fork to poke a few small holes in the crust to allow steam to escape.

Preheat one side of the grill to medium. Place pasties on a baking sheet on the grill over indirect heat, cooking until the dough is browned. Serve with a dipping sauce, such as mustard or your favorite barbecue sauce.

GRILLED PORTOBELLO MUSHROOMS WITH PEPPERONI & CHEESE

4 SERVINGS • PREP: 5 MIN. • GRILL: 10 MIN.

4 large portobello mushrooms, stems removed, cleaned with paper towel
2 tablespoons butter
½ cup mozzarella, shredded
½ cup Parmesan cheese, shredded
Italian seasoning
16 slices pepperoni

Preheat grill to medium. Lightly butter a baking sheet lined with foil. Place mushrooms on baking sheet; add a bit of butter to each; pile shredded cheeses (generously); sprinkle with herbs; and arrange pepperoni on top. Grill until mushrooms are slightly softened and cheese is golden brown, about 10 minutes. Cut in wedges or serve whole.

These mushrooms taste like a pepperoni-and-cheese pizza—and you don't have to fling dough.

MINI ONION BLOSSOMS

4 SERVINGS

4 large sweet onions, peeled
6 tablespoons butter, divided
Garlic salt to taste
Salt and pepper to taste

Preheat grill to high heat. Cut each onion into quarters, keeping sections of each onion together. Place 1½ tablespoons butter and desired amount of garlic salt in the center of each onion. Wrap each onion in a double layer of aluminum foil. Place wrapped onions directly on the grill and cook for 30 to 45 minutes. Carefully remove onions from grill. Using a hot pad or oven mitt, slowly unwrap onions and season with salt and pepper.

It's important for me who is at the table with me;
the moment when everyone speaks to each other and everyone
listens. If there's good food, it's much better.

–Andrea Bocelli

HOT CORN DIP

6 SERVINGS • PREP: 10 MIN. • GRILL: 10–20 MIN.

2 tablespoons unsalted butter

2 cups corn kernels (from 2 ears corn)

Salt and pepper to taste

½ cup yellow onion, chopped

¼ cup red bell pepper, chopped

¼ cup chopped green onions (green and white parts)

1 jalapeño, chopped

2 teaspoons garlic, chopped

¼ cup mayonnaise

½ cup Monterey Jack cheese, grated

¼ teaspoon cayenne

½ cup sharp cheddar, grated

Melt one tablespoon of the butter in a pan. Add the corn; season with salt and pepper; and sauté until the corn starts to turn golden brown, about 5 minutes. Remove from the pan and set aside.

Melt the remaining tablespoon of butter in the same pan. Add the onion and pepper, and sauté until softened, about 2 minutes.

Add the green onions, jalapeño, and garlic; sauté until softened, about 2 minutes. Mix the corn, onions, peppers, mayonnaise, Monterey Jack, and cayenne in a bowl. Pour the mixture into an 8 x 8-inch baking dish or aluminum pan and top with the cheddar cheese.

Place on the top rack of a grill that has been preheated to medium and cook until bubbling and golden brown on top, about 10 to 20 minutes.

SMOKED PECANS & GOUDA

4–6 SERVINGS • PREP: 10 MIN. • SMOKE: 35–60 MIN.

1 pound pecan halves, walnuts,
    or almonds
⅓ cup butter, melted
Seasoned salt to taste
1½ pounds Gouda, shredded

With a small wooden skewer, punch several small holes in the bottom of a foil pan.

Add pecans to melted butter and spread in an even layer in pan. Sprinkle with seasoned salt. Add cheese to a second pan. Place both pans on top rack of smoker. Smoke for 35 to 60 minutes. About halfway through cooking time, stir nuts and sprinkle with additional seasoned salt. Serve warm nuts and cheese with fruits and crackers.

GRILLED SWEET-POTATO CHIPS

4 SERVINGS • PREP: 10 MIN. • GRILL: 30 MIN.

2 medium sweet potatoes,
    preferably red-skinned
Olive oil
Kosher salt

Peel sweet potatoes and slice into ¼- to ½-inch-thick slices. Brush or spray lightly with olive oil. (For large quantities, place in a plastic zip-top bag; add the oil; and massage to coat all surfaces.) Season liberally with salt just before grilling.

Place potatoes directly on cooking grate over direct heat and grill 3 minutes on each side or until seared. Move to indirect heat for about 20 minutes until tender; turn halfway through cooking time. When soft and tender, remove from grill; sprinkle with salt to taste; and serve immediately.

GRILLED NACHOS

4–6 SERVINGS • PREP: 10 MIN. • GRILL: 10–12 MIN.

1 bag corn tortilla chips
1 small can sliced green
    chili peppers
4 ounces Monterey Jack cheese
4 ounces extra-sharp
    cheddar cheese
Sour cream
Salsa

Preheat grill to medium. Place tortilla chips in foil pan. Sprinkle chili peppers and cheeses on top.

Grill chips over medium heat with lid closed until melted, 10 to 12 minutes. Serve with sour cream and salsa.

My two essential ingredients are chiles, any kind, dried or fresh, and acid, whether it's citrus—lemon, lime, yuzu—or vinegars. Food has to pop.
–Jean-Georges Vongerichten

FRIED PICKLES

4–6 SERVINGS • PREP: 10 MIN. • DEEP-FRY: UNTIL DONE

Oil for frying
1 cup flour
1 cup yellow cornmeal
2 tablespoons favorite
   barbecue rub
¼ cup prepared yellow mustard
2 tablespoons beer
15–20 dill pickle slices

Heat oil in deep fryer to 350°F. In wide, flat pan, combine flour and cornmeal. Season mixture with barbecue rub. In a small bowl, mix mustard and beer. Dip pickle slices in mustard mixture and then in flour/cornmeal mix. Using tongs, carefully slip individual pickle slices into hot oil. Deep-fry until batter is browned. Pickles will float to top of hot oil when done. Remove from oil with tongs, and drain pickles on paper towels on a shallow plate. Serve hot.

These delicious snacks, great with ice-cold beer, hail from the southern United States.

EASY SMOKY CHICKEN DRUMETTES PARTY PLATTER

4–5 SERVINGS • PREP: 15 MIN. • SMOKE: 20 MIN.

This recipe is from Barry "CB" Martin, on Twitter: @BarryCBMartin.

20 chicken wing drumettes
2 tablespoons garlic powder
1 teaspoon ground ginger
1 teaspoon ground mustard
1 pinch ground cumin
Coarse salt & pepper to taste
¼ cup peanut or canola oil
¼ cup white wine
¼ cup favorite barbecue sauce
    for dipping

Rinse and pat dry chicken drumettes, and place them in a large mixing bowl. Add the next five ingredients, and mix thoroughly. Drizzle oil onto drumettes, and mix until chicken is lightly coated with oil and spices.

Preheat grill to high. Place small packet of moist wood chips on grill; when they begin to smoke, reduce heat to medium.

Grill chicken approximately 8 to 10 minutes, turning to prevent burning. Keep lid closed between turns to ensure that the smoke permeates the meat. After drumettes have browned sufficiently, remove them from grill, and place them in the center of a large sheet of aluminum foil. Fold foil around the drumettes, leaving a small opening. Pour wine into opening, and loosely seal foil. Place foil packet with drumettes back onto grill until wine begins to steam. Remove drumettes, and garnish with lettuce, celery, or parsley. Serve with your favorite barbecue sauce.

SPICY MAPLE GRILLED WINGS

6–8 SERVINGS • PREP: 10 MIN. • GRILL: 25 MIN.

This recipe comes from Adam Byrd, a self-taught grilling and cooking enthusiast from Round Rock, Texas. He regularly participates in new-product testing for Char-Broil.

1 package (18–24) chicken wings
½ teaspoon each of salt, pepper, and paprika
¼ cup pure maple syrup
3 tablespoons brown sugar
1 tablespoon butter
3 tablespoons Thai chili sauce

Mix together salt, pepper, and paprika, and then season wings. Preheat one side of grill to medium, the other side to low. In small saucepan, add syrup, sugar, butter, and chili sauce. Bring to simmer, whisking briskly. Remove from heat. Grill wings for 2 to 3 minutes per side over medium heat and then transfer them to low-heat burner. Continue cooking over this burner, turning occasionally, for about 20 minutes or until skin is nicely browned and crisp. About 2 minutes before removing them from grill, brush wings with maple glaze. Serve.

BUFFALO DRUMSTICKS

4 SERVINGS

8 large chicken drumsticks
3 tablespoons hot pepper sauce
1 tablespoon vegetable oil
1 clove garlic, minced
¼ cup mayonnaise
3 tablespoons sour cream
1½ tablespoons white
    wine vinegar
¼ teaspoon sugar
⅓ cup crumbled blue cheese
Celery sticks

Place chicken drumsticks in a large zippered bag. In a small bowl, combine hot pepper sauce, vegetable oil, and minced garlic. Pour mixture over chicken in bag. Marinate chicken in refrigerator at least 1 hour or up to 24 hours, turning occasionally. To make blue cheese dressing, in a small bowl, combine mayonnaise, sour cream, white wine vinegar, and sugar. Mix well and stir in crumbled blue cheese. Store dressing and celery sticks in airtight containers until ready to serve.

At tailgate, preheat grill to high heat. Remove chicken from bag and discard marinade. Place chicken on grate and grill, covered, for 25 to 30 minutes, turning three to four times during grilling time. Chicken is done when it is tender and no longer pink in middle. Serve drumsticks with blue cheese dressing and celery sticks.

BACON-WRAPPED BARBECUED SHRIMP

4–6 SERVINGS • PREP: 20 MIN. • GRILL: 2–5 MIN.

1 pound large, giant, or jumbo
    shrimp, shelled and deveined
1 slice of bacon per shrimp,
    partially cooked, cut in half
1 each red and yellow bell
    pepper, seeded, cleaned, and
    cut in 1-inch chunks
1 small olive per shrimp
1 cup favorite barbecue
    sauce
Grilling basket, or 8 bamboo
    skewers, soaked for 2 hours
Fresh lime juice

Place an olive in center of each shrimp and then wrap a piece of bacon around each shrimp. Place one or two pieces of pepper on each skewer, followed by one bacon-wrapped shrimp. Coat with barbecue sauce and place over direct heat for 3 minutes. If using larger shrimp, you may need to cook an additional 2 to 3 minutes until shrimp turns opaque. Drizzle with lime juice. Serve.

BASIC PIZZA DOUGH

4 SERVINGS • PREP: 3 HR.

½ cup cold milk
½ cup hot water
1 package active dry yeast
Pinch sugar
2¼ teaspoons kosher salt
1 tablespoon extra-virgin olive oil
¼ cup cornmeal
2¾ cups flour

Combine milk and water in a large bowl. Add yeast and sugar; set aside until yeast foams. Stir in salt, oil, and cornmeal. Gradually stir in flour until soft dough forms. Turn dough out onto floured surface; knead until smooth and shiny, about 10 minutes. Return dough to greased bowl; cover tightly with oiled plastic wrap; and let rise about 2 hours or until doubled in size.

Press dough down gently and proceed with your favorite grilled pizza or grilled bread recipe. Yields two pizzas.

HOT tip! Be sure to work on a well-floured surface and to flour rolling pin to prevent dough from sticking. Shape pie as evenly and thinly as possible but not so thin that holes appear in dough. Some prefer crust that is less than ¼-inch thick; others prefer it thicker. When set on grill, dough firms up immediately and thickens slightly. Not all pies will conform to a perfectly round shape. Free-form shapes are completely acceptable when making homemade pizza.

HERBED MARGHERITA FLATBREAD

6 SERVINGS

Flatbread, cut into 6 serving-
size pieces
½ (4 to 5.2 ounces) container
semisoft cheese with garlic
and herbs
1 medium Roma tomato,
thinly sliced
½ cup halved or quartered
cherry tomatoes
1 tablespoon olive oil
Fresh basil leaves, chopped

Preheat grill to medium heat. Grill one side of flatbread until
browned. Remove from grill and spread browned side with cheese
and tomatoes. Drizzle with oil and return to grill until bottom side is
browned. Remove from grill, sprinkle with basil, and cut into wedges
to serve.

SIMPLE APPETIZER CHEESE PIZZA

8 SERVINGS

1 can (13.8 ounces) refrigerated pizza crust dough
Pizza sauce
Mozzarella cheese

Preheat grill to medium heat. Spray pizza pan with nonstick cooking
spray (a pizza pan with small holes works well). Unroll pizza dough on
pan; add pizza sauce and cheese. Grill about 10 to 20 minutes or until
crust is baked and cheese is melted.

BEST GRILLED PIZZA

4 SERVINGS • PREP: 20 MIN. • GRILL: 3–5 MIN.

Courtesy of Barry "CB" Martin, on Twitter: @BarryCBMartin.

1 pizza dough recipe (see page 88), or premade dough

Cornmeal for dusting pan

¼ cup extra-virgin olive oil

4 cloves garlic, minced

¼ cup Parmesan cheese, freshly grated

1 cup mozzarella cheese, shredded

1 cup Italian-style tomato sauce

Fresh basil leaves, cut into strips

Scatter a handful of cornmeal over pizza pans. On a lightly floured surface, divide dough into two portions; form each into a smooth ball and then press each ball with hands to flatten. Gently stretch each round into a disk about ½ inch thick and 8 inches across. Using a flour-dusted rolling pin, roll out each disk to about ⅛ inch thick—dusting surface with additional flour if necessary—until dough measures 12 to 14 inches in diameter.

Place dough on pizza pans and shake to cover bottoms with cornmeal. If dough sticks anywhere, lift edge gently and sprinkle more cornmeal underneath.

Preheat grill to medium. Slide first pan onto grill and cook until lightly browned, about 4 minutes. Pop any bubbles with tongs. Remove pan from grill; flip dough over. Return to grill and cook about 30 seconds more until just set. Remove from grill and repeat steps with second pizza.

Brush both pizzas with olive oil; scatter on garlic; sprinkle on cheeses; dab on tomato sauce; and sprinkle on basil. Return to grill, and close lid. Cook about 4 minutes or until cheese is melted and bottom crust is browned.

VARIATIONS

- Sliced pepperoni and Canadian bacon
- Grilled portobello mushrooms and asparagus
- Sautéed peppers and onions
- Fresh or frozen spinach with ground sausage or prosciutto
- Crisp bacon or grilled ham cubes and artichoke hearts
- Goat cheese and sun-dried tomatoes or cherry tomatoes
- Smoked salmon, chives, and sour cream
- Grilled eggplant and goat cheese
- Cooked ground beef, shrimp, scallops, or clams, with chopped fresh tomatoes, garlic, and basil

People want honest, flavorful food,
not some show-off meal that takes days to prepare.
–Ted Allen

5

Instead of going out to dinner, buy good food.
Cooking at home shows such affection.
–Ina Garten

Poultry

FIRST TIME COOKING WITH A

Kiddo Chef? Get ready to see through a child's eyes the fun and creativity of turning separate ingredients into something new to eat—kind of like magic! Be prepared for the process to take longer than usual and the messes to be more abundant than usual. A plastic tablecloth on the floor below the workstation may help catch anything that misses the bowl. Kids enjoy touching and tasting the food as they help you cook. Teach them which foods are safe to eat raw and the importance of washing hands. You'll have a Kiddo Chef ready for adventurous eating!

DO-AHEAD MINCED-CHICKEN BURGERS

24 SERVINGS • PREP: 25 MIN. • MARINATE: 2 HR. • GRILL: 1 HR.

12 chicken-leg quarters
1 quart apple-cider vinegar
⅓ cup low-sodium chicken broth
⅓ teaspoon onion salt

1 teaspoon coarsely ground fresh pepper
2 bay leaves
24 sandwich buns
1 cup Dijon mustard

In a large saucepan, mix together the vinegar, chicken broth, onion salt, pepper, and bay leaves. Bring to a boil over high heat. Place the chicken in a bowl, and pour the hot vinegar mixture over it. Cover, and marinate in the refrigerator for at least 2 hours.

Preheat the grill to medium. Place the chicken on the grill, skin side up. Pour 2 cups of the marinade in a small saucepan, and bring to a boil on the grill. Grill the chicken, turning and basting with the boiled marinade every 10 to 15 minutes for about 1 hour or until the internal temperature reaches 165°F.

Remove the chicken from the grill, and let it cool for about 10 minutes. Cut the chicken from the bone; discard the bones and skin. Place the meat, four quarters at a time, into a food processor and pulse 3 or 4 times until the chicken is coarsely chopped. (Chop with a knife if a processor is not available.) Repeat this with the remaining chicken. (There should be about 9 cups.)

Boil the remaining marinade to reduce it to 1¼ cups; pour over the minced chicken. Serve on toasted buns spread with mustard. Garnish with a dill pickle slice if desired.

CHEF TASKS

KIDDO CHEF

- Measure the ingredients for the saucepan.
- Spread the mustard on the buns.
- Add a dill pickle slice to each sandwich, if desired.

TEENAGE SOUS CHEF

- Mix and boil the marinade in the saucepan.
- Cover the chicken with the marinade and refrigerate.
- Mince the grilled chicken in a food processor or chop with a knife.
- Add the marinated minced chicken to the buns.

HEAD CHEF (AKA THE GROWN-UP)

- Keep an eye on your helpers!
- Preheat the grill to medium.
- Grill the chicken for about 1 hour, or until the internal temperature reaches 165°F.
- Toast the buns on the grill.
- Cut the chicken from the bone, discarding the bones and skin.

ISLAND GRILLED JERK CHICKEN

8 SERVINGS • PREP: 15 MIN. • MARINATE: 1 HR.–OVERNIGHT • GRILL: UNTIL DONE

2 pounds boneless, skinless
   chicken breasts
⅓ cup soy sauce
2 tablespoons sesame oil
3 cloves garlic, chopped
3 scallions, chopped
3 tablespoons fresh thyme leaves
1½ teaspoons ground allspice
1½ teaspoons freshly
   ground pepper
½ teaspoon ground cinnamon
½ teaspoon ground red pepper
16 wooden skewers, soaked
   in water

MANGO-PAPAYA RELISH

(makes 1½ cups)
1 ripe mango, peeled and diced
1 ripe papaya, peeled and diced
2 scallions, minced
¼ cup minced fresh cilantro
2 teaspoons brown sugar
1 tablespoon lemon juice
Hot sauce to taste

Combine all relish ingredients in medium bowl; cover; and refrigerate at least 1 hour before serving.

Preheat the grill to medium-high. Wash the chicken and pat it dry. Cut each chicken breast in half lengthwise, and then into four strips; place the strips in a plastic storage bag. Combine the soy sauce and next eight ingredients in a blender; blend until smooth. Pour the mixture over the chicken and tightly seal the bag. Turn the bag gently to coat the chicken. Marinate in the refrigerator for at least 1 hour and up to 24 hours. Thread chicken strips on skewers. Grill on each side until cooked. Serve with mango-papaya relish.

GRILLED CHICKEN CACCIATORE

4 SERVINGS • PREP: 25 MIN. • GRILL: 3–4 HR.

Courtesy of Barry "CB" Martin, on Twitter: @BarryCBMartin.

2 to 3 pounds chicken thighs
　and drumsticks
Kosher salt and freshly ground
　black pepper
3 tablespoons canola oil or spray
1 yellow onion, sliced
2 medium shallots, diced
2 cups diced red, yellow, and/or
　green peppers
3 cloves garlic, minced
3 tablespoons flour
½ pound mushrooms, quartered
1 cup baby carrots
15-ounce can diced tomatoes
2 cups chicken broth
⅓ cup red wine
2 tablespoons chopped
　fresh cilantro
2 tablespoons chopped
　fresh parsley
1 tablespoon dried thyme
¼ teaspoon red pepper flakes
Dash Tabasco® sauce
Sliced black olives, if desired

Preheat grill to high. Season chicken with salt and pepper. Brush or lightly spray chicken with oil. Place on hot grill skin side down. Cook until browned on one side, and then turn and brown the other side, but do not cook completely. Set aside.

Turn grill's side burner to high. In a large, nonreactive pan over the burner, heat the oil. Then reduce heat to medium and add onion. Sauté for 2 to 3 minutes; add shallots. Continue to cook for 1 minute before adding bell peppers. When shallots and onions begin to caramelize and peppers soften, add garlic, making sure that mixture does not burn.

Add the flour to mixture, 1 tablespoon at a time. Add mushrooms and the remaining ingredients.

Reduce heat to low and add chicken. Cover and cook over indirect heat on grill for 3 to 4 hours.

Grilling the chicken adds a rich flavor that's even better if you use some wood chips to impart a bit of smoke. To get a head start, grill the chicken the day before.–CB

CHICKEN SALAD BOATS

18 SERVINGS

4 packages of about 20 precooked chicken tenders
18 hard rolls
3 cups finely chopped celery
1 medium onion, peeled and finely chopped
4 tablespoons mayonnaise
1 large bottle Italian salad dressing
Salt and pepper to taste
18 slices provolone cheese

Preheat grill to medium heat and cover the grate with aluminum foil. Grill chicken tenders until heated through, remove from grill, and cut into small pieces. Meanwhile, hollow out hard rolls by cutting a hole in top of each roll and pulling out bread, leaving bottom intact to make a boat shape. In a medium bowl, combine chicken tender pieces, chopped celery, chopped onion, mayonnaise, Italian salad dressing, salt, and pepper. Mix well and spoon mixture into hollowed rolls. Place rolls in a metal 9 x 13-inch baking dish. Place 1 slice of provolone cheese over each roll in baking dish. Place baking dish over heated grill until cheese melts and rolls are slightly browned. Remove from grill and serve warm.

PACIFIC-RIM CHICKEN BURGERS WITH GINGER MAYO

8 SERVINGS • PREP: 20 MIN. • GRILL: 10–15 MIN.

¼ cup soy sauce
1 tablespoon hoisin sauce
1 tablespoon honey
1 tablespoon red chili paste
2 pounds ground chicken
2 green onions, thinly sliced
2 jalapeño peppers, minced
4 cloves garlic, minced
1 cup finely chopped cilantro
1 cup finely chopped
    tarragon leaves
1 egg, lightly beaten
⅔ to 1 cup panko or other
    unseasoned bread crumbs
Vegetable oil
8 pineapple rings (fresh or canned)
1 cucumber, peeled and
    thinly sliced
8 hamburger buns

GINGER MAYONNAISE

½ cup mayonnaise
2 cloves garlic
1- to 2-inch knob of ginger
Juice of 1 lime
¼ teaspoon salt

Put all mayonnaise ingredients into a blender or food processor, and blend until smooth. Refrigerate.

In a pot over medium heat, warm the soy sauce, hoisin, and honey for 5 minutes, stirring periodically to dissolve the honey and hoisin. Mix in the chili paste, and let the sauce simmer for a few minutes. Remove from heat, and let cool. In a large bowl, combine ground chicken with vegetables and herbs.

After the marinade has cooled, add the egg. Work this mixture gently into the ground chicken. Gently mix in the bread crumbs. Form the mixture into 8 patties by coating your hands (in food-safe gloves) liberally with vegetable oil. (The chicken mixture will be very sticky.)

Rub each patty with a bit of oil on all sides. Chill patties briefly in the refrigerator while you preheat the grill to medium-high. Cook about 5 minutes per side, turning when underside has browned and releases easily from the grill. (Be careful that you don't scorch the patties; the sugar in the marinade can burn.)

Cook the pineapple on the grill for roughly 2 minutes per side, or until grill marks appear. To serve, place each burger on a toasted bun, and top with ginger mayo, pineapple, and cucumber slices.

BARBECUED CHICKEN THIGHS AU VIN

6 SERVINGS • PREP: 15 MIN. • MARINATE: 3 HR.–OVERNIGHT
GRILL: 35 MIN. (UNTIL MEAT TEMP. IS 180°F)

6 chicken thighs (about
     1½ pounds)
1 tablespoon vegetable oil
1 tablespoon butter
2 tablespoons finely
     chopped shallots
1 clove garlic, minced
¼ cup red-currant jelly
½ cup red wine
¼ cup chicken stock or
     orange juice
1 teaspoon grated orange rind
½ teaspoon dry mustard
½ teaspoon ground ginger

Place chicken thighs in a plastic bag or large bowl. In saucepan, heat oil and butter; add shallots and garlic; and cook over medium heat for 5 minutes or until softened. Add jelly, wine, stock, orange rind, mustard, and ginger. Heat only until jelly has melted. Remove from heat; let cool to room temperature.

Pour marinade over chicken. Press air out of bag and secure with twist tie. Marinate at least 3 hours to overnight in refrigerator. Pour marinade into saucepan; bring to a boil; simmer 5 minutes; reserve.

Place chicken thighs, skin side up, on greased grill heated to medium-high. Cook for 20 minutes, with lid closed, brushing occasionally with marinade once most of fat is rendered from chicken pieces. Turn each thigh and cook 10 to 15 minutes longer or until juices run clear when chicken is pierced with fork (180°F).

GRILLED TEQUILA CHICKEN

4 SERVINGS • MARINATE: 2–8 HR.

4 boneless, skinless
   chicken breasts
⅓ cup lime juice
2 tablespoons jalapeno
   pepper jelly
2 tablespoons fresh
   chopped cilantro
2 tablespoons tequila
2 tablespoons olive oil
1 teaspoon fresh minced garlic
¼ teaspoon salt
¼ teaspoon pepper

Rinse chicken breasts and pat dry. Arrange chicken breasts in an 8-inch square baking dish and set aside. In a small bowl, combine lime juice, jalapeno pepper jelly, fresh chopped cilantro, tequila, olive oil, minced garlic, salt, and pepper. Mix well and pour over chicken in baking dish. Cover baking dish and let marinate in refrigerator 2 to 8 hours.

Preheat grill to medium-high heat. Place marinated chicken over grill and heat until chicken is cooked through.

The secret to using the Secret Ingredient is knowing when not to use it.
–Alex Guarnaschelli

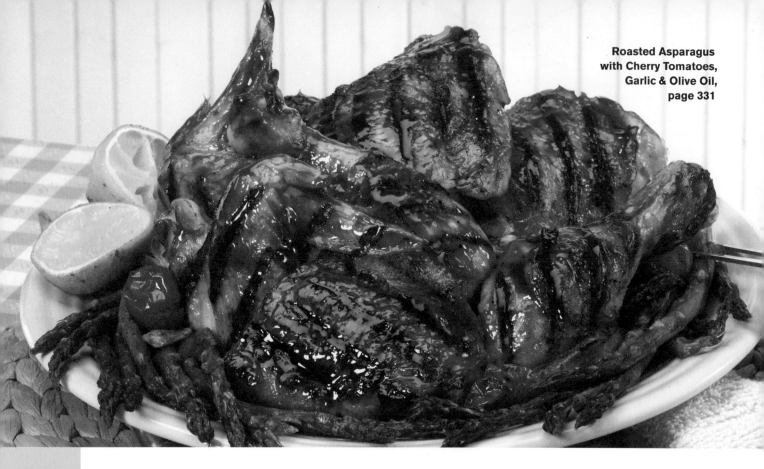

Roasted Asparagus
with Cherry Tomatoes,
Garlic & Olive Oil,
page 331

V8® CHICKEN

4 SERVINGS • PREP: 15 MIN. • MARINATE: 18–24 HR.
GRILL: 40–50 MIN. (UNTIL THIGH TEMP. IS 180°F)

Courtesy of Barry "CB" Martin, on Twitter: @BarryCBMartin.

1 fryer chicken, cut into 8 pieces
1 12-ounce can V8® vegetable
   juice cocktail
½ to 1 cup water
Barbecue sauce for glaze

Sometimes the ingredients for great-tasting marinades are already made and ready for the using. By accident, I discovered this idea, and the flavors were very tasty!–CB

Trim chicken pieces of excess fat and place in a nonreactive bowl or plastic food bag. Add V8® juice and water until meat is covered. Cover bowl or seal bag and refrigerate overnight.

One hour before cooking, remove chicken from marinade; rinse chicken; and pat dry with paper towels. Allow chicken to rest a bit at room temperature.

Preheat half of grill to high. Spray or lightly brush chicken parts with canola oil. Sear over high heat. Because wings and legs tend to cook faster, add them to grill after starting breasts and thighs. Use tongs to turn chicken when skin is seared and releases from grill.

As pieces are seared and begin to brown, place them in a pan away from direct heat. Cover loosely with foil or another pan. Allow chicken to finish cooking in pan until breasts reach an internal temperature of 165°F; thighs, 180°F.

During final 5 to 10 minutes of indirect cooking, brush on a light coating of barbecue sauce. Serve.

CLASSIC CHICKEN

6 SERVINGS • GRILL: 45–50 MIN.

1 (3½ pounds) whole frying
   chicken, quartered
¼ cup lemon juice
¼ cup olive oil
2 tablespoons soy sauce
2 large cloves garlic, minced
½ teaspoon sugar
½ teaspoon ground cumin
¼ teaspoon pepper

Rinse chicken under running water and pat dry with paper towels. In a heavy-duty extra-large zippered bag, combine lemon juice, olive oil, soy sauce, minced garlic, sugar, ground cumin, and pepper. Place chicken in bag and seal. Let chicken marinate in a cooler filled with ice for 1 hour or overnight.

Preheat grill. Remove chicken pieces from bag. Place chicken on hot grate, skin side down, for about 25 minutes. Turn chicken pieces and cook for an additional 20 to 25 minutes, or until the juices run clear and chicken is cooked throughout.

BBQ ORANGE CHICKEN

4–5 SERVINGS • PREP: 15 MIN. • GRILL: 35 MIN.

2½ pounds chicken parts

BBQ SAUCE
¼ cup vegetable oil
¼ cup frozen orange
   juice concentrate
½ cup white wine vinegar
¼ cup tomato paste
Zest from 1 orange

Preheat grill to high. In a medium bowl, mix together all sauce ingredients until smooth. Reduce heat to medium on one side; turn off heat on the other side. Place chicken pieces on grill away from heat, skin side down; cook 15 minutes. Turn chicken and grill for 10 additional minutes. Brush chicken pieces with sauce, and turn occasionally, cooking for additional 10 minutes.

Good food is a global thing, and I find that there is always something new and amazing to learn.

–Jamie Oliver

SOUTHWEST CHICKEN

4 SERVINGS • GRILL: 8–10 MIN.

2 tablespoons olive oil
1 clove garlic, pressed
1 teaspoon chili powder
1 teaspoon ground cumin
1 teaspoon dried oregano
½ teaspoon salt
1 pound skinless boneless
    chicken breast halves
    or thighs

Preheat grill. In a small bowl, combine olive oil, pressed garlic, chili powder, ground cumin, dried oregano, and salt. Brush mixture over both sides of chicken breasts or thighs. Place chicken on hot grate and cook over grill for 8 to 10 minutes, turning once, until chicken is cooked throughout.

FAMILY-PLEASING GRILLED CHICKEN

8 SERVINGS • GRILL: 40–60 MIN.

1 teaspoon salt
1 teaspoon black pepper
¾ teaspoon brown sugar
¾ teaspoon garlic powder
¾ teaspoon onion powder
1 (3½ to 4 pounds) whole
    chicken, cut up*

Lightly oil grate and preheat grill to medium heat. In a small bowl, combine salt, black pepper, brown sugar, garlic powder, and onion powder; mix well. Sprinkle mixture over chicken pieces and pat evenly over skin.

To cook, place chicken on grate over indirect heat, skin side up. Cover grill and cook for 15 to 20 minutes. Turn chicken, cover grill, and cook for 20 to 40 minutes longer, turning occasionally, or until juices run clear and internal temperature reaches 165°F–170°F for breasts and 165°F–180°F for thighs and legs.

Choose legs, thighs, breasts, wings, or quarters, adjusting cooking times for the size and type of pieces being grilled. The white meat of chicken breasts cooks more quickly than the dark meat of quarters, legs, or thighs.

MASTUR-K'S CHICKEN ON A STICK

2 SERVINGS • PREP: 30 MIN. • GRILL: 20–25 MIN.

Mastur-K, also known as Kevin W., is a "Sizzle on the Grill" reader and contributor.

1 medium to large boneless,
   skinless chicken breast
Garlic-pepper mix
2 wooden skewers, soaked for at
   least 30 minutes

GARLIC-PEPPER MIX
2 tablespoons black peppercorns
1 tablespoon powdered garlic
1 tablespoon paprika
1 tablespoon Mrs. Dash® spice
   mix (original flavor)

Put all the garlic-pepper mix ingredients into a spice or coffee grinder, and process until fine. Put the mixture in a shaker, and use it as you please. Note: This recipe does not contain salt. You may add a tablespoon or two if desired.

Preheat grill to medium-low. Trim any fat from the chicken. Cut the fillet down the middle into two long strips. (Each piece should look like a chicken tender.) Place tenders in a clean kitchen towel, and pat them dry. Run skewers through both pieces, starting with smaller end. Place the skewers on a placemat or over the sink, and shake on as much garlic-pepper mix as desired. Grill skewers for 10 minutes on each side or until chicken is no longer pink in center. (Note: The small end of the chicken should be farther away from the center of the grill so that the larger end can cook evenly.) Serve with rice and vegetables.

GRILLED CHICKEN SKEWERS WITH GRILLED CAESAR SALAD

2 SERVINGS • PREP: 25 MIN. • MARINATE: 1 HR.–OVERNIGHT
GRILL: 8–10 MIN. COMBINED

Provided by Erik Lind, 2006 Char-Broil Grilling Team Chef

2 4-ounce boneless, skinless
   chicken breasts
1 cup barbecue sauce of
   your choice
2 whole heads romaine lettuce
½ cup extra-virgin olive oil
½ cup minced shallot
½ cup minced fresh garlic
Salt and pepper
Bamboo skewers soaked in white
   wine for 1 hour
1 prepared log herbed polenta
1 cup balsamic vinegar
1 jar favorite Caesar dressing

Cut the chicken breasts lengthwise into four equal slices. Place chicken in a plastic bag with the barbecue sauce; seal; and marinate for 1 to 2 hours or overnight. Cut the romaine heads in half lengthwise. Drizzle the olive oil over both sides. Spread the shallot, garlic, salt, and pepper over the cut side of the heads. Set lettuce aside.

Preheat grill to high. Place chicken on skewers, and grill until the meat reaches 165°F. Slice the polenta into ¼-inch slices, and spray with nonstick cooking spray. Grill polenta 5 to 8 minutes on each side to ensure even grill marks. To make the balsamic reduction, place vinegar in a pan over medium heat, and cook until it reduces into syrup. Cool, and reserve. Grill the romaine heads on both sides for 2 to 3 minutes until just wilted. Remove and slice lengthwise, and then roughly chop. Toss lettuce very lightly with Caesar dressing. Place a small amount on each plate. Cut the polenta circles in half, and arrange them across the salad. Place the chicken skewers in an "X" over the salad, and drizzle with the balsamic reduction.

MOROCCAN-SPICE GRILLED CHICKEN & PEACHES

4 SERVINGS • PREP: 15 MIN. • GRILL: 30 MIN.

Courtesy of Barry "CB" Martin, on Twitter: @BarryCBMartin.

2 large boneless chicken breasts
1 15-ounce jar peaches in natural
 juice (about 1 cup)
3 tablespoons curry powder
Kosher or sea salt to taste
Cooking oil spray
2 tablespoons olive oil
1 clove garlic, finely chopped
1 tablespoon brown sugar
2 tablespoons balsamic vinegar
3 tablespoons chopped mint
 or parsley

Strain peaches, and reserve the juice. Rinse the chicken; pat it dry; and season with salt and curry powder. Let chicken reach room temperature, about 15 minutes.

Preheat one side of grill to high; reduce to medium-high when grilling. Preheat the other side to medium low. Spray cooking oil on the chicken, and place it on the hot side of the grill for about 4 minutes per side. When both sides have dark grill marks, remove the chicken from the hot side of the grill, and place on the other side to "roast" until done, about 8 to 10 minutes.

In the meantime, warm the oil in a medium pan over medium-low heat. Add the garlic, and sauté until it begins to brown, about 1 to 2 minutes. Add the sugar, vinegar, and peach juice; reduce sauce while chicken cooks.

Using tongs, place the peach slices on hot side of grill to form grill marks. Turn the peaches just once to ensure uniform grill marks. When chicken is cooked to an internal temperature of approximately 150°F, remove and place on a warm plate until the internal temperature is 160°F–170°F. Cut chicken into pieces; place the grilled peaches on top; and pour the sauce over both.

CHICKEN WITH GOAT CHEESE & ROASTED RED PEPPERS

4 SERVINGS • PREP: 15 MIN. • GRILL: 15–20 MIN. • BAKE: 5 MIN.

4 boneless, skinless
    chicken breasts
¼ cup plus 2 tablespoons olive oil
2 red bell peppers, roasted
3 ounces fresh, soft goat cheese,
    sliced into rounds
1 teaspoon chopped onion
1 teaspoon chopped garlic
½ cup white wine
2 teaspoons chopped
    fresh rosemary
½ stick unsalted butter
Salt and pepper to taste
Sliced almonds, toasted

Preheat grill to medium-high. Wash chicken and pat it dry. Brush chicken with 2 tablespoons of olive oil. Grill for 10 minutes or until no longer pink. Remove chicken to a baking dish and top with roasted pepper strips and cheese rounds. Bake at 350°F for 5 minutes or just until cheese is heated through.

Sauté onion and garlic in ¼ cup olive oil in a heavy skillet over high heat. Add wine and rosemary. Cook for approximately 3 minutes. Gradually whisk in butter. Season mixture with salt and pepper; spoon over chicken. Top with toasted almonds.

GRILLED CHICKEN IN OLIVE OIL-CHIVE VINAIGRETTE

2–4 SERVINGS • PREP: 45 MIN. • MARINATE: 4 HR.–OVERNIGHT • GRILL: 45–60 MIN.

4 bone-in chicken breasts

OLIVE OIL-CHIVE VINAIGRETTE

6 tablespoons olive oil, divided
4 tablespoons red wine
  vinegar, divided
1 teaspoon salt, divided
½ teaspoon pepper, divided
¼ teaspoon dry mustard
1 clove garlic
Peel of 1 lemon
1 tablespoon chopped chives

In food processor or blender, place 1 tablespoon oil, 1 tablespoon vinegar, and ¼ teaspoon each salt, pepper, and mustard. Process 15 seconds. While processor is running, add 2 teaspoons olive oil; process 10 seconds. Add remaining 3 tablespoons vinegar, remaining 3 tablespoons oil, garlic, lemon peel, and chopped chives. Process 15 seconds more.

Dip each piece of chicken in vinaigrette (see recipe at left), and coat well. Marinate in refrigerator for a minimum of 4 hours or overnight.

Preheat grill to medium. Place chicken on grill, skin side up. Sprinkle with remaining ¾ teaspoon salt and ¼ teaspoon pepper. Grill, turning and basting with sauce every 10 minutes for about 1 hour or until internal temperature reaches approximately 160°F.

GRILLED BEER-CAN CHICKEN

4–6 SERVINGS • PREP: 15 MIN. • MARINATE: 1 HR.–OVERNIGHT • GRILL: 1½–2 HR.

1 whole chicken (4 to 5 pounds)
2 teaspoons vegetable oil
1 16-ounce can beer

RUB 1

1 teaspoon dry mustard
¼ cup minced onion
1 teaspoon paprika
1 teaspoon kosher salt
4 small cloves garlic, minced
½ teaspoon ground coriander
½ teaspoon ground cumin
½ teaspoon freshly ground
    black pepper

RUB 2

3 tablespoons paprika
2 tablespoons sugar
1 tablespoon salt
2 teaspoons coarsely ground
    black pepper
1 teaspoon onion powder
1 teaspoon garlic powder
1 teaspoon ground red pepper
    (cayenne)

In a small bowl, combine rub ingredients (see recipes at left). Wash the chicken and pat it dry. Coat the entire chicken with vegetable oil and season it with the rub, inside and out.

Preheat the grill to medium. Pour half of the beer out of the can and carefully place the half-full can inside the cavity of the chicken. Note: The can will be almost completely covered by the chicken. Transfer the bird to the grill, keeping the can upright. Grill for 1½ to 2 hours or until the internal temperature reaches 180°F in the thickest part of the thigh and the meat is no longer pink. Carefully remove the chicken with the can from the grill, using protective mitts. Let the chicken rest for about 10 minutes before lifting it from the can. Discard the beer. Cut the chicken into serving pieces.

TANDOORI SPICE-RUBBED CHICKEN

4 SERVINGS • PREP: 10 MIN. • REST/SUFFUSE: 15–30 MIN. • GRILL: 10–15 MIN.
(UNTIL INTERNAL TEMP. IS AT LEAST 165°F) • REST: 5 MIN OR MORE

4 skinless, boneless
   chicken breasts
4 tablespoons paprika, smoked
   variety preferred
2 tablespoons kosher salt
2 tablespoons freshly
   ground coriander
2 tablespoons freshly
   ground cumin
1 tablespoon light brown sugar
1 teaspoon freshly ground
   black pepper
1 teaspoon turmeric
1 teaspoon ground ginger
½ teaspoon ground cinnamon
½ teaspoon cayenne pepper
   (optional)
Cooking spray as needed

Mix all of the spices together in a bowl. Coat the chicken and let it sit for 15–30 minutes.

Preheat grill to medium-high. Lightly spray the chicken with cooking spray and grill it until it reaches an internal temperature of at least 165°F. Remove the chicken from the heat; let it rest for at least 5 minutes and then slice and serve.

PINEAPPLE TERIYAKI CHICKEN

4 SERVINGS • MARINATE: 24 HR.

1½ cups pineapple juice
½ cup soy sauce
1 teaspoon ground ginger
½ teaspoon garlic powder
¼ teaspoon white pepper
4 boneless, skinless chicken
  breast halves

In a large bowl, combine pineapple juice, soy sauce, ground ginger, garlic powder, and white pepper. If desired, reserve a small amount for dipping sauce while serving. Place chicken in a large, sealable plastic bag or container with lid. Pour pineapple mixture over chicken and add enough water to cover. Close or cover container. Refrigerate for 24 hours to marinate.

Place charcoal in an outdoor grill and light the flame. Remove chicken from container and discard remaining marinade. Place chicken on grill over medium-high heat. Grill for 10 to 15 minutes or until juices run clear when chicken is pierced with a fork. Turn chicken once during grilling time. Serve with reserved dipping sauce, if desired.

BRICK CHICKEN

4 SERVINGS • PREP: 5–10 MIN.
GRILL: 10–15 MIN. (UNTIL INTERNAL TEMP. IS AT LEAST 165°F)

1 3–4-pound broiler-fryer
   chicken, quartered
2 tablespoons olive or canola oil
¼ cup chopped thyme leaves
Salt and pepper to taste
1 lemon, quartered
Cooking spray as needed

Preheat grill to high. Place two large cast-iron pans on the grill to preheat. Rub the chicken with the oil, thyme, salt, and pepper. Place the chicken, skin side down, in the pan, and place the other pan on top to press the chicken down. (You can instead use the more traditional method: a brick wrapped in aluminum foil, below; hence, the name of the recipe.) When the first side develops a crust, flip the chicken in the pan and continue to cook until it reaches an internal temperature of at least 165°F. Remove the chicken from the heat and serve with a squeeze of lemon juice on each piece of chicken.

SHREDDED CHICKEN WITH GRILLED CORN CAKES

4 SERVINGS • PREP: 15–20 MIN. • GRILL: 30–35 MIN. (UNTIL INTERNAL TEMP. OF
CHICKEN IS AT LEAST 165°F) • REST: 5 MIN.

4 chicken thighs, fat trimmed
⅛ teaspoon cumin
Pinch cayenne pepper
½ teaspoon smoked sweet paprika
⅛ teaspoon onion powder
½ teaspoon garlic powder
¼ teaspoon ancho chili powder
¼ teaspoon salt
¼ teaspoon black pepper

CHIPOTLE SOUR CREAM
½ cup fat-free sour cream
1 tablespoon chipotle sauce
1 tablespoon chopped cilantro

CORN CAKES
1½ ears corn, husk removed
3 chives, chopped (plus some
    additional for garnish if desired)

½ cup all-purpose flour
½ teaspoon salt
¼ teaspoon baking soda
½ teaspoon Old Bay® seasoning
1 egg white
¼ cup buttermilk
¼ cup 2-percent milk

Preheat grill to high heat. Cook the corn until it develops grill marks, not burned (about 5 minutes on each side). Take corn off grill and set aside to let cool. While the corn is cooling, rub spices onto the chicken thighs, making sure to evenly cover each piece. Put it in the refrigerator until it's ready to grill.

Cut corn off cob; put in a large bowl; and then mix in all of the other ingredients for the corn cakes. Form pancakes and sear the cakes in a hot skillet on the grill (using cooking spray to keep the cakes from sticking) until each side is nice and crispy (not burned), with the inside fluffy and soft. Place them on a baking sheet in an oven at 200°F to keep warm.

Take the chicken out of the refrigerator and grill it until the internal temperature of each piece is at least 165°F. Take the chicken off the grill and let it cool for 5 minutes. Using two forks, shred the chicken and then mix ingredients for the chipotle sour cream together in a bowl. Divide the shredded chicken into four portions; place each portion on top of a corn cake; top with a small dollop of chipotle sour cream; and garnish with chopped chives if desired.

CHIPOTLE CHICKEN FAJITAS

5 SERVINGS • MARINATE: 1–4 HR.

1 (12 ounces) bottle chili sauce
¼ cup lime juice
4 chipotle peppers in adobo
    sauce (or to taste)
1 pound chicken tenders, sliced
    into thin strips
½ cup cider vinegar
⅓ cup brown sugar
⅓ cup molasses
4 green bell peppers, cut into
    1-inch pieces
1 onion, cut into 1-inch pieces
1 tablespoon olive oil
⅛ teaspoon salt
⅛ teaspoon black pepper
10 (8-inch) flour tortillas
1½ cups chopped tomatoes
1 cup shredded Mexican
    cheese blend

In a food processor, combine chili sauce, lime juice, and chipotle peppers; cover and process until blended. Transfer ½ cup of mixture to a large resealable plastic bag. Add chicken tenders, seal bag, and turn to coat well. Refrigerate bag to marinate chicken for 1 to 4 hours. Pour remaining marinade into a small bowl. Add vinegar, brown sugar, and molasses; mix well. Cover and refrigerate.

To cook, lightly oil grate and preheat grill to medium heat. On six metal or soaked wooden skewers, alternately thread pieces of chicken, green pepper, and onion. Brush with oil and sprinkle with salt and black pepper. Place on the grate and cover grill; cook for 10 to 16 minutes, turning occasionally, or until chicken is no longer pink inside and juices run clear. Remove chicken and vegetables from skewers and place in a large bowl. Add ½ cup chipotle-molasses mixture and toss to coat; keep warm. Grill tortillas, uncovered, over medium heat for 45 to 55 seconds on each side or until warmed. Top each tortilla with a portion of chicken mixture, tomatoes, cheese, and remaining chipotle-molasses mixture; roll up and serve.

JALAPEÑO CHICKEN FAJITA

4 SERVINGS • PREP: 20–25 MIN. • MARINATE: 15–60 MIN. • GRILL: 15–20 MIN. (UNTIL INTERNAL TEMP. IS AT LEAST 165°F) • REST: 15 MIN.

4 4–6-ounce chicken breasts, skin removed
½ cup rough-chopped cilantro
¼ cup lime juice, fresh squeezed
3 cloves garlic, crushed and rough chopped
1 jalapeño pepper, seeded and rough chopped
4 tablespoons olive or canola oil
1 teaspoon ground coriander

1 teaspoon ground cumin
1 red bell pepper, cut into ¼-inch strips
1 green bell pepper, cut into ¼-inch strips
1 red or white onion, cut into ¼-inch strips
Salt and pepper to taste
Cooking spray as needed

OPTIONAL AS-NEEDED INGREDIENTS

Whole-grain tortillas
Low-fat or fat-free sour cream
Fresh salsa or pico de gallo salsa
Shredded lettuce
Brown rice
Guacamole

Mix cilantro, lime, garlic, jalapeño, 2 tablespoons oil, coriander, cumin, salt, and pepper in a bowl. Add chicken and let it marinate for 15 minutes to 1 hour.

Preheat grill to medium-high. Toss red and green peppers, onions, 2 tablespoons oil, salt, and pepper in a bowl. Grill chicken breasts to at least 165°F, and grill onions and peppers in a perforated grilling pan to desired doneness. Set chicken aside once done to rest for 15 minutes or so.

To assemble fajitas, slice chicken and mix it with grilled onions and peppers. Place mixture on your favorite tortilla and top with your preferred ingredients. (See above.)

TERIYAKI CHICKEN SLIDERS

8 SERVINGS • PREP: 15–20 MIN.
REFRIGERATE/SUFFUSE: 30 MIN.–OVERNIGHT • GRILL: 6–10 MIN.

1 pound lean ground chicken
½ cup egg substitute or 2
    whole eggs
½ cup puréed vegetables (per
    note below)
½ cup low-sodium teriyaki sauce
¼ cup thinly sliced green onions
    (scallions)
1 tablespoon minced garlic
Whole-wheat bread crumbs,
    couscous, or instant oatmeal
    as needed
2 heads baby bok choy, split into
    quarters lengthwise
2 tablespoons canola or
    peanut oil
¼ cup brown-rice vinegar
Salt and pepper to taste
Cooking spray as needed
Whole-wheat buns, bread, or
    English muffins (optional)

Mix the chicken, eggs, vegetable purée, teriyaki, onions, garlic, salt, and pepper in a bowl. (The mixture may be very soft and moist at this point.) Add the desired binder (bread crumbs, etc.) a little at a time until the mixture becomes malleable and you can form patties. Form the mixture into eight slider-size burgers and let them rest for 30 minutes to overnight (in the refrigerator).

Preheat grill to medium-high. Place the quartered bok choy pieces in a bowl and toss them with the oil, vinegar, salt, and pepper. Lightly mist the sliders with the cooking spray to prevent sticking. Cook the sliders (to at least 165°F internal temperature, about 3 to 5 minutes per side) and the bok choy together to desired doneness. Place each slider on your bread of choice (optional) and top it with the bok choy and your favorite burger condiments.

For the vegetable purée, the kind of vegetable is not really important. The vegetables will mimic some of the properties of the missing fat, giving you a moist, tender product. When considering which vegetable to use, reflect on what is available, what flavors you like on the burgers (mushroom, onion, or wilted spinach, etc.), or what you have left over in your refrigerator.

CHICKEN SOUVLAKI WITH CUCUMBER SAUCE ON WHOLE-WHEAT PITA

4 SERVINGS • PREP: 10–15 MIN. • MARINATE: 1 HR. • GRILL: 15–20 MIN. (UNTIL INTERNAL TEMP. IS AT LEAST 165°F)

¾ pound boneless, skinless chicken breast, cut into
    1-inch cubes
½ cup brown-rice vinegar
¼ cup olive oil
¼ cup lemon juice
1 tablespoon chopped fresh oregano
1 teaspoon chopped fresh mint
Salt and pepper to taste
4 pieces whole-wheat pita bread
Tomato, cut into wheels, as needed
White onion as needed

SAUCE
1 cup low-fat Greek yogurt
½ cup peeled, seeded, and diced cucumber
2 tablespoons brown-rice vinegar
1 tablespoon lemon Juice
1 tablespoon olive oil
¼ cup chopped fresh dill
1 teaspoon chopped garlic
Salt and pepper to taste

Combine ½ cup brown-rice vinegar, ¼ cup oil, ¼ cup lemon juice, oregano, mint, salt, and pepper in a bowl. Add the chicken and let it marinate for 1 hour.

Preheat grill to high. Spray the chicken lightly with cooking spray and then sear the breasts until grill marks appear. Then turn down the heat to low and cook until the breasts reach an internal temperature of at least 165°F.

Fold all of the sauce ingredients together in a bowl and adjust the seasonings. Toast the pita bread on the grill; place desired amount of fresh onion and tomato on top; and cover with the grilled chicken and cucumber sauce.

CHICKEN MEATBALL KEBABS WITH MANGO-PAPAYA SAUCE

6 SERVINGS • PREP: 15–20 MIN. • CARAMELIZE: 5–10 MIN. • GRILL: 30–35 MIN.
(MAKE SURE INTERNAL TEMP. OF MEATBALLS IS AT LEAST 165°F)

1½ pounds ground chicken
10 cloves garlic, skin on
½ large yellow onion
1 teaspoon ground cumin
½ teaspoon ground coriander
2 tablespoons chopped
    fresh cilantro
½ cup whole-wheat panko
    bread crumbs
Salt and pepper to taste
4 metal skewers
Cooking spray as needed

SAUCE
1 cup frozen mango chunks
1 cup frozen papaya chunks
½ teaspoon chili-garlic sauce
1 tablespoon rice-wine vinegar

Preheat grill to medium-high. Place the garlic cloves in aluminum foil; seal the foil, making a closed pouch; and poke a small hole in middle of the pouch. Place the garlic foil pouch on the grill for 20–25 minutes.

In the meantime, caramelize the onions in a small pan with some cooking spray. This can be done on the grill or a stove. Cook the onions until they are brown, soft, and sweet. When both the garlic and the onions are done, chop them up and combine them in a large bowl. Mix in all other ingredients for the meatballs in the same bowl.

After all of the ingredients are well mixed, make the meatballs. Spray each meatball generously with cooking spray; assemble three or four (depending on the size) meatballs onto each skewer; and put the skewers on the grill. Cook about 5 minutes each side, until the middle is at least 165°F.

While the meatballs are on the grill, combine all of the ingredients for the sauce in a saucepan. Cook the sauce until the frozen mango and papaya become soft and the sauce comes to a boil. Take the sauce off the heat and purée it using a blender. Serve the meatballs with the mango-papaya sauce drizzled on top (about 1½–2 tablespoons per skewer).

Try a Thai green papaya salad for a refreshing side dish that aids in digestion. Papayas, especially the green variety, are high in the digestive enzymes papain and chymopapain.

FIRST-PRIZE GRILLED TURKEY BREAST

6 SERVINGS • PREP: 25 MIN. • MARINATE: OVERNIGHT • GRILL: 1¼–1¾ HR.

This recipe by Tye Rinner won first prize in the Autumn 2000 Iowa Farm Bureau Cookout Contest.

1 bone-in turkey breast (3½ to
    4 pounds)

MARINADE
¾ cup orange juice
¾ cup soy sauce
¼ cup honey
½ cup scallions, chopped
4 cloves garlic, crushed
2 teaspoons freshly ground
    black pepper
2 teaspoons ground ginger

MANGO-PAPAYA RELISH
(makes 1½ cups)
1 mango, peeled and diced
1 papaya, peeled and diced
2 scallions, minced
¼ cup cilantro, minced
2 teaspoons brown sugar
1 tablespoon lemon juice
Hot sauce to taste

Combine all relish ingredients; cover; and refrigerate the mixture for at least 1 hour before serving.

Mix the orange juice, soy sauce, honey, scallions, garlic, and seasonings together. Reserve ¼ cup of marinade. Place the remaining marinade in a large plastic bag. Add the turkey breast; seal; and marinate in refrigerator for 12 to 24 hours, turning the sealed bag every few hours. Remove the turkey from the marinade and then drain.

Prepare the grill for indirect-heat cooking. Place the turkey, breast side up, on grill over a drip pan. Cover and grill the turkey breast for 1¼ to 1¾ hours. During last 30 minutes, brush the turkey breast with the reserved ¼ cup of marinade. Cook until a meat thermometer inserted in the thickest portion of the breast registers 170°F. Remove the turkey breast from the grill and let stand for 15 minutes before carving. Serve with mango-papaya relish.

BBQ TURKEY DRUMSTICKS

4 SERVINGS • PREP: 20 MIN. • MARINATE: 2 HR. • GRILL: 1 HR. 15 MIN.

4 pounds turkey drumsticks

BBQ SAUCE
½ clove garlic, minced
1 cup chili sauce or ketchup
¼ cup vegetable oil
⅓ cup cider vinegar
¼ cup onion, chopped
1 tablespoon
    Worcestershire sauce
½ teaspoon salt
¼ teaspoon freshly
    ground pepper
½ teaspoon dried thyme

Combine all sauce ingredients in a small saucepan. Simmer, uncovered, over low heat for 15 to 20 minutes.

Arrange the turkey drumsticks in a foil-lined roasting pan. Pour the BBQ sauce (see opposite page) over the drumsticks; cover; and marinate them for 2 hours in the refrigerator. Turn the drumsticks occasionally in the sauce. Remove them from the refrigerator.

Preheat grill to low. Grill the drumsticks until browned, about 7 minutes on each side. Turn and baste them frequently. Continue to grill over low heat for about 1 hour or until the internal temperature registers 180°F.

ALL-AMERICAN TURKEY BURGERS

4 SERVINGS • PREP: 10 MIN. • GRILL: 10–15 MIN.

1 pound ground turkey
½ cup onion, chopped
1 clove garlic, minced
¼ cup ketchup
⅛ teaspoon pepper
4 kaiser rolls, sliced
4 leaves lettuce
4 slices red ripe tomato
4 thin slices onion

Preheat the grill. In a medium-size bowl, combine the turkey, onion, garlic, ketchup, and pepper. Evenly divide the turkey mixture into four burgers, approximately 3 inches in diameter. Grill the turkey burgers 5 to 6 minutes per side until they reach 165°F on a food thermometer and the turkey is no longer pink in the center. To serve, place each turkey burger on the bottom half of a kaiser roll and top it with lettuce, tomato, and onion and the remaining half of the roll.

No one is born a great cook. One learns by doing.
–Julia Child

BURRITO TURKEY BURGERS

8 SERVINGS • PREP: 15 MIN. • GRILL: 5–10 MIN.

Vegetable cooking spray
2 pounds ground turkey
4 ounces green chiles, chopped
    and drained
1 cup onion, chopped
1 ounce taco seasoning mix
8 8-inch flour tortillas
16 ounces refried beans
Lettuce, shredded
½ cup cheddar cheese, grated
    and divided
2 cups salsa

Preheat the grill to medium-high. In a medium bowl, combine the turkey, chiles, onion, and seasoning mix. Evenly divide the turkey into eight rectangular burgers. Grill the burgers for 3 to 4 minutes; turn them; and continue cooking for 2 to 3 minutes or until they reach 165°F on a meat thermometer and the turkey is no longer pink in the center.

Remove the burgers and keep them warm. Heat the tortillas according to the package directions. Spread each tortilla with ¼ cup refried beans and sprinkle with lettuce. Place the burgers in the center of each tortilla and sprinkle 1 tablespoon of cheese over the top. Fold the sides of the tortilla over the burger to create a burrito. Serve with salsa.

TURKEY-CRANBERRY SLIDER WITH GREEN-BEAN PESTO

8 SERVINGS • PREP: 20–25 MIN.
REFRIGERATE/SUFFUSE: 30 MIN.–OVERNIGHT • GRILL: 10–15 MIN.

1 pound lean ground turkey
½ cup egg substitute or 2
    whole eggs
½ cup puréed vegetables
    (see note on page 132)
½ cup dried cranberries
¼ cup finely chopped celery
2 tablespoons chopped fresh thyme
2 tablespoons chopped
    fresh rosemary
1 tablespoon chopped fresh sage
Salt and pepper to taste

Whole-wheat bread crumbs,
    couscous, or instant oatmeal
    as needed
Cooking spray as needed
Tomato and red onion, sliced,
    as needed
Romaine or iceberg lettuce
    as needed
Whole-wheat toast, buns, or
    English muffins (optional)

GREEN-BEAN PESTO

2 ounces green beans, trimmed
    and blanched
1 clove garlic
1 teaspoon extra-virgin olive oil
1–2 tablespoons water (blanching
    liquid or tap water) as needed
    to make mixture smooth
2 tablespoons oregano leaves
¼ cup picked basil leaves
1 tablespoon Parmesan cheese
Salt and pepper to taste

In a bowl, mix the turkey, eggs, vegetable purée, cranberries, celery, herbs, salt, and pepper. (The mixture may be very soft and moist at this point.) Add the binder you choose (bread crumbs, etc.) until the mixture becomes malleable and you can form patties. Make eight slider-size burgers and let them rest for 30 minutes to overnight (in the refrigerator).

Put all of the pesto ingredients, except the water, in a food processor. Pulse for 10–20 seconds. If a chunky paste does not form, add water, 1 tablespoon at a time, until it does.

Preheat grill to medium-high. Mist the sliders lightly with the cooking spray and cook them to 165°F internal temperature or to your liking. Serve with the pesto, your favorite burger condiments, and toast or a bun if you choose.

TEA-SPICE DUCK BREAST

4 SERVINGS • PREP: 5–10 MIN. • GRILL: 15–20 MIN. • REST: 5 MIN.

4 4–6-ounce duck breasts,
　　skin removed
Contents of 2 tea bags (approx.
　　2 tablespoons), cherry, lemon,
　　or raspberry flavored
1 teaspoon orange zest
½ teaspoon salt
½ teaspoon freshly
　　ground pepper
½ teaspoon ground
　　ginger powder
½ teaspoon onion powder
Cooking spray as needed

Preheat grill to high. Place the tea and all of the spices in a spice grinder or coffee grinder, and grind until it becomes a fine powder. Lightly dust the duck breasts with the tea spice. Grill the breasts on high until a crust forms, and then immediately turn the heat as low as possible and continue to cook to the desired doneness.

Let the duck breast rest, off the heat, for 5 minutes; slice; and serve.

DUCK WITH CHERRY-PORT-WINE SAUCE

4 SERVINGS • PREP: 20–25 MIN. • GRILL: 10–15 MIN. • REST: 5 MIN.

4 4–6-ounce duck breasts,
    skin removed
Salt and pepper to taste
4 green onions, thinly sliced on
    the bias
Cooking spray as needed

SAUCE

1 teaspoon olive or canola oil
1 cup halved pitted cherries
½ cup tawny (preferred) or
    ruby port
1 cup low-sodium chicken stock
½ tablespoon low-sodium
    soy sauce
1 fresh ginger-root slice (to be
    removed at the end)
1 thyme sprig (to be removed at
    the end)

Preheat grill to high. Add the oil and cherries to a saucepan, and cook to soften. Remove the pan carefully from the heat and add the port. At this point, any flames can cause the port to ignite. Be cautious of this.

When the port reduces by one-fourth, add the chicken stock, soy sauce, ginger, and thyme, and simmer to reduce by another one-fourth. Remove the ginger and thyme, and set aside for plating.

Season the duck and lightly mist it with the cooking spray. Grill on high until just marked, and then immediately reduce the heat to as low as possible and cook to desired doneness. Let the duck breast rest, off the heat, for 5 minutes; slice; and serve topped with the port wine sauce. Garnish with the green onions, ginger, and thyme.

DUCK WITH PLUM SAUCE

4 SERVINGS • PREP: 30–35 MIN. • GRILL: 15–20 MIN. • REST 5 MIN.

4 4–6-ounce duck breasts, skin removed
1 teaspoon kosher salt
½ teaspoon Chinese five-spice powder
¼ teaspoon freshly ground black pepper
4 ripe plums
1 teaspoon olive or canola oil
¼ cup finely diced red onion
2 cloves garlic, minced
1 jalapeño pepper, seeded & finely diced (optional)
¼ cup white wine
¼ cup applesauce
¼ cup orange juice
¼ cup low-sodium soy sauce
Cooking spray as needed

Preheat grill to high. Add the oil, onions, garlic, and peppers to a preheated saucepan, and sauté until the onions become translucent. Add the white wine, and reduce until almost dry. Reduce the heat. Dip the plums in boiling water for 30 seconds to a minute and then immediately remove to a bowl of ice water. This should allow you to easily peal off the skin. Dice the plums and add them to the pan with the applesauce, juice, and soy sauce. Simmer the sauce to desired consistency and set aside.

Combine the salt and spices in a bowl, and lightly coat the duck breasts. Grill the duck on high until just marked, and then immediately reduce the heat as low as possible and cook to desired doneness. Let the duck breast rest, off the heat, for 5 minutes; slice; and serve topped with the plum sauce.

OSTRICH OPEN-FACED SANDWICH WITH SUN-DRIED TOMATOES & CHIMICHURRI SAUCE

8 SERVINGS • PREP: MIN. • MARINATE: OVERNIGHT
GRILL: 10–12 MIN. (UNTIL INTERNAL TEMP. IS ABOUT 150°F) • REST: 10 MIN.

8 4-ounce ostrich steaks (about ¾ inch thick)

3 sun-dried tomatoes, sliced thinly

½ small French multigrain baguette (sliced into 8 thin, even diagonal slices)

MARINADE

2 cups red wine

1 tablespoon finely chopped fresh thyme

2 tablespoons finely chopped garlic

1 tablespoon chopped rosemary leaves

2 tablespoons olive oil

1 teaspoon salt

1 teaspoon black pepper

CHIMICHURRI SAUCE

½ white onion, chopped finely

1 bunch cilantro leaves, chopped finely

2 limes, juiced

Salt and pepper to taste

Mix all of the ingredients for the marinade in a bowl. Pour the marinade from the bowl into one large, sealable plastic bag. Place the steaks into the bag; close the bag; and lay it flat in the refrigerator to marinate overnight.

Preheat grill to high. Combine and mix all of the ingredients for the chimichurri sauce in a small bowl and set aside. Place the ostrich steaks on the grill, mark each side, and then turn down heat to medium and cook until ostrich is medium, about 4–5 minutes on each side (should reach an internal temperature of at least 150°F).

Take the steaks off of the grill and let them rest for 10 minutes. Slice the ostrich into ½-inch slices. Slice the bread on a bias into eight equal slices and then toast the bread on the grill for about 2 minutes each side.

To assemble the open-face sandwiches, fan the ostrich slices on the toast; sprinkle thin slices of sun-dried tomatoes over the meat; and finish with a teaspoon of chimichurri sauce.

Ostrich meat is leaner than almost any meat you will cook, so be sure not to overcook it. Although ostrich is a bird, its taste and texture are much more similar to those of beef. It is higher in iron than beef, so it is very red in color, even when properly cooked.

OSTRICH WITH JICAMA SLAW

4 SERVINGS • PREP: 15–20 MIN. • MARINATE: 30 MIN. (SLAW) 15–60 MIN. (MEAT)
GRILL: 15–20 MIN. (UNTIL INTERNAL TEMP. IS ABOUT 150°F) • REST: 5 MIN.

1½ pounds ostrich thigh fan
½ cup brown-rice vinegar
1 tablespoon olive or canola oil
2 cloves garlic, minced
2 tablespoons chili powder
2 tablespoons paprika
1 tablespoon ground cumin
Salt and pepper to taste
Cooking spray as needed

JICAMA SLAW

1 small jicama, peeled and
 thinly sliced
½ small cabbage head,
 thinly sliced
2 carrots, shredded or
 thinly sliced
1 small red onion, thinly sliced
½ cup finely chopped cilantro
1–2 limes, juiced
2 tablespoons rice vinegar
2 tablespoons olive or canola oil
Salt and pepper to taste

Mix the vinegar, oil, garlic, chili, paprika, cumin, salt, and pepper together in a bowl. Pour this over the ostrich fan and let it marinate for 15 minutes to 1 hour.

In a separate bowl, add all of the slaw ingredients and let it sit for at least 30 minutes.

Preheat grill to high. Sear the meat just until you have marked both sides with grill marks, and then turn down the heat to medium or low and continue to cook to desired doneness. (For medium, it should reach an internal temperature of 150°F.) Let the fan rest for at least 5 minutes, off the heat, and then slice and serve, topped with the jicama slaw.

FUN fact! Jicama is considered part of the legume family; it is also known as the yam bean.

Jicama is low in sodium and high in potassium and fiber, and it comes in at just 23 calories per ½ cup. Most people say that jicama is a cross between an apple and a potato because of its slightly sweet taste and crunchy texture (almost like water chestnuts). You can enjoy jicama raw or cooked, but peel it first; the tan skin is inedible. It's great in salads and slaw, or use it sliced for dipping.

6

It is important to experiment and endlessly seek after creating the best possible flavors when preparing foods.
–Rocco DiSpirito

Beef, Lamb, Venison & Bison

ALL HANDS ON DECK!

YOU KNOW WHAT THEY SAY:
the family that cooks together . . . enjoys a fantastic meal together! And everyone who takes part in preparing the meal will savor the food so much more because they helped make it. Even if the youngest members of the family aren't able to help with the cooking, they can help set the table and decorate it with their own drawings and crafts.

INSIDE-OUT & UPSIDE-DOWN BURGERS

3 SERVINGS • PREP: 50 MIN. • GRILL: 15 MIN.

Courtesy of Barry "CB" Martin, on Twitter: @BarryCBMartin.

1 pound lean ground beef
6 strips lean bacon, cooked but not crisp, chopped
1 cup shredded cheese mix, such as cheddar and jack cheese
3 tablespoons olive oil

½ teaspoon Worcestershire sauce
1 clove garlic, minced
4 tablespoons unsalted butter
2 teaspoons sea salt or kosher salt
Freshly ground black pepper

In a large mixing bowl, gently fold together ground beef, bacon, cheese, olive oil, Worcestershire sauce, and garlic. Form mixture into three round balls. Gently press burger balls into 1- to 2-inch-thick patties. Chill for at least 30 minutes.

Preheat grill to high. Melt butter in a small saucepan. Remove burgers from the refrigerator; season with salt and pepper to taste.

Lightly brush one side of each burger with melted butter; place, buttered-side down, on one side of grill; and reduce heat on that side to medium, leaving other side of grill on high. Cook for approximately 7 minutes with lid closed.

Open lid and brush top of burgers with remaining butter. Using an oiled spatula, gently lift patties; place, buttered side down, on opposite side of grill over high heat. Reduce heat on that side to medium and close lid. Cook for 5 minutes. Let patties rest, covered with foil, for approximately 2 minutes. Place on buns and serve.

CHEF TASKS

KIDDO CHEF

- Shred 1 cup of cheese.
- Measure the Worcestershire sauce and olive oil.
- Make the ground-beef balls. (Be sure to wash up afterwards!)
- Place the condiments on the table.

TEENAGE SOUS CHEF

- Fold the ground-beef mixture in a large bowl.
- Melt the butter in a small saucepan.
- Season the patties with salt and pepper.
- Brush the melted butter on one side of the raw burgers.
- Place the grilled burgers on buns.

HEAD CHEF (AKA THE GROWN-UP)

- Keep an eye on your helpers!
- Cook and chop the bacon.
- Mince 1 clove of garlic.
- Preheat the grill to high.
- Grill the burgers for a total of around 15 minutes.

PIZZA BURGER

---
4 SERVINGS

¼ cup pizza sauce,
  warmed, divided
12 to 20 thin slices
  pepperoni, divided
½ cup shredded mozzarella
  cheese, divided
4 toasted hamburger buns

On each hot grilled hamburger patty, spread approximately 1 tablespoon pizza sauce; arrange 3 to 5 pepperoni slices and 2 tablespoons mozzarella cheese over sauce. Serve on toasted buns.

I believe that anyone can cook a great meal. Basically, all you need to do is get your hands on some fresh ingredients and not be afraid to make a mess in the kitchen.

–Nadia Giosia

BACON MUSHROOM BURGER

4–5 SERVINGS • GRILL: 10–12 MIN.

1 can (4 ounces) mushrooms,
    drained
1 pound lean ground beef
4 bacon strips, cooked
    and crumbled
2 tablespoons diced green onions
1 teaspoon Worcestershire sauce
1 teaspoon soy sauce
½ teaspoon salt
4 to 5 hamburger buns
Tomato slices, optional

Preheat grill to high heat and lightly oil grate. Cut drained mushrooms into small pieces. In a large bowl, mix mushroom pieces, ground beef, crumbled bacon, diced green onions, Worcestershire sauce, soy sauce, and salt until well blended. Form mixture into 4 or 5 patties. Place patties on prepared grill and cook for 5 to 6 minutes on each side or until internal temperature of burgers reaches 160°F on a meat thermometer. Serve patties on hamburger buns. If desired, top each burger with a few tomato slices.

CAJUN BURGERS

6–8 SERVINGS • PREP: 20 MIN. • GRILL: 15 MIN.

2 pounds ground beef
1 cup seasoned bread crumbs
2 tablespoons ground coriander
2 tablespoons Cajun spice
¼ teaspoon dried steak seasoning
¼ teaspoon dried oregano
1 teaspoon Worcestershire sauce
¼ teaspoon garlic powder
2 jalapeño peppers, seeded
    and diced

Combine all ingredients in a large mixing bowl with ground beef; form into patties (6–8 ounces each).

Cook on high heat until desired doneness, 6–8 minutes per side for medium.

THE CHEDDAR BURGER

4 SERVINGS

1 pound ground beef
⅓ cup steak sauce, divided
4 (1-ounce) slices cheddar
    cheese
1 medium onion, peeled and cut
    into strips
1 medium green or red bell
    pepper, cut into strips
1 tablespoon butter
4 hamburger buns, split
4 slices tomato

Preheat grill to medium-high heat. In a medium bowl, combine ground beef and 3 tablespoons steak sauce. Mix lightly but thoroughly. Divide mixture into four equal parts. Shape each part into a patty, enclosing one slice of cheddar cheese inside each burger and set aside. Place a skillet on hot grate and cook onion and bell pepper strips in butter, heating until vegetables are tender. Stir in remaining steak sauce and keep warm. Place burgers on hot grate. Cook burgers over grill for 8 to 10 minutes, turning once, until cooked to desired doneness. Remove burgers from grate and place on buns. Top each burger with a tomato slice and some cooked onions and peppers.

BIG RANCH BURGERS

4 SERVINGS • GRILL: 8–10 MIN.

1 cup sliced onion
⅓ cup sliced green bell
    pepper strips
⅓ cup sliced red bell
    pepper strips
1 tablespoon butter or margarine
3 tablespoons A.1. Steak Sauce
2 teaspoon prepared horseradish
1 pound ground beef
4 hamburger buns, split

Preheat grill or place grilling grate over campfire. Place a skillet on hot grate and cook sliced onions, green bell pepper strips, and red bell pepper strips in butter, heating until vegetables are tender but crisp. Stir in steak sauce and horseradish. Shape ground beef into 4 burgers and place burgers on hot grate. Cook burgers over grill for 8 to 10 minutes, turning once, until thoroughly cooked to desired doneness. Remove burgers from grate and place on buns. Top each burger with ¼ cup cooked onions and peppers.

Beef, Lamb, Venison & Bison

BEER BURGERS SMASHED WITH FRESH GOAT CHEESE

6 SERVINGS • PREP: 15 MIN. • GRILL: 15 MIN.

1½ pounds ground beef
1 teaspoon salt
2 tablespoons onion, minced
6 slices goat cheese, chilled
    until firm
⅓ can beer
3 tablespoons steak sauce
⅓ cup ketchup
1 tablespoon prepared mustard
1 tablespoon sugar
6 hamburger or potato
    buns, buttered

Combine first three ingredients and shape meat into half patties. Place slice of goat cheese on one half and then put another half patty on top to form whole burger.

Combine next five ingredients and heat in a saucepan until mixture thickens. Keep warm.

Preheat grill to high. Place patties in an oiled grill basket; grill 4 to 6 minutes on each side. Toast hamburger buns on edge of grill, turning once, for approximately 2 minutes. Place beef patties in buns and top with warm sauce before serving.

GUACAMOLE BURGERS

6 SERVINGS • PREP: 20 MIN. • GRILL: 10 MIN.

2 to 3 heads of garlic, roasted
    (see page 282)
Vegetable oil
2 cups mayonnaise
½ teaspoon lemon juice
2 pounds ground chuck
1 tablespoon
    Worcestershire sauce
1 teaspoon coarse salt
½ teaspoon freshly ground
    black pepper
2 tablespoons Tex-Mex rub
    (see below)
6 thick slices ripe tomato
6 lettuce leaves
6 large hamburger buns
Guacamole (see page 283),
    or premade
Salt and freshly ground pepper
    to taste

TEX-MEX RUB
2 tablespoons chili powder
4 teaspoons garlic salt
2½ teaspoons onion powder
2 teaspoons ground cumin
1½ teaspoons dried oregano
¾ teaspoon cayenne pepper

Mix all ingredients for Tex-Mex rub in a small bowl. Set aside.

For garlic mayonnaise, squeeze one bulb of roasted garlic from its skin into a medium bowl. Using fork, mash garlic, pressing against side of bowl. Add mayonnaise and lemon juice, and mix well. Refrigerate mixture until ready to serve burgers.

Place second bulb of roasted garlic in a large bowl and mash with fork against side of bowl. Add ground chuck, Worcestershire sauce, salt, and pepper, and mix with hands until just combined. Gently form six patties approximately ½ to ¾ inches thick. Coat patties with dry rub.

Preheat grill to high. Grill burgers for approximately 1 minute on each side. Reduce grill temperature to medium and continue cooking burgers for 4 to 5 minutes more per side. Toast buns at edge of grill. Spread garlic mayonnaise on one half of each bun and top with lettuce, burger, guacamole, and tomato slice. Sprinkle with salt and pepper.

STEAK & POTATO KEBABS

4 SERVINGS • PREP: 20 MIN. • GRILL: 15 MIN.

1 pound all-purpose potatoes
1 medium yellow or
    zucchini squash
1 pound boneless top sirloin
    steak, cut into 1-inch-
    thick cubes

SAUCE
¾ cup Heinz 57 Sauce
2 large cloves garlic, minced

Cut potatoes into 1½-inch pieces. Place in a microwave-safe dish; cover with vented plastic wrap. Microwave on high 6 to 8 minutes or until just tender, stirring once. Cool slightly.

Combine sauce ingredients in 1-cup glass measuring cup. Microwave on high 1½ minutes, stirring once.

Cut steak and squash into 1¼-inch pieces. Combine beef, squash, potatoes, and ⅓ cup sauce in a large bowl; toss. Alternately thread beef and vegetables onto metal skewers.

Place kebabs on grill over medium heat. Grill, uncovered, approximately 10 to 12 minutes for medium rare to medium, turning occasionally. Brush kebabs with remaining sauce during last 5 minutes.

CARNE ASADA

4 SERVINGS • GRILL: 13–17 MIN.

4 (¾-inch thick) beef rib eye
    steaks, trimmed
2 tablespoons fresh lime juice
4 (6-inch) flour tortillas
1 cup shredded Colby and
    Monterey Jack cheese, divided
Salsa

Preheat grill or place grilling grate over campfire. Sprinkle half of lime juice onto one side of each steak and rub into surface. Turn steaks and repeat with remaining lime juice. Wrap tortillas in aluminum foil. Place steaks on hot grate and grill for 12 to 15 minutes, turning once, or until steaks reach desired doneness. During last 5 minutes of cooking time, place aluminum-wrapped tortillas on outer edge of grate, turning once. Top each steak with ¼ cup shredded cheese and grill for an additional 1 or 2 minutes. Remove steaks from grill and top each steak with salsa. Serve steaks with heated tortillas on the side.

HAPPY "HOLLA" BRANDY PEPPER STEAK

6 SERVINGS • PREP: 20 MIN. • GRILL: 15 MIN.

Ed Roith, of the Happy "Holla" Bar-B-Q team of Shawnee, Kansas, created this steak recipe, which is cooked in a skillet on top of the grill.

1 2-pound sirloin steak, 1½ to 2 inches thick
2 teaspoons coarsely ground pepper
½ cup beef bouillon
1½ teaspoons salt
½ cup Slivovitz (plum brandy) or regular brandy
1 teaspoon cornstarch
2 tablespoons water
8 ounces mushrooms, cleaned and sliced (optional)

Trim excess fat from steak and reserve. Render some of fat in a large skillet that has been preheated on grill over high heat.

Reduce heat to medium-high. Sprinkle both sides of steak with pepper and add to skillet. Cook until browned on each side. Reduce heat and cook for 8 to 10 minutes. Remove steak to warm platter.

Drain pan drippings, reserving 2 teaspoons. Combine reserved drippings, bouillon, salt, and brandy in skillet. Add mushrooms and cook until reduced by one quarter, stirring constantly. Stir in cornstarch mixed with water. Cook until thickened, continuing to stir. Slice steak thinly across grain. Pour mixture over steak.

EASY BARBECUE FLANK STEAK

4 SERVINGS • PREP: 20 MIN. • MARINATE: 4 HR.–OVERNIGHT • GRILL: 15 MIN.

Flank steak (1½ pounds)
½ cup any hickory-flavored
 barbecue sauce
¼ cup red wine

Place steak in a large zip-top plastic bag. Combine barbecue sauce with red wine; pour mixture over steak. Seal bag and turn several times to coat steak. Marinate 4 to 24 hours in refrigerator, turning several times.

Discard marinade. Grill steak over medium heat to desired doneness, turning and brushing with additional barbecue sauce.

**Grilling takes the formality out of entertaining.
Everyone wants to get involved.**
–Bobby Flay

BALSAMIC-MARINATED FLANK STEAK

6 SERVINGS • MARINATE: 1 HR. OR OVERNIGHT • GRILL: 6–8 MIN.

1 red onion, quartered
⅓ cup balsamic vinegar
¼ cup capers, drained
2 tablespoons chopped
    fresh oregano
3 cloves garlic, minced
¼ teaspoon salt
¼ teaspoon pepper
1½ pounds flank steak

Sliver one quarter of onion and place it in a bowl; cover and set aside. Chop remaining onion sections. In a medium bowl, combine chopped onion, vinegar, capers, oregano, and minced garlic. Add one quarter of mixture to slivered onions; cover and set aside. Sprinkle salt and pepper over both sides of the steak. Using a fork, pierce holes into surface of steak. Place steak in a large sealable plastic bag or container with lid. Add remaining chopped onion mixture. Place both containers in refrigerator. Marinate steak for 1 hour or overnight, turning occasionally. Remove steak container from refrigerator. Place steak on grill over direct heat; discard marinade. If using an oven broiler, position broiler rack so meat will be 4 inches from heat source. Grill for 3 to 4 minutes. Turn steaks over and grill for 3 to 4 additional minutes or until meat is cooked to desired doneness (for rare, 145°F; for medium, 160°F; for well done, 170°F). Let stand for 5 minutes before slicing. Remove slivered onion mixture from refrigerator. Place meat on a platter and pour reserved onion mixture over steak.

GRILLED SKIRT STEAK

4-6 SERVINGS • MARINATE: 4–24 HR. • GRILL: 5–8 MIN.

1½ to 2 pounds beef skirt steak*
Sea salt and black pepper
    to taste
2 teaspoons onion powder
2 teaspoons garlic powder
2 tablespoons white wine vinegar
2 tablespoons olive oil

Trim fat and cut steak into 4 to 6 even pieces. Rub a generous amount of salt and pepper into both sides of each steak. Pat some of onion powder and garlic powder into each piece. Place steaks in a shallow glass dish and sprinkle vinegar over the tops; brush each piece with some of the oil. Cover and refrigerate to marinate meat at least 4 hours or up to 24 hours.

To cook, lightly oil the grate and preheat the grill to medium heat. Remove steaks from dish and place them on the grate; grill for 5 to 8 minutes, or to desired doneness, turning once halfway through cooking. Remove from the grill and let rest for 5 minutes before serving. If desired, slice the steaks thinly across the grain before serving. Drizzle with sauce or top with fruit salsa, if desired.

* *You may substitute other less tender steaks, such as flank or round steak.*

INDIVIDUAL STEAK PIZZAS

8 SERVINGS • GRILL: 14–20 MIN.

1 pound boneless beef
    sirloin steak
2 teaspoons steak
    seasoning, divided
1 onion
1 green, red, or yellow bell pepper
1 tablespoon plus 1 teaspoon
    olive oil, divided
1 tube (13.8 ounces) refrigerated
    pizza dough
1 cup prepared pizza sauce
2 cups shredded mozzarella or
    Monterey Jack cheese, divided
8 ounces crumbled blue
    cheese, optional

Lightly oil the grate and preheat grill to medium heat. Sprinkle both sides of steak with seasoning. Place steak on the grate and cook for 5 to 7 minutes on one side. Meanwhile, cut the onion and bell pepper into thick slices and brush with 1 teaspoon oil. Arrange vegetables on the grate to cook. Turn steaks and cook for 5 to 7 minutes longer or to desired doneness while vegetables continue to cook until tender-crisp. Remove steak and vegetables from the grill and cut into bite-size pieces; set aside.

Unroll dough and cut into four equal pieces. On a floured board, pat out each piece to larger rectangles about ¼ inch thick; brush top of each piece with remaining tablespoon oil. Place dough on the grate, oiled side down. Close lid and cook for 1 to 2 minutes or until grill marks show on crusts. Use tongs or a large spatula to carefully flip each crust over on the grate, moving it to indirect heat. Spread a portion of the sauce on each crust. Sprinkle about half of the mozzarella cheese over the four pizzas. Top each pizza with grilled steak, vegetables, and optional blue cheese. Sprinkle remaining mozzarella cheese on top. Close grill lid and cook pizzas for 3 to 4 minutes longer or until cheese is melted and crust is browned. Check pizzas often and rotate as needed for even baking. Slide pizzas onto a clean baking sheet before serving.

TAILGATE CHEESESTEAKS

4 SERVINGS • PREP: 10 MIN. • GRILL: 10 MIN.

Courtesy of Barry "CB" Martin, on Twitter: @BarryCBMartin.

2 onions, thinly sliced 1 pound
    sirloin steak (you can also use
    lamb, pork, or chicken)
4 cups shredded cheddar, jack, or
    havarti cheese
Salt and pepper
4 hoagie rolls
4 sheets heavy-duty foil

Preheat grill to medium-high. Spray foil with nonstick cooking spray and place one-quarter of onion slices on each sheet.

Cut meat into strips ⅛ inch thick; season with salt and pepper. Add one quarter of steak strips, followed by one quarter of cheese to onions on each foil sheet. Fold foil over mixture, sealing edges firmly. Leave some space for food to expand during cooking.

Grill 10 minutes on covered grill, turning once. Serve on hoagie rolls, topped with favorite barbecue sauce.

> This is a great preparation method for picnics, tailgating, or any time you have a large group of folks to serve. Prepare the foil packets in advance, keep cool, and place on the grill as you need them.–CB

"EAGLES" TAILGATING STEAK

4 SERVINGS • PREP: 10 MIN. • MARINATE: OVERNIGHT • GRILL: 10 MIN.

Philadelphia Eagles fan and tailgater Kevin Gibbons provided this easy recipe.

⅓ cup Worcestershire sauce
¼ tablespoon dry red wine
¼ tablespoon red wine vinegar
½ tablespoon dark brown sugar
2 cloves garlic, minced
½ tablespoon steak sauce
1½ pound flank steak

Combine first six ingredients in a bowl. Place steak in a plastic bag or container, and pour marinade over meat. Let marinate in refrigerator overnight.

Remove steaks from marinade; reserve marinade. Cook steak over hot grill, approximately 5 minutes per side. While steak is grilling, bring reserved marinade to a boil in a saucepan until mixture is reduced by one-third. Let steak rest 10 minutes.

Cut on the grain and serve with sauce.

LIME-MARINATED STEAK

4 SERVINGS

¼ cup vegetable oil
6 dried chili peppers, cut
   into strips
1 cup coarsely chopped onion
1½ teaspoon minced fresh garlic
½ cup beef broth
2 tablespoons fresh lime juice
2 teaspoons cumin seed
1½ teaspoons salt
1 teaspoon brown sugar
4 New York steaks, tenderized
Juice from 2 limes

In a medium skillet over medium-low heat, combine vegetable oil, chili pepper strips, chopped onion, and minced garlic; sauté until onion is tender. Pour onion mixture in a blender and add beef broth, lime juice, cumin seed, salt, and brown sugar. Process until blended. Place tenderized steaks in a large zippered bag and pour half of the marinade over steaks in bag and seal. Place remaining marinade in an airtight container. Place bag with steak and container with remaining marinade in refrigerator or cooler until ready to prepare.

Preheat grill to medium heat. Place steaks over grill and baste with reserved marinade. Grill to desired doneness. Before serving, brush with additional marinade and generously squeeze lime juice over cooked steaks.

POMSEY'S TAILGATE SIRLOIN TIPS

10 SERVINGS • PREP: 20 MIN. • MARINATE: 24–30 HR. • GRILL: 15 MIN.

9 pounds sirloin tips or rib-
eye cubes
French rolls
American cheese
Vidalia onion, grilled

SAUCE
1 cup ketchup
⅛ tablespoon molasses
⅓ teaspoon spicy brown or
Dijon mustard
⅙ teaspoon soy sauce
⅓ teaspoon garlic powder
⅓ teaspoon hot pepper sauce
1 teaspoon black pepper

Trim any excess fat (keeping in mind that meat needs some fat to remain juicy throughout grilling process), and cut meat into 2-inch cubes. Place tips in a large plastic container or bag.

In a large mixing bowl, combine sauce ingredients. Set aside some sauce for basting if you desire, and pour remaining sauce over tips. Mix well so that meat is completely coated. Refrigerate for 24 to 30 hours.

Preheat grill to medium-high heat. Grill tips to your desired doneness. Serve on rolls with cheese and onions. Note: To avoid a messy grill, coat your tips well the day before so that there's no need to slather on extra sauce.

"Sizzle on the Grill" contributor Greg from Quincy, Massachusetts, writes that his gang enjoys these tips on fresh French rolls with American cheese and grilled Vidalia onions. This recipe feeds 10 if other main courses are served.

HICKORY BEEF RIBS

4 SERVINGS • PREP: 3 HR. • GRILL: 10 MIN.

2 racks beef ribs (8–10 ribs each)

RIB MIXTURE
½ cup soy sauce

1 tablespoon steak spice

1 tablespoon garlic salt

1 tablespoon fresh
    garlic, chopped

1 teaspoon chili flakes

SAUCE
1 large onion, diced

1 tablespoon olive oil

3 28-ounce cans tomato sauce

1 19-ounce jar apple sauce

2 cups brown sugar

1 cup honey

½ cup soy sauce

½ cup white vinegar

4 tablespoons molasses

1¼ teaspoon liquid smoke

Salt and pepper

Fill a large pot with water and add rib mixture. Bring water to a boil. Add ribs; boil for 1 hour.

Sauté diced onion in olive oil until soft. Add remaining ingredients to a large sauce pot; bring to a boil and then continue to simmer over medium heat for 30 minutes. Remove ribs from water and pat dry with paper towels. Coat with enough sauce to cover; let stand 30 minutes. Grill ribs on medium-high for 8 to 10 minutes, basting and turning often to avoid burning.

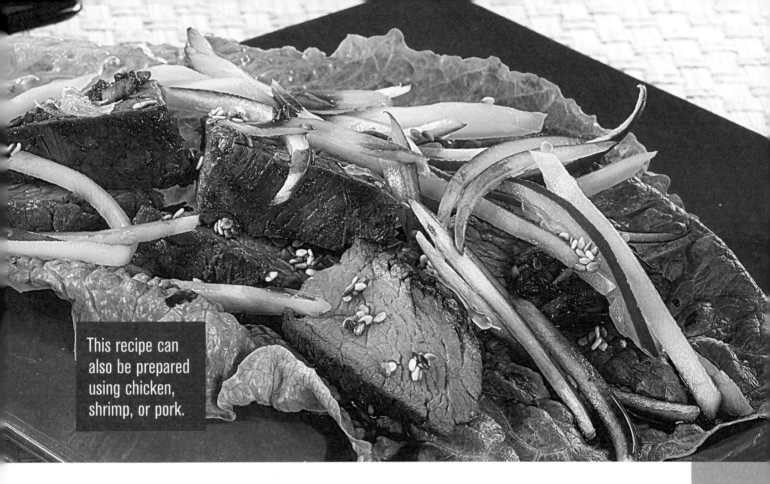

This recipe can also be prepared using chicken, shrimp, or pork.

ASIAN STEAK IN LETTUCE WRAPS

6–8 SERVINGS • PREP: 30 MIN. • MARINATE: 30 MIN. • GRILL: 5–10 MIN.

¾ cup soy sauce

¼ cup rice vinegar

2½ tablespoons sugar

2 tablespoons fresh
ginger, minced

1 tablespoon Asian sesame oil

1 teaspoon Asian chili paste

3 garlic cloves, minced

2 scallions, chopped

1 flank steak, approximately
1½ pounds

1 ripe mango, peeled
and julienned

1 small red onion, julienned

3 tablespoons lime juice

24 lettuce leaves (Bibb
or romaine)

2 tablespoons toasted
sesame seeds

Combine first eight marinade ingredients in a bowl. Reserve approximately one-quarter of the marinade. Place the steak in a plastic bag, and pour the larger portion of marinade over it. Seal the bag tightly and turn to distribute the marinade. Let rest at room temperature for 30 minutes.

Remove steak from marinade and grill over high heat for approximately 2 to 4 minutes per side, until seared on the surface but still pink at the center. Let steak rest for 5 minutes.

Meanwhile, combine the mango, onion, and lime juice in a bowl. Slice the steak across the grain into very thin strips approximately ¼ inch thick. Cut the strips into thirds. Coat the steak with the reserved marinade and arrange on a platter. Surround with a plate of lettuce leaves, the mango mixture, and the sesame seeds.

To assemble, allow guests to spoon some strips of the steak onto each lettuce leaf, topping with mango mixture and sprinkling with sesame seeds.

SMOKED BEEF BRISKET

8–10 SERVINGS • PREP: 20 MIN. • DRY RUB: OVERNIGHT • GRILL: 1 HR. PER LB.

1 beef brisket (10 to 12 pounds)
16 ounces beer
1 orange, thinly sliced
1 lemon, thinly sliced

BRISKET RUB

½ cup paprika
¼ cup black pepper
¼ cup salt
¼ cup turbinado or brown sugar
2 tablespoons chili powder
1 tablespoon onion powder
1 tablespoon dry mustard
1 tablespoon celery salt
1 teaspoon red pepper

BRISKET BASTING SPRAY

1 cup apple-cider vinegar
1 can beer
1 tablespoon Worcestershire sauce
1 tablespoon olive oil
1 pound thinly sliced bacon

Combine rub ingredients and massage into brisket. Seal meat in a plastic bag, and refrigerate overnight.

Remove brisket from the refrigerator and let stand at room temperature for 1 hour before grilling. Prepare a smoker and bring temperature to 220°F. Fill water pan with hot water and 16 ounces of beer. Float orange and lemon in pan. Combine basting ingredients, and pour into clean, empty spray bottle.

Place brisket in center of grill over water pan, fat side up. Loosely place bacon on top of brisket. Cook brisket 1 to 1½ hours per pound, for a minimum of 12 hours, basting every hour with brisket spray. Brisket is done when internal temperature reaches 190°F–200°F. Meat will shrink dramatically and turn almost black. Remove meat from grill; spray once more; and let rest, sealed in aluminum foil. Slice across the grain and serve with your favorite barbecue sauce.

SMOKED RIB ROAST

4–6 SERVINGS • PREP: 20 MIN. • MARINATE: 6 HR.–OVERNIGHT
GRILL: 1 HR. PER LB.

1 medium onion, diced
1 bay leaf
Sprig each of fresh thyme,
    marjoram, and oregano
2 tablespoons oil
2 cloves garlic, finely chopped
2 cups red wine
3-pound boneless cross rib roast

Combine onion, bay leaf, herbs, oil, garlic, and red wine to make marinade. Trim excess fat from the meat. Place roast in a large plastic bag or airtight container, and pour in the marinade. Seal bag tightly and turn gently to distribute the marinade. Refrigerate overnight, turning occasionally.

Remove roast from marinade and pat dry with paper towels. Preheat smoker to 220°F. Place roast on the upper grate of the smoker. Using your favorite flavored wood chips, smoke the roast for 7 to 8 hours or until internal temperature reaches 150°F. Let rest 10 minutes before carving.

Enjoy with roasted potatoes, gravy, horseradish, and Yorkshire pudding, or slice for sandwiches the next day.

HAWAIIAN-STYLE TRI-TIP

6–8 SERVINGS • PREP: 15 MIN. • REST: 1 HR. • GRILL: 15–20 MIN. • REST AFTER COOKING: 15–20 MIN.

Courtesy of Barry "CB" Martin, on Twitter: @BarryCBMartin.

2½ pounds tri-tip roast (triangular tip of sirloin)
Pineapple slices
Vegetable oil spray

DRY RUB

2 tablespoons coarse salt
½ tablespoon cracked black pepper
1 tablespoon minced garlic

GLAZE

1 tablespoon brown sugar
2 tablespoons butter, melted
1 tablespoon light soy sauce
1 tablespoon finely grated fresh ginger

Combine dry-rub ingredients; apply to all surfaces of meat; wrap meat in plastic; and allow meat to rest at room temperature for 1 hour.

Preheat one side of grill to high. Remove meat from plastic and lightly spray with vegetable oil on all sides. Place on hot side of grill to sear for about 2 to 3 minutes on each side, using tongs to turn.

Thoroughly combine glaze ingredients in a small bowl. Place seared roast in pan on cool half of grill; apply glaze with silicon brush; and close hood. Cook until internal temperature of meat reaches 145°F for medium rare, 160°F for medium. (Tri-tip is best enjoyed medium rare.) Transfer roast to carving board; tent with foil; and let stand for 15 to 20 minutes. Grill pineapple slices 2 to 3 minutes on each side.

PITA POCKET LAMB BURGERS WITH SPINACH & FETA

4 SERVINGS • PREP: 20 MIN. • GRILL: 10 MIN.

1 tablespoon unsalted butter
1 10-ounce package frozen
   spinach, thawed
1 teaspoon minced garlic
1 teaspoon chopped
   fresh oregano
1¼ cups crumbled feta cheese
2 tablespoons cottage cheese
2 pounds ground lamb
1½ teaspoons minced garlic
1 tablespoon chopped parsley
½ teaspoon sweet paprika
1 teaspoon freshly ground
   black pepper
4 pita pockets
1 lemon

Melt butter in a saucepan over medium heat. Add spinach, garlic, and oregano. Cook, stirring constantly, until all liquid evaporates, approximately 4 minutes. Keep warm.

Combine lamb with next four ingredients. Mix well and form four patties, approximately ¾ inch thick. Grill burgers over medium-high heat, 4½ minutes per side for medium rare or until desired doneness.

Cut lemon in half and squeeze juice over burgers a few minutes before removing them from grill. Place a dollop of spinach mixture on top of each burger and then place burgers inside pita pockets.

MUSTARD-AND-MINT GROUND LAMB WITH FETA-YOGURT SAUCE

8 SERVINGS • PREP: 15–20 MIN. • REFRIGERATE/SUFFUSE: 30 MIN.–OVERNIGHT
GRILL: 10–12 MIN.

1 pound lean ground lamb

½ cup egg substitute or 2 whole eggs

½ cup puréed vegetables (see note at right, below)

2 tablespoons Dijon mustard

¼ cup chopped fresh mint

¼ cup chopped fresh rosemary

Whole-wheat bread crumbs, couscous, or instant oatmeal as needed

Salt and pepper to taste

Cooking spray as needed

Tomato and red onion, sliced, as needed

Romaine or iceberg lettuce as needed

Whole-wheat buns, bread, or English muffins (optional)

SAUCE

1 cup low-fat or fat-free Greek yogurt

¼ cup crumbled feta cheese

¼ cup grated cucumber

Salt and pepper as needed

First, fold all of the sauce ingredients together in a bowl. Next, mix the lamb, eggs, vegetable purée, herbs, salt, and pepper in a separate bowl. (The mixture may be very soft and moist at this point.) Add the desired binder (bread crumbs, etc.) a little at a time until the mixture becomes malleable and you can form patties. Make eight slider-size burgers and let them rest for 30 minutes to overnight (in the refrigerator).

Preheat grill to medium-high. Mist the sliders lightly with the cooking spray to prevent sticking, and cook them for 5–6 minutes per side for medium rare (145°F internal temperature) or to desired doneness. Mix the sauce ingredients together in a small bowl. Place the sliders on toasted buns or another bread of your choice if desired; top them with the yogurt sauce; and serve with your favorite burger condiments.

Note: For the vegetable purée, the kind of vegetable is not really important. The vegetables will mimic some of the properties of the missing fat, giving you a moist, tender product. When considering which vegetable to use, reflect on what is available, what flavors you like on the burgers (mushroom, onion, or wilted spinach, etc.), or what you have left over in your refrigerator.

ROTISSERIE-ROASTED LEG OF LAMB

8–10 SERVINGS • PREP: 40 MIN.
GRILL: UNTIL INTERNAL TEMP. REACHES 140°F (RARE)

4-pound boneless leg of lamb
4 cloves of garlic, peeled and cut
   into slivers
3 tablespoons dried oregano
3 tablespoons dried rosemary
1 teaspoon dried thyme
5 tablespoons olive oil
Salt and freshly ground
   black pepper
Olive oil for basting
Juice of 2 lemons

Using a knife, create six to eight deep slashes at various points in roast and insert garlic pieces. Combine the herbs, oil, salt, and pepper, and rub the meat with the seasonings. Allow meat to rest for 20 minutes.

Preheat the grill. Insert spit rod lengthwise through center of the lamb; secure with holding forks on each side.

Grill for 45 minutes to 1 hour, basting lamb with olive oil and lemon juice every 10 to 15 minutes. Allow the lamb to rest for 20 minutes, and then carve and serve.

LAMB CHOPS WITH COUSCOUS

4 SERVINGS • PREP: 1 HR. • GRILL: 10 MIN.

1 cup chicken stock
½ cup couscous, uncooked
¼ cup tomato, chopped
    and seeded
1 green onion, chopped
2 tablespoons parsley, chopped
2 tablespoons red wine vinegar
6 tablespoons olive oil
Salt and pepper to taste
1 sprig fresh rosemary, chopped
8 baby lamb chops or
4 shoulder lamb chops

In a saucepan, bring chicken stock to a boil; stir in couscous. Simmer 5 minutes; remove from heat. Let stand, covered, for 20 minutes. Spoon into serving bowl. Chill for one hour.

Stir couscous and add tomato, green onion, parsley, vinegar, 3 tablespoons olive oil, salt, and pepper. Mix well. Place in microwaveable bowl and warm 1 minute in microwave until heated through.

Preheat the grill; oil grill grates. Rub lamb with additional olive oil; sprinkle with rosemary and pepper. Grill chops for 5 minutes on each side. Serve with warm couscous.

Beef, Lamb, Venison & Bison

GRILLED CERVENA VENISON CHOPS

4 SERVINGS • PREP: 10 MIN. • GRILL: 5 MIN. (UNTIL INTERNAL TEMP. IS 180°F)

1 8-rib rack of Cervena venison
2 tablespoons vegetable oil
Salt and pepper

Preheat grill to high. Remove the outside sliver skin, using a sharp knife, and season the meat well. Cut the rack into four double cutlets, or cook it as a whole piece. Either way, first sear the venison over high heat to get a nice browning. Remove the whole venison rack to the internal cooking rack in the grill hood or to indirect heat and cook for 35 minutes, or cook the double chops for 10 minutes over medium heat.

Slice the venison into individual chops and serve with your favorite fresh tomato salsa or tomato chutney.

Maldon salt is a flavorful salt from the UK that you can find in specialty stores, but you can also use kosher salt.

CERVENA VENISON SLIDERS WITH THREE TOPPINGS

16 SERVINGS • PREP: 10–15 MIN. • COOK: 30–60 MIN. • GRILL: 2–4 MIN.

2 pounds Cervena venison from leg

1 teaspoon dried oregano

1 teaspoon ground cinnamon

8 stems flat leaf parsley, leaves removed and finely chopped

2 teaspoons extra-virgin olive oil

2 teaspoons Maldon salt (see note above)

½ teaspoon freshly ground pepper

Small egg buns or whole-wheat buns, bread, or English muffins (optional)

TOPPING 1: SHERRY VINEGAR ONIONS

1 red onion, peeled and cut into ½-inch rounds

1 bay leaf

1 stem rosemary

½ teaspoon dried oregano

1 clove garlic, flattened with side of knife

3½ tablespoons sherry vinegar

3 tablespoons extra-virgin olive oil

1 tablespoon dark brown sugar

½ tablespoon Maldon or kosher salt

TOPPING 2: SWEET & SOUR TOMATOES

1-pound can peeled and crushed tomatoes

½ thumb ginger, peeled and finely chopped

3 cloves garlic, minced

2 teaspoons Tabasco® sauce

¾ cup sugar

1 tablespoon fish sauce

5 tablespoons cider vinegar

TOPPING 3: PICKLED BEETS

1 pound beets

1 red chili, deseeded and finely chopped

5 cloves garlic, finely chopped

1 knob ginger, peeled and finely chopped

¾ cup muscovado or dark brown sugar

2 cups Greek red wine vinegar

1 cup cider vinegar

Salt and black pepper to taste

4 eggs

Once the meat mixture is ground, separate it into 16 equal portions. Lightly form the meat into slider-size patties, taking care not to pack them too tightly.

Preheat the grill to medium. Grill the sliders to medium rare (145°F internal temperature), about 1–2 minutes on each side. Be careful not to overcook the sliders, as the meat cooks very quickly. If desired, use small egg buns or drizzle olive oil over the buns and grill them to get richer, moister bread.

TOPPING 1: SHERRY VINEGAR ONIONS

Preheat an oven to 350°F. Place the onion slices in an even layer in an oven-safe dish. Combine the remaining ingredients in a mixing bowl and whisk them together. Pour the mixture over the onions.

Cover the oven-safe dish with foil and place it in the preheated oven for about 40 minutes. The onions will have softened, turned a pale red, and absorbed most of the liquid. Remove the onions from the oven and allow them to cool. You will end up with more than you need, but they keep well in the refrigerator.

TOPPING 2: SWEET & SOUR TOMATOES

Combine all of the ingredients in a saucepan and then place the pan over medium heat. Bring the sauce to a boil, and reduce the heat to a simmer. Cook the sauce on a low simmer for 30 minutes or until it becomes thick and glossy. Remove the sauce from the heat and allow it to cool. This also keeps very well in the refrigerator.

TOPPING 3: PICKLED BEETS

Preheat the oven to 375°F. Wash the beets and wrap them in aluminum foil. Place the foil-wrapped beets on a baking tray and place the tray in the oven for about 40–60 minutes, depending on size, or until you can easily insert and remove a sharp knife.

Allow the beets to cool; peel them; and cut them into thin slices. Combine all of the remaining ingredients in a saucepan. Place the pan over medium heat and bring the contents to a boil. Reduce the heat to a medium simmer and continue to cook until the volume of liquid is reduced by about one quarter. Pour the liquid over the sliced beets and refrigerate.

Note: Cervena is farm-raised venison from New Zealand that is available throughout North America and in New Zealand. Because the venison is farm raised, there is no gamey taste. It is very lean red meat, providing all of the benefits of vitamins and minerals but with a much healthier fat profile.

JERK BISON SLIDER WITH FRUIT SALSA

8 SERVINGS • PREP: 15–20 MIN.
REFRIGERATE/SUFFUSE: 30 MIN.–OVERNIGHT • GRILL: 6–10 MIN.

1 pound lean ground bison
    or beef
½ cup egg substitute or 2
    whole eggs
½ cup puréed vegetables
    (see note at right, below)
¼–½ cup wet jerk seasoning (not
    powdered), mild, medium,
    or spicy
Whole-wheat bread crumbs,
    couscous, or instant oatmeal
    as needed
Salt and pepper to taste
Cooking spray as needed
Shredded romaine or iceberg
    lettuce as needed
Whole-wheat buns, bread, or
    English muffins (optional)

SALSA

½ cup small-diced papaya
½ cup small-diced mango
½ cup finely julienned red onion
½ cup small-diced green
    bell pepper
½ cup small-diced tomato
1 lime, juiced
¼ cup finely chopped cilantro
Salt and pepper to taste

> Fruit may not be
> the first thing you'd
> think of to pair
> with a burger, but
> give it a try. You
> will be pleasantly
> surprised!

Mix the ground bison, eggs, vegetable purée, jerk seasoning, salt, and pepper in a bowl. (The mixture may be very soft and moist at this point.) Add the binder of your choice (bread crumbs, etc.) a little at a time until the mixture becomes malleable and you can form patties. Make eight slider-sized burgers and let them rest for 30 minutes to overnight (in the refrigerator).

Mix all of the salsa ingredients together in a bowl; season to taste; and set aside.

Preheat grill to high. Lightly mist the sliders with the cooking spray to prevent sticking to the grill. Cook the slider to 145°F for medium rare or to desired doneness. Place the sliders on your choice of bread if desired; top each with the salsa; and serve with your favorite burger condiments.

Note: For the vegetable purée, the kind of vegetable is not really important. The vegetables will mimic some of the properties of the missing fat, giving you a moist, tender product. When considering which vegetable to use, reflect on what is available, what flavors you like on the burgers (mushroom, onion, or wilted spinach, etc.), or what you have leftover in your refrigerator.

BISON SIRLOIN TIP WITH GARLIC-BALSAMIC BEET SAUCE

4 SERVINGS • PREP: 15 MIN. • COOL: 10–20 MIN. • GRILL: 14–20 MIN. • REST: 5 MIN.

1 pound bison top sirloin tip
2 tablespoons olive or canola oil
1 cup balsamic vinegar
1 cup beet juice (note below)
2 tablespoons extra-virgin olive oil
2 cloves garlic, roasted
1 teaspoon Dijon mustard
    (optional, but it will
    improve texture)
1 tablespoon picked and rough-
    chopped fresh rosemary
2 tablespoons fresh lemon juice
Salt and pepper to taste

Preheat grill to high. Rub the sirloin tip with 2 tablespoons oil, salt, and pepper, and set it aside. Now heat the balsamic vinegar in a saucepan on the grill and reduce it by one-half. Add the beet juice and reduce that mixture by one-quarter. Set the reduction aside to cool to room temperature.

Sear the bison tip on each side for 2 minutes, rotating it after 1 minute to create diamond grill marks. Reduce the heat to medium and grill the bison to your desired doneness (155°F for medium). Once it's done, set it aside to rest for at least 5 minutes.

Combine the beet-balsamic reduction, extra-virgin olive oil, garlic, mustard (optional), rosemary, lemon, salt, and pepper in a blender, and purée until smooth. (If the rosemary doesn't completely blend into the sauce, consider straining the sauce before serving it.)

Cut the sirloin tip into thin slices. Top each serving with 1–2 tablespoons of the balsamic beet sauce.

Note: Beet juice can be difficult to find, and juicers are expensive. You can substitute one roasted beet and ¾–1 cup of water or beef stock, puréed smooth in a blender, for conventional beet juice. Depending on the size of the beet, this may make your sauce thicker than desired. Have some extra water or beef stock on hand to help you adjust the texture.

7

Cooking with kids is not just about ingredients, recipes, and cooking. It's about harnessing imagination, empowerment, and creativity.
–Guy Fieri

Pork

ALL HANDS ON DECK!

HAVING THE WHOLE CREW—
grandparents, aunts, uncles, cousins, and friends who are like family—over for a big meal calls for special planning. Huddle with the home team and divvy up chores and shopping before the gathering. If weather and space allow, dine outside for an extra-festive feeling. Add strings of lights or lanterns and background music to add that relaxed vibe when the sun goes down.

GRILLED PORK WITH AVOCADO SALSA

4 SERVINGS • PREP: 20–25 MIN. • GRILL: 14–20 MIN.
(UNTIL INTERNAL TEMP. IS AT LEAST 145°F) • REST: 5 MIN.

¾–1 pound boneless top-loin pork chops,
    thick cut (or pork tenderloin)
½ cup rough-chopped Spanish onions
½ cup freshly squeezed lime juice
2 tablespoons extra-virgin olive oil
¼ cup seeded and chopped jalapeño peppers
2 teaspoons ground cumin
1 teaspoon salt
1 teaspoon ground black pepper
Water as needed

SALSA

1 avocado, peeled, pit removed, and
    medium diced
1 cup halved cherry or pear tomatoes
½ cup seeded and medium-diced cucumber
¼ cup finely diced red onion
¼ cup chopped cilantro
1 tablespoon extra-virgin olive oil
1–2 tablespoons freshly squeezed lime juice
Salt and pepper to taste

Create a marinade by combining the Spanish onions, ½ cup of lime juice, 2 tablespoons oil, jalapeño, cumin, and 1 teaspoon each salt and pepper in a blender and blending on high until smooth. If the marinade does not blend properly, add water, a little at a time, until the mixture purées. Put the pork and the marinade in a sealable plastic bag and marinate for 1 hour to overnight.

Preheat grill to high. Mix all of the salsa ingredients together in a bowl close to the time you will serve the dish to prevent browning (enzymatic oxidation) of the avocado. Mist the pork with the cooking spray to prevent sticking. Sear the pork on all sides, and then lower the heat to medium and cook the meat to an internal temperature of at least 145°F or more, according to taste. Remove the tenderloin from the heat and let it rest for a minimum of 5 minutes. Slice and serve with a generous serving of the salsa.

CHEF TASKS

KIDDO CHEF

- Squeeze the lime juice for the marinade and salsa.
- Measure the marinade ingredients and put them in the blender.
- Mix the salsa ingredients.

TEENAGE SOUS CHEF

- Chop the Spanish onions and jalapeño peppers.
- Prep the avocado, tomatoes, cucumber, red onion, and cilantro.
- Combine the marinade ingredients in the blender.

HEAD CHEF (AKA THE GROWN-UP)

- Keep an eye on your helpers!
- Preheat the grill to high.
- Mist the pork with cooking spray.
- Grill the pork for about 14–20 minutes, until the internal temperature reaches 145°F.

TAILGATE GRILLED BABY BACK RIBS

SERVINGS: 1 RACK PER PERSON • PREP: 5 MIN. • MARINATE: 2 HR.
GRILL: 2 HR. AT HOME, 15–30 MIN. ON SITE

Courtesy of Barry "CB" Martin, on Twitter: @BarryCBMartin.

1-pound rack of baby back ribs
    per person
¼ cup brown sugar per rack
    of ribs
¼ cup apple-cider vinegar
    per rack
¼ cup your favorite barbecue
    sauce per rack
Coarse salt and fresh ground
    pepper to taste

Have the butcher remove the thin membrane from the back of the ribs. Rinse the ribs and pat dry. Rub each rack with salt and pepper and then the ½ cup of brown sugar—make sure it's all rubbed in. Note: It's a good idea to use food-safe gloves during this process.

Place the ribs meat-side down in a nonreactive bowl or pan, and pour cider vinegar over them. Cover ribs with plastic wrap and refrigerate. Marinate for a minimum of 2 hours.

Remove the ribs from the refrigerator and discard the marinade.

Preheat one side of the grill to medium-high; reserve the other side for indirect cooking. You can add wood chips for smoke flavor for the first hour.

Place the ribs on the hot side and sear for about 5 minutes, and then use tongs to transfer to the side without direct heat. Close hood; reduce heat to low and roast for about 2 hours. You want to maintain an even temperature of about 225°F–250°F.

Note: You can also finish the ribs in the oven. Just place them on a baking sheet in an oven set to about 225°F–250°F for about 1½ hours to 2 hours. Use tongs to grab each rack. If the rib rack bends and starts to separate, ribs are ready!

To transport: Up to 1 hour in advance, baste ribs with barbecue sauce and seal in aluminum foil. Place in insulated carrier. Once on site, you can place one or two of the foil packages on the grill, heated to low, and close the lid to warm the ribs. When the ribs have warmed, remove them from foil and turn grill to medium-high. Sear ribs on direct heat, brushing on remaining sauce, if needed. To serve, slice individual ribs and pile on platter with more sauce if desired

This is an easy recipe to prepare at home and finish at a tailgate party.

BEER-BASTED BABY BACK RIBS

4–6 SERVINGS • PREP: 60 MIN. • GRILL: 12 MIN.

8 pounds baby back pork ribs, cut
   into 4-rib sections
6 cups beer
2½ cups brown sugar
1½ cups apple-cider vinegar
1½ tablespoons chili powder
1½ tablespoons ground cumin
1 tablespoon dry mustard
2 teaspoons salt
2 teaspoons dried crushed
   red pepper
2 bay leaves

Bring first nine ingredients to a boil in a large pot. Reduce heat and simmer about 1 minute to blend flavors. Add half of ribs to sauce. Cover pot and simmer until ribs are tender, turning frequently, about 25 minutes. Transfer ribs to baking dish. Repeat with remaining ribs. Boil barbecue sauce until reduced to 3 cups, about 40 minutes. Discard bay leaves. (Note: Sauce can be prepared 1 day ahead. Cover ribs and sauce separately, and refrigerate. Warm sauce before continuing.)

Preheat grill to medium; oil grill grates. Brush ribs with some of sauce; sprinkle with salt. Grill ribs until heated through, browned, and well-glazed, brushing occasionally with sauce, about 6 minutes per side.

COLA RIBS

6 SERVINGS • PREP: 10 MIN. • MARINATE: 4 HR. • SMOKE: 3 HR. • REST: 10 MIN.

2 racks baby back ribs, approx.
    3 pounds each
3 sweet potatoes
3 ears corn
Canola oil

MARINADE

2 cups cola
½ cup bourbon
½ cup brown sugar
2 tablespoons mustard powder
2 tablespoons chili flakes
1 tablespoon garlic, minced
3 sprigs fresh rosemary
½ bag char wood (⅔ soaked in
    cool water for 2 hours or
    until saturated)

Place ribs in nonreactive glass dish. Mix marinade ingredients in medium-size bowl. Pour marinade over ribs and cover with plastic wrap. Allow ribs to marinate for 4 hours.

Preheat grill to medium heat for indirect cooking. Add two thirds of drained, soaked wood and remaining dry char wood to smoking tray. Mix, and allow wood to smoke. Once smoke is achieved, reduce heat to low and add more wet chips.

Place ribs over side of grill without direct heat. Close lid and smoke for 3 hours or until ribs are falling off the bone. While cooking, continue to add wet chips to tray. Remove ribs from grill, and loosely tent them with foil. Let ribs rest for 10 minutes before serving.

Spray potatoes with canola oil. Sear potatoes 3 minutes on each side. Move to tray over indirect heat, and cook for 20 minutes or until tender; grill corn over direct heat turning often, for about 5 minutes.

SEASONED PORK RIBS

4 SERVINGS • MARINATE: 2–8 HR.

1 tablespoon chili powder
1 tablespoon dried parsley flakes
2 teaspoons onion powder
2 teaspoons garlic powder
2 teaspoons dried oregano
2 teaspoons paprika
2 teaspoons pepper
1½ teaspoons salt
4 pounds pork spareribs, cut into
    4 racks
BBQ Sauce (recipe below)

BBQ SAUCE
Makes 3½ cups
3 cups prepared barbecue sauce
¼ cup cider vinegar
¼ cup honey
2 teaspoons onion powder
2 teaspoons garlic powder
Dash of hot pepper sauce

In a small bowl, combine chili powder, dried parsley flakes, onion powder, garlic powder, dried oregano, paprika, pepper, and salt. Mix well and rub over ribs. Cover ribs and let marinate in refrigerator 2 to 8 hours. Preheat oven to 350°F and place ribs in a shallow roasting pan. Bake ribs 30 minutes.

In a medium bowl, whisk together barbecue sauce, vinegar, honey, onion powder, garlic powder and hot pepper sauce until well mixed.

Preheat grill to medium heat. Place ribs over grill and heat 10 minutes, brushing frequently with barbecue sauce. Continue to grill until ribs are tender.

BABY BACK RIBS WITH MUSTARD SAUCE

8 SERVINGS • GRILL: 1–1½ HR.

⅓ cup brown sugar

¼ cup minced onion

¼ cup white vinegar

¼ cup yellow mustard

½ teaspoon celery seed

½ teaspoon garlic powder

4 pounds pork
    spareribs, separated

In a medium saucepan, combine brown sugar, minced onion, vinegar, mustard, celery seed, and garlic powder. Bring mixture to a boil, stirring until sugar is completely dissolved; set aside.

Preheat grill and adjust heat for indirect cooking. Place ribs on grill rack over medium heat; cover and grill for 1 to 1½ hours or until ribs are tender and no pink remains. Brush occasionally with sauce during the last 15 minutes of grilling time.

NUT-CRUSTED RIBS WITH BOURBON MOP SAUCE

8–10 SERVINGS • PREP: 30 MIN. • MARINATE: 3 DAYS TOTAL • SMOKE: 3½–4 HR.

Courtesy of Barry "CB" Martin, on Twitter: @BarryCBMartin.

2 whole racks (about 4 to 5 pounds) pork spareribs
½ cup apple-cider vinegar
½ cup dark porter beer, or stout
3 to 4 cups finely chopped pecans, walnuts, or almonds

DRY RUB

1 tablespoon garlic powder
1 tablespoon chili powder
1 tablespoon onion powder
1 tablespoon mustard powder
1 tablespoon cumin
1 teaspoon kosher salt
1 teaspoon freshly ground black pepper
1 cup dark brown sugar

BOURBON MOP SAUCE

¼ pound butter
1 cup dark brown sugar
4 cups ketchup
½ cup apple-cider vinegar
6 garlic cloves, crushed and finely minced
2 teaspoon curry powder
Contents of 1 Earl Grey tea bag
1 tablespoon stone-ground mustard
4 ounces Worcestershire sauce
1 ounce Tabasco® sauce
2 cups Kentucky bourbon

Combine and briefly simmer the mop-sauce ingredients, except bourbon. Add bourbon and then remove from heat. Refrigerate, covered, for at least 2 days. The night before cooking, remove the cover and air dry the ribs in the refrigerator for 1 hour. Next, coat them with a mixture of vinegar and beer; massage them with the dry rub; wrap tightly in plastic; and refrigerate overnight.

Preheat grill and prepare a smoker box using the chips of your choice. Smoke ribs for 2½ hours in low (225°F) indirect heat and then place them on heavy aluminum foil; coat with warmed mop sauce and the nuts; wrap; and cook for at least 1 hour with the grill lid closed. When meat easily pulls away from the bone, place the ribs on the grates to finish, adding more sauce and nuts.

CHEESE-STUFFED BRATS

5 SERVINGS • GRILL: 5–10 MIN.

5 fully cooked bratwurst
¼ cup shredded Monterey
    Jack cheese
2 green onions, thinly sliced
5 strips bacon
5 French-style rolls or brat buns
Ketchup, mustard, chopped
    onions and/or relish, optional

Preheat grill to medium heat. Cut a ½-inch wide slit lengthwise in each bratwurst. Fill the slit in each bratwurst with shredded Monterey Jack cheese, dividing cheese evenly among the bratwursts. Repeat with sliced green onions. Wrap 1 strip of bacon around each bratwurst to enclose the green onions and cheese. Secure bacon strips with toothpicks. Place bratwursts, cut side up, over grill and heat for 5 to 10 minutes, until bacon is crisp and cheese is melted. Place bratwursts in buns and, if desired, top with ketchup, mustard, chopped onions and/or relish.

INDIAN TANDOORI RIBS

4 SERVINGS • PREP: 15 MIN. • MARINATE: OVERNIGHT • GRILL: 1½ HR.

2 slabs pork spareribs

MARINADE
2 8-ounce cartons plain yogurt
2 garlic cloves, crushed
3 tablespoons ginger root, grated
2 jalapeño chiles, seeded
½ cup fresh cilantro leaves
1 tablespoon cumin, ground
Red food coloring

Tandoori refers to the Indian traditional red-orange tint of tandoor-oven cooking. Serve with flatbread or naan, seasoned rice mixed with peas, and cucumber salad.

In a blender, combine yogurt, garlic, ginger, chiles, cilantro, and cumin, and purée. Reserve a small amount for dipping sauce if desired. Add a few drops of red food coloring. Place ribs in large plastic bag; coat with marinade; seal bag; and refrigerate overnight.

Preheat grill to medium. Drain ribs and discard marinade. Place ribs over drip pan; close grill hood; and cook for 1½ hours over indirect heat, until ribs are tender.

SOUTH-OF-THE-BORDER BARBECUED RIBS

4 SERVINGS • GRILL: 30 MIN.

1 cup ketchup
¼ cup cider vinegar
2 tablespoons
   Worcestershire sauce
2 teaspoons dry mustard
2 teaspoons crushed red pepper
½ cup brown sugar
3 to 4 pounds spareribs

In a small saucepan over medium-low heat, combine ketchup, vinegar, Worcestershire sauce, dry mustard, crushed red pepper, and brown sugar; heat to boiling. Reduce heat, cover, and simmer for 15 minutes. Reserve half of sauce for serving.

Place ribs on grill over medium-high heat. Close lid and grill for 10 minutes. Baste with sauce and continue to grill, uncovered. Baste and turn every few minutes. Discard sauce. Grill for an additional 20 minutes or until done. Serve with reserved sauce.

PORK SPARERIBS WITH COCONUT-PEANUT SAUCE

3–4 SERVINGS • PREP: 10 MIN. • GRILL: 1½ HR.

3 to 4 pounds pork spareribs

COCONUT-PEANUT SAUCE

⅓ cup light coconut milk

¼ cup creamy peanut butter

2 tablespoons soy sauce

1 tablespoon sesame oil

1 tablespoon ginger, minced

1 tablespoon cilantro, snipped

¼ to ½ teaspoon red pepper, crushed, to taste

1 garlic clove, minced

Grill ribs over indirect medium heat for 1 hour. Stir together sauce ingredients until well combined; reserve half of sauce to serve with finished ribs. Brush remaining sauce on ribs; grill for 30 minutes longer until ribs are tender and meat pulls from the bone. Warm reserved sauce and serve with ribs.

Why make the same old barbecued ribs? Try this sauce for your next cookout. Serve with tropical fruit salad and rice.

GARLIC-LIME PORK TENDERLOIN

6 SERVINGS • PREP: 45 MIN. • MARINATE: OVERNIGHT & UP TO 2 DAYS
GRILL: 15–20 MIN.

6 cloves garlic, chopped

2 tablespoons soy sauce

2 tablespoons fresh
    ginger, grated

2 tablespoons Dijon mustard

⅓ cup fresh lime juice

½ cup olive oil

⅛ teaspoon cayenne or to taste

6 pork tenderloin steaks

Blend first seven ingredients with salt and pepper to taste in blender or food processor. Trim any excess fat and skin from tenderloins. Combine steaks with marinade in large plastic storage bag. Seal bag and marinate pork in refrigerator, turning occasionally, at least 1 day and up to 2 days.

Preheat grill to medium-high. Remove steaks from refrigerator and let stand at room temperature about 30 minutes. Remove steaks from marinade and grill 15 to 20 minutes, turning every 5 minutes. Pork is done when internal temperature reaches 155°F and center is barely pink.

MEDITERRANEAN GRILLED PORK ROAST

4–6 SERVINGS • PREP: 15 MIN. • GRILL: 1–1¼ HR.

4-pound boneless pork loin roast
Zest of 2 lemons
5 garlic cloves, peeled
⅓ cup fresh rosemary leaves
¼ cup fresh sage leaves
¼ cup coarsely ground
    black pepper
Salt to taste

Pat pork roast dry. In bowl of food processor, place remaining six ingredients and process until fairly smooth. Pat seasoning mixture over all surfaces of roast. Place roast on medium-hot grill over indirect heat. Close grill lid and grill for about 1 to 1¼ hours or until internal temperature reaches about 155°F. Remove pork from grill and let rest about 10 minutes before slicing to serve.

GREEK PORK LOIN ROAST

6–8 SERVINGS • PREP: 45 MIN. • MARINATE: OVERNIGHT • GRILL: 1–1½ HR.

3 pounds boneless
    pork tenderloin
1 cup plain yogurt
1 cucumber, peeled and chopped
½ teaspoon garlic, crushed
½ teaspoon coriander
    seeds, crushed
¼ cup red onion, minced
¼ teaspoon crushed red pepper

MARINADE
(Combine ingredients in a bowl.)
¼ cup olive oil
¼ cup lemon juice
1 teaspoon oregano
1 teaspoon salt
1 teaspoon pepper
6 cloves garlic, minced

Trim any excess fat and skin from tenderloin. Place pork tenderloin in large plastic storage bag. Pour marinade over tenderloin in bag. Seal bag and marinate pork in refrigerator overnight. Remove from marinade; discard marinade.

Preheat grill to medium-high. Combine remaining six ingredients in a bowl; cover and refrigerate until ready to serve with pork roast. Place drip pan in grill under tenderloin. Grill 1 to 1½ hours over indirect heat in covered grill. Pork is done when internal temperature reaches 155°F and center is barely pink. Let meat rest 10 minutes before slicing thinly.

PORK LOIN BEER-B-QUE

12 SERVINGS • MARINATE: OVERNIGHT • GRILL: 1 HR.

1 boneless pork loin (3 pounds)
1 can beer (12 ounces)
½ cup dark corn syrup
½ cup finely chopped onion
⅓ cup yellow mustard
¼ cup vegetable oil
2 tablespoons chili powder
2 cloves garlic, minced

Place pork loin in a shallow glass baking dish; set aside. In a medium bowl, combine beer, corn syrup, chopped onion, mustard, oil, chili powder, and minced garlic; mix well. Pour mixture over pork loin, turning the pork loin to coat with marinade. Cover dish with lid or aluminum foil and refrigerate overnight, turning occasionally.

Remove pork loin from baking dish. Discard marinade. Grill pork loin over medium-high heat for 1 hour or until a meat thermometer inserted into center of loin reads 145°F. Let rest for 10 minutes before slicing. Slice thin to serve.

SPICY TAILGATER'S POCKETS

8 SERVINGS • GRILL: 45 MIN.

1 package (1.25 ounces) Caribbean-flavored marinade mix

¼ cup water

2 tablespoons pineapple or orange juice

1 tablespoon brown sugar

1 tablespoon distilled white vinegar

1 pound kielbasa, cut into ¼-inch slices

1 large red bell pepper, cut into strips

1 medium onion, peeled and sliced

1 package pita bread or burrito-style tortillas

Preheat grill to medium-high heat. In a small bowl, combine marinade mix, water, pineapple juice, brown sugar, and vinegar. Mix well and set aside.

Cut aluminum foil into four 18-inch squares. Place an even amount of kielbasa slices, red bell pepper strips, and onion slices in center of each aluminum foil square. Roll aluminum foil to loosely enclose ingredients and fold up one end, leaving one end open. Divide marinade evenly among packets and seal packets by folding down remaining open end of aluminum foil. Shake packets to coat mixture inside. Place packets on preheated grill and cook for 45 minutes, turning once. Carefully remove packets from grill and open one end. Let mixture cool for 2 to 3 minutes while letting steam escape. To serve, divide grilled mixture into four pita bread pockets or spoon on tortillas.

"GREEN BAY" TAILGATING KIELBASA

20 SERVINGS • PREP: 10 MIN. • GRILL: 15–20 MIN.

Courtesy of grilling fan Vincent and his fellow tailgaters from Hofstra University in New York.

10 horseshoe-shaped kielbasa
½ pound deli-style white American
   cheese, sliced
10 crusty French or Italian rolls
Favorite barbecue sauce

Preheat grill to medium-high. Split each sausage lengthwise, taking care not to slice all the way through. Place kielbasas on grill, split sides down. After a few minutes, turn sausages over; place cheese on cut sides; fold kielbasas closed; and baste with barbecue sauce. Cook, turning occasionally, until sausages brown and cheese melts. Split open French rolls; toast rolls on edge of grill, if desired. Slather each roll with sauce, and place one sausage in each roll. Serve immediately.

Cooking is the ultimate giving.
–Jamie Oliver

ITALIAN SAUSAGE & PEPPERS

4 SERVINGS • GRILL: 5–6 MIN.

½ cup olive oil
¼ cup red wine vinegar
2 tablespoons fresh
    chopped parsley
1 tablespoon dried oregano
2 cloves garlic, crushed
1 teaspoon salt
1 teaspoon pepper
4 hot or sweet Italian
    sausage links
1 large onion, peeled and sliced
    into rings
1 large red bell pepper, quartered

In a small bowl, combine olive oil, vinegar, chopped parsley, dried oregano, crushed garlic, salt, and pepper. Place sausages, sliced onion, and quartered red bell peppers in a large zippered bag and pour marinade over ingredients in bag. Close bag and place in refrigerator or cooler until ready to prepare.

Preheat grill to medium heat. Place a heavy skillet over heated grill. Empty contents of bag into skillet and heat, covered, about 4 to 5 minutes. Continue to grill until sausages are cooked through. To serve, spoon cooked sausages and some of the onions and peppers onto each serving plate.

BACON-WRAPPED PORK & APPLE PATTIES

4 SERVINGS • PREP: 15 MIN. • GRILL: 8–10 MIN.

¾ cup quick-cooking rolled oats
½ teaspoon ground sage
½ teaspoon salt
¼ teaspoon pepper
¼ teaspoon dried thyme, crushed
⅓ cup applesauce
1 egg, slightly beaten
¼ cup scallion, minced
1 pound lean ground pork
4 slices bacon
1 large tart green apple, cored
    and cut into thin wedges
½ medium onion, cut in
    small wedges
1 tablespoon olive oil

Preheat grill to medium. In large bowl, combine oats, sage, salt, pepper, and thyme. Stir in applesauce, egg, and scallion; mix well. Stir in ground pork until well blended. Be sure not to overmix ground meat. Form into four patties about ¾ to 1 inch thick. Wrap bacon strip around each patty; secure with toothpick. Grill 4 to 5 minutes on each side.

Meanwhile, in small skillet, cook and stir apples and onions in hot oil until tender. Sprinkle lightly with salt. Serve with pork and apple patties.

Applesauce helps keep these burgers moist and flavorful. Remind diners to be careful of the toothpicks!

FIVE-SPICE PORK CHOPS

4 SERVINGS • PREP: 10 MIN. • GRILL: 20 MIN.

Courtesy of Barry "CB" Martin, on Twitter: @BarryCBMartin.

4 thick-cut bone-in pork chops
2 tablespoons Chinese five-
    spice powder
Coarse salt and freshly ground
    black pepper to taste
1 teaspoons garlic powder
Vegetable oil spray

FRESH CITRUS SALSA

2 large navel oranges,
    peeled and cut into cubes
2 kiwi fruits, peeled and
    cut into cubes

Combine five-spice powder, salt, and pepper with garlic powder. Dry pork chops with paper towel and then rub them with spice mixture.

Spray chops with oil and place them on clean grates of preheated medium-high grill. Cook about 5 minutes or until meat browns and sear mark appear. Use tongs to turn. When chops have sear marks on both sides, remove to a holding pan to finish over indirect heat. Serve with rice and fresh citrus salsa.

Most large supermarkets carry Chinese five-spice powder, which is usually composed of cinnamon, clove, fennel seed, star anise, and peppercorns.

GRILLED PORK CHOPS WITH GARLIC, CITRUS & CILANTRO

4 SERVINGS • PREP: 25 MIN.
GRILL: 15–20 MIN. (UNTIL MEAT TEMP. IS 155°F–160°F)

Courtesy of Barry "CB" Martin, on Twitter: @BarryCBMartin.

4 pork chops (center-cut pork
   chops or the cut you prefer)
Canola oil spray
Coarse salt to taste

SAUCE

6 to 8 large garlic cloves,
   finely minced
⅓ cup fresh orange juice with pulp,
   rind reserved for grating or
   slicing at presentation
⅛ cup fresh lime juice with pulp,
   rind reserved for grating or
   slicing at presentation
⅛ cup olive oil
4 tablespoons chopped fresh
   cilantro, several sprigs reserved
   for garnish
½ teaspoon coarse salt
⅓ teaspoon red pepper flakes
⅓ teaspoon anchovy paste
1 teaspoon butter to finish sauce
   prior to serving

For the sauce, mix together all of the ingredients except the butter and citrus rinds in a large glass or nonreactive bowl, and let rest for 3 hours so that flavors will meld. Prior to use, heat on low until vapors appear and then lower to a simmer. Just before serving, add the butter. Ladle over chops and serve with grated or sliced citrus to taste.

Preheat one side of your grill to medium-high for direct grilling, and reserve the other side of the grill for indirect cooking in a tray or pan.

Season chops on both sides with pinches of salt and spritz with canola oil.

Grill chops over direct heat for 3 to 4 minutes per side until grill marks appear. To finish cooking, remove chops from direct heat and finish in the pan. Serve on platter with sauce. Garnish with grated or sliced citrus rinds.

GRILLED PORK CHOPS MARSALA

2–3 SERVINGS • PREP: 15 MIN. • GRILL: 20 MIN. (UNTIL MEAT TEMP. IS 150°F)

Courtesy of Barry "CB" Martin, on Twitter: @BarryCBMartin.

1 pound pork chops (about 2 or 3
    double-thick cut)
Coarse salt to taste
¼ cup Parmesan cheese
⅛ cup Italian flat leaf
    parsley, chopped

SAUCE
1 tablespoon butter
1 tablespoon virgin olive oil
1 shallot, finely chopped
Lemon-pepper seasoning
¼ cup Marsala wine

For the sauce, melt butter and olive oil in small skillet over medium heat on the side burner. Add shallots and allow to cook until translucent. Add lemon-pepper seasoning. Reduce heat and warm for a few minutes. Add Marsala wine; remove mixture from heat; and pour into a holding pan placed on the warming rack of the grill over indirect heat.

Dry pork chops on both sides with paper towels and then lightly season with salt. Allow to rest while you preheat grill to medium-high. Spray the chops on both sides with canola oil and place on clean, hot grates. Sear for about 3 to 4 minutes per side. If the chops are very thick, you may wish to cross-hatch sear marks.

When the chops are seared, place in a foil pan or tray with the Marsala sauce to finish over indirect heat. The pork is done when it reaches at least 150°F internal temperature. Arrange the chops on a platter; drizzle Marsala sauce over them; and top with Parmesan cheese and chopped parsley.

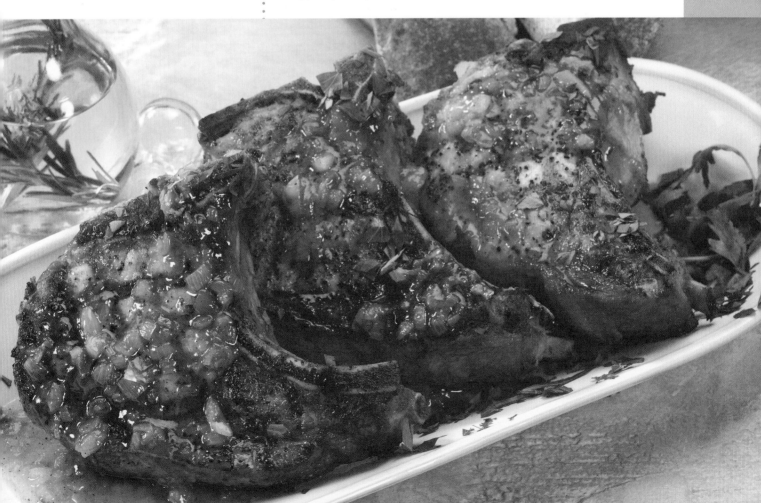

A *paillard* is a piece of meat that has been pounded thin and grilled.

GRILLED PORK PAILLARDS WITH TWO-MUSTARD SAUCE

4 SERVINGS • PREP: 10 MIN. • CHILL: 30 MIN. • GRILL: 5–10 MIN.

Courtesy of Barry "CB" Martin, on Twitter: @BarryCBMartin.

4 boneless pork loin chops, about
    1 inch thick
¼ cup olive oil
2 tablespoons apple-cider vinegar
1 clove garlic, minced
1 tablespoon coarse-
    grain mustard
1 tablespoon Dijon-style mustard
1 teaspoon brown sugar
Coarse salt and freshly ground
    black pepper to taste
Toasted baguettes

Place pork chops between two pieces of plastic wrap. Using flat end of a meat cleaver, pound and tenderize them. When all chops are pounded, season with salt and pepper to taste. Refrigerate chops in a plastic bag until ready to grill.

After seasoned pork has rested for at least 30 minutes, remove from bag while you preheat grill to medium-high. Spray meat surfaces with canola oil and, using tongs, place on grill just long enough to sear on both sides. Be careful not to overcook meat, or it will be too dry.

For sauce: Mix olive oil, vinegar, garlic, mustard, and brown sugar in a nonreactive bowl, and set aside.

Remove pork from grates when seared on both sides. Fold into toasted baguettes and serve along with sauce.

GRILLED PORK & PINEAPPLE TACOS

4 SERVINGS • PREP: 10 MIN. • MARINATE: 1 HR.
GRILL: 35–40 MIN. (UNTIL MEAT TEMP. IS 150°F)

Courtesy of haleysuzanne.wordpress.com

1 pork tenderloin (about 1 pound), trimmed
¼ cup onion, chopped
¼ cup fresh pineapple, chopped
3 garlic cloves, minced

3 chipotles in adobo sauce, sliced, with 1 tablespoon sauce reserved
1 tablespoon red wine vinegar
⅓ cup olive oil
¼ teaspoon cayenne pepper

1 tablespoon cumin
1 teaspoon pimento (smoked paprika)
½ teaspoon ancho chili powder
1 teaspoon coriander
1 teaspoon dried oregano

In bowl of a food processor, combine all ingredients except for pork tenderloin. Pulse until a thick paste forms. Place pork tenderloin in a large plastic bag and add marinade. Place in the refrigerator for 1 hour before grilling.

Grill tenderloin over medium heat for 35 to 40 minutes, until center of tenderloin registers 150°F. Let meat rest for 5 minutes before slicing into thin medallions. Serve in soft tortillas with pineapple salsa, guacamole, and a little fresh cilantro.

Serve with pineapple salsa, guacamole, tortillas, and fresh cilantro.

GRILLED PORK PATTIES

3-4 SERVINGS • PREP: 15 MIN.
CHILL: 30 MIN. • GRILL: 15–30 MIN. (UNTIL MEAT TEMP. IS 160°F)

1 pound ground
    pork, unseasoned
1 red onion, finely diced
¾ cup saltine cracker crumbs
½ cup buttermilk
2 eggs, lightly beaten
Coarse salt and freshly ground
    pepper to taste
Canola oil

Mix all of the ingredients in a large bowl, using your hands and food-safe gloves. Form 3 or 4 large meat patties with a slight indentation in the middle of each one. Place on a wax paper-covered plate and set in freezer for up to 30 minutes to chill—but not freeze.

Preheat your grill to high. Remove the pork patties from the freezer and spritz both sides with canola oil. Place the patties on clean grates. "Where they hit, they sit" until the side sears. Flip the patties to a clean section of the grates and sear that side.

When both sides of the pork patties are seared, remove to a holding pan on the warming rack (not over direct heat) and finish to an internal temperature of 160°F.

These pork patties are delicious on lightly toasted rye bread with mustard and grilled onions.

GRILLED BREADED PORK CHOPS

8 SERVINGS • PREP: 15 MIN. • GRILL: 10–15 MIN. (UNTIL MEAT TEMP. IS 160°F)

Recipe courtesy of amandascookin.com.

8 ¾-to-1-inch-thick bone-in
   center-cut pork chops
   (4½ pounds)
4 cups fresh bread crumbs,
   finely grated
⅔ cup Parmigiano-Reggiano,
   finely grated
Rounded ½ teaspoon salt
¼ teaspoon black pepper
1 cup olive oil (not extra-virgin)

Toast bread crumbs in a 350°F oven for 7 to 10 minutes until dry. Cool bread crumbs completely.

Mix bread crumbs with cheese, salt, and pepper in a shallow bowl or a 9-inch pie plate. Lightly season pork chops with salt and pepper.

Line a baking sheet with wax paper. Pour oil in another shallow bowl. Dip each chop in oil, letting excess drip off, and then dredge both sides of chops in bread-crumb mixture, pressing gently to help crumbs adhere, and transfer to baking sheet.

Preheat grill to medium-high. Grill chops, turning over once or twice, until pork is cooked through and crumbs are golden brown, about 10 minutes or until a thermometer reads 160°F.

8

I love the culture of grilling. It creates an atmosphere that is festive but casual.
–Bobby Flay

Seafood

SUCCULENT SHRIMP . . .

smoked salmon . . . Seafood and grilling are a match made in grilling heaven! Gather the family to join in the fun of prepping these tasty dishes. Check out this sample recipe to get an idea of how to divide and conquer the cooking responsibilities among every family member.

GRILLED SHRIMP & VEGETABLE KEBABS

2–4 SERVINGS • PREP: 20 MIN. • MARINATE: 1 HR. • GRILL: 4–6 MIN.

Courtesy of www.cookthink.com

2 pounds shrimp, peeled and deveined
4 to 6 wooden skewers
2 medium zucchini, cut into ½-inch half-rounds
2 medium yellow squash, cut into ½-inch half-rounds
1 medium onion, cut into ½-inch pieces

MARINADE
2 garlic cloves, minced
1 tablespoon chopped fresh oregano
2 teaspoons lemon juice
1 teaspoon lemon zest
¼ cup olive oil

Soak the skewers in water for 20 minutes. For the marinade, whisk together the garlic, oregano, lemon juice, zest, and oil.

Thread each skewer with alternating shrimp and vegetables. Place the skewers in a large baking dish, and pour the marinade over them. Turn the skewers to coat with the marinade, and refrigerate up to 1 hour.

Preheat one side of the grill to high. Lightly spray the hot side of grill with vegetable oil.

Shake any excess marinade off the skewers, and place them on the hot side of the grill. Leave them alone to brown on the one side, a minute or so. Turn skewers, and brown the vegetables on all sides until the shrimp is cooked, about 4 to 6 minutes.

CHEF TASKS

COOKING RULES FOR ROOKIES & PROS!

- Wash your hands.
- Tie back long hair.
- Clean up any messes right away.
- Ask before you taste test.
- Always listen to the Head Chef!

KIDDO CHEF

- Soak the skewers in water.
- Measure the ingredients.
- Whisk the garlic, oregano, lemon juice, zest, and oil for the marinade.
- Thread each skewer with shrimp and vegetables (with the Sous Chef's assistance).

TEENAGE SOUS CHEF

- Cut the zucchini, yellow squash, onion, and fresh oregano.
- Mince the garlic cloves.
- Zest a lemon.
- Help the Kiddo Chef thread the skewers.
- Pour the marinade over the loaded skewers.

HEAD CHEF (AKA THE GROWN-UP)

- Keep an eye on your helpers!
- Preheat one side of the grill to high.
- Grill the loaded skewers for about 4–6 minutes.

ROSEMARY & GARLIC GRILLED SHRIMP

3–4 SERVINGS • PREP: 10 MIN. • MARINATE: OVERNIGHT
GRILL: 6–10 MIN. COMBINED

1 pound raw shrimp, peeled,
   tails on
1 clove garlic, minced or chopped
1 teaspoon crushed dried
   rosemary, or 2 teaspoons
   finely chopped fresh rosemary
1 teaspoon dried basil, or 2
   teaspoons finely chopped
   fresh basil
1 teaspoon freshly ground pepper
⅛ teaspoon kosher or sea salt
1 to 2 teaspoons extra-virgin
   olive oil

Marinating time can be overnight if preparing on a stove or 1 hour before grilling.

Mix first five ingredients together in a large bowl; marinate shrimp in refrigerator 1 hour or overnight. Preheat grill to medium heat. Just before grilling, add salt and 1 to 2 teaspoons of extra-virgin olive oil to shrimp mixture; mix to coat well.

Place shrimp on grill and cook for 3 minutes on each side. Serve.

THAI SHRIMP

4 SERVINGS • PREP: 5 MIN. • GRILL: 7–10 MIN.

15 to 20 shrimp, tails on
1 tablespoon Cajun spice mix
1 cup white wine
1 teaspoon chopped
   fresh cilantro
1 teaspoon Tabasco® sauce
½ teaspoon chili paste
½ teaspoon lime juice
1 pinch of chili flakes

Preheat grill to medium-high. Place shrimp in medium-size bowl. Sprinkle Cajun spice on shrimp and toss until lightly coated. Add remaining six ingredients to medium saucepan.

Grill shrimp over medium-high heat, turning once, for 4 to 5 minutes or until pink. Place saucepan containing sauce ingredients over heat. Place shrimp in sauce; bring to a boil for about 2 minutes. Serve.

I love grilling. Grilling is an incredible way to keep healthy.
–Curtis Stone

GRILLED SHRIMP & BLUE CHEESE GRITS

10 SERVINGS • PREP: 30 MIN. • MARINATE: 1 HR. • GRILL: 5 MIN.

5 pounds shrimp, peeled and
    deveined, tails on
¼ cup olive oil
¼ cup soy sauce
¼ cup white wine
2 teaspoons Cajun seasoning or
    seasoned salt
5 pounds assorted vegetables
    (peppers, zucchini,
    onions, mushrooms)
½ cup olive oil
¼ cup sliced fresh basil
Salt and pepper to taste
4 cups stone-ground grits
1 cup crumbled blue cheese
10 skewers

Combine oil, soy sauce, wine, and Cajun seasoning. Add shrimp. Refrigerate and marinate for 1 hour. While the shrimp marinate, dice or julienne the vegetables. Heat a pan over high heat; add oil; and sauté vegetables until softened, about 5 minutes. Add basil and remove from heat. Season vegetables with salt and pepper.

Cook grits following package directions, about 20 minutes. Add blue cheese and simmer until thick. Cover to keep warm.

Preheat grill to high. Skewer shrimp and place on grates. Cook until just opaque, turning once, about 5 minutes. To serve, place grits in center of platter. Top with vegetables. Surround with shrimp.

CREOLE SHRIMP & SAUSAGE

6 SERVINGS • PREP: 10 MIN. • GRILL: 7–10 MIN.

1 pound Andouille sausage
1 pound jumbo Gulf prawns
    (about 23 per pound), cleaned
Canola oil

CREOLE SAUCE

⅓ cup Creole or stone-
    ground mustard
1 tablespoon orange marmalade
    or preserves
2 teaspoons Tabasco® sauce

For sauce, combine sauce ingredients and set on grill away from direct heat to warm.

Preheat one section of grill to high and one section to low. Sear sausages on hot side of grill and move to a pan on the low side to finish.

When sausages are just about done (160°F internal temperature), spray prawns with canola oil and place over direct heat to sear. When grill marks appear, remove them to pan with sausages. Add Creole sauce to coat prawns and sausages; serve with mac and cheese (page 237) or over white rice.

LEMONGRASS SHRIMP "LOLLIPOPS"

---

4 SERVINGS • PREP: 15–20 MIN. • GRILL: 7–15 MIN.

---

1 pound shrimp, small to medium
  in size
2 garlic cloves, roughly chopped
1 shallot, roughly chopped
1 tablespoon grated ginger
1 tablespoon olive oil
1 teaspoon salt

1 teaspoon finely grated
  black pepper
¼ cup shredded coconut,
  unsweetened, toasted until
  light brown
¼ cup chopped cilantro
2 jalapeño peppers, seeded,
  finely diced

1 lime, juiced
Rice flour or cornstarch as needed
8–10 lemongrass stalks, trimmed
  so that only white part remains
Cooking spray as needed
Soy sauce, low sodium, as needed
  (optional)

Purée shrimp, garlic, shallots, ginger, oil, salt, and pepper in a food processor until just slightly chunky. Transfer to a bowl, and fold in coconut, cilantro, peppers, and lime. Add rice flour or cornstarch, a little at a time, until mixture starts to hold form of a meatball. Mold a portion of shrimp mix around each lemongrass stalk, leaving just enough of lemongrass to hold like a stick.

Preheat one side of grill on high, leaving other half off or on low. Place a piece of aluminum foil on cool side of grill; spray with oil; and arrange lollipops so that all of them fit. Cover grill and cook for 5-10 minutes, or until shrimp starts to "set." Reapply spray and transfer lollipops from aluminum foil to hot side of grill to sear. Cook to desired doneness and serve lightly drizzled with soy sauce.

GRILLED HONEY & LIME GULF PRAWNS

3–4 SERVINGS • PREP: 1 HR. • MARINATE: 1 HR. • GRILL: 7–10 MIN.

Courtesy of Barry "CB" Martin, on Twitter: @BarryCBMartin.

1 pound jumbo Gulf prawns
   (about 21 per pound),
   cleaned, tails on

MARINADE

2 tablespoons Italian salad
   dressing
2 tablespoons dry white vermouth
⅓ cup Worcestershire sauce
1 garlic clove, finely minced
2 tablespoons finely
   chopped cilantro
1 teaspoon ground ginger

BASTING SAUCE

2 tablespoons Worcestershire
   sauce
¼ cup olive oil
¼ cup honey

Combine marinade ingredients in a sealable plastic bag and add Gulf prawns. Refrigerate for up to 1 hour. Combine basting-sauce ingredients in a nonreactive bowl and set aside.

Preheat grill to medium-high. Place marinated prawns on hot grates. Use tongs to turn, and sear all sides. When seared, remove the prawns to a holding pan away from direct heat. Brush with basting sauce and allow to finish cooking, about 3 to 5 minutes. Prawns may be served as a main course over rice or pasta or with a salad.

GARLIC-LIME ALASKA PRAWNS WITH AVOCADO CREAM

8 SERVINGS • PREP: 30 MIN. • MARINATE: 1 HR. • GRILL: 3–5 MIN.

1 ½ pounds peeled Alaska Spot
　　Prawns, or large shrimp,
　　tails on
1 ½ tablespoons kosher salt
1 ½ tablespoons sugar
¼ cup olive oil
¼ cup chopped fresh cilantro
3 cloves garlic, peeled
　　and minced
2 teaspoons grated lime peel
½ teaspoon fresh-ground pepper
Wooden or metal skewers
Avocado cream (see page 289)

In a bowl, combine salt and sugar. Rinse prawns; pat dry. Add prawns to salt-sugar mixture; stir gently to coat. Cover and refrigerate for up to 1 hour. For avocado cream, see page 289.

Rinse prawns well and drain. Preheat grill to high. In another bowl, combine olive oil, cilantro, garlic, lime peel, and pepper. Add prawns and mix to coat. Thread prawns on metal or soaked wooden skewers, running them through each prawn at the tail and head to form a C-shape.

Lay skewers on well-oiled grill grates. Close lid on grill. Cook, turning once, just until prawns are opaque throughout, about 3 to 5 minutes total. Slide prawns off skewers and arrange on platter. Set avocado cream alongside.

Note: A brief cure in salt and sugar adds flavor to prawns and makes them more tender. You can cure and marinate the prawns up to 1 day ahead. Chill in an airtight container.

PRAWNS WITH PARMESAN-HERB BASTE

6 SERVINGS • PREP: 30 MIN. • MARINATE: 30 MIN. • GRILL: 6–8 MIN.

24 Alaska Spot Prawns or jumbo
    shrimp, peeled, tails on
12 wooden skewers
¼ cup freshly grated
    Parmesan cheese
2 tablespoons olive oil
2 tablespoons red wine vinegar
1½ teaspoons dried basil
1 teaspoon coarsely ground
    black pepper

Soak skewers in water for at least 30 minutes. Blend grated cheese, olive oil, vinegar, basil, and pepper. Place two prawns on each skewer, carefully piercing through both head and tail sections. Transfer skewers to baking tray; brush each prawn with parmesan mixture; cover and refrigerate for 30 minutes. Reserve any remaining baste.

Preheat grill to medium-high. Place skewers directly over heat on well-oiled grill; cook for 3 to 4 minutes. Turn once; brush with remaining baste; and continue to cook for 3 to 4 minutes or until prawns turn pink and are opaque throughout.

LOBSTER TAILS WITH BROWN SUGAR SAUCE

4 SERVINGS • PREP: 30 MIN. • GRILL: 4–6 MIN.

4 lobster tails
3 tablespoons brown sugar
¼ cup butter
¼ cup bread crumbs

DIPPING SAUCE
¼ cup butter
2 cloves garlic, crushed
1 teaspoon chopped parsley
Salt and pepper

Combine lobster, brown sugar, butter, and crumbs in a small saucepan. Place pan over medium heat, stirring occasionally, until butter is melted and sugar is dissolved.

Preheat grill to medium. Cook lobster tails on grill for 4 to 6 minutes.

In a separate saucepan, combine ingredients for dipping sauce. Heat until butter is melted. Remove lobster from grill and baste with lobster mixture. Serve with dipping sauce.

GRILLED SEA SCALLOPS WITH LEMON & FENNEL SAUCE

6 SERVINGS • PREP: 10 MIN. • GRILL: 10–15 MIN. COMBINED

Courtesy of Barry "CB" Martin, on Twitter: @BarryCBMartin.

10 large sea scallops, fresh
    or thawed
1 large lemon with
    unblemished peel
2 egg yolks
2 teaspoons canola oil, or
    cooking oil spray
1 medium-large fennel bulb,
    sliced lengthwise and cut into
    bite-size strips
1½ cups dry white wine,
    champagne, or dry vermouth
1 cup unsalted chicken broth
⅛ teaspoon cinnamon or nutmeg
½ tablespoon corn starch
2 teaspoons sea salt or
    kosher salt
2 teaspoons freshly ground
    black pepper

Using a citrus zester or grater, zest the lemon rind. Juice remainder of lemon and reserve.

In a small bowl, add egg yolks and about 1 tablespoon of lemon juice. Mix using a whisk–do not froth.

Preheat oven to medium-high. In a medium-size saucepan, add 1 tablespoon of canola oil. Add fennel, heat slightly, and then add wine and lemon zest. Bring mixture to a boil; cook until reduced by half. Blend in broth and nutmeg or cinnamon. Return to boil and then reduce heat to medium. Cook until sauce is reduced by about half.

Add some of the sauce reduction to the egg-and-lemon-juice mixture; stir and then add the rest. Continue to cook on medium heat until creamy. If sauce is not coming together, add a very small amount of cornstarch. Add lemon juice and sea salt to taste.

Preheat grill to medium-high. Spray scallops with cooking oil; grill for about 3 minutes and then turn, placing scallops on another section of grates for approximately 3 minutes. Remove to a covered dish and set aside. Ladle a generous portion of sauce on each plate and top with three to five scallops.

CILANTRO-PESTO SNAPPER WITH RED-PEPPER SAUCE

4 SERVINGS • PREP: 20 MIN. • GRILL: 8–12 MIN.

4 snapper or mahi-mahi or
    swordfish fillets (1½ pounds)
2 tablespoons shredded
    Parmesan cheese
2 fresh garlic cloves
⅓ cup chopped walnuts
1 tablespoon extra-virgin olive oil
¼ cup fresh cilantro
¾ teaspoon pepper, divided
1 medium shallot
½ cup white wine
1 (12-ounce) jar roasted red
    peppers, drained
¾ teaspoon salt, divided
1 tablespoon butter

Preheat grill to medium-high. Make pesto: place cheese, garlic, and walnuts in food processor; process 15 to 20 seconds or until finely chopped. Add olive oil, cilantro, and ⅛ teaspoon of the pepper. Process until smooth; remove from food processor and set aside.

Mince shallot finely; combine with wine in saucepan. Bring to boil; reduce heat to medium; and cook about 4 minutes, stirring occasionally, or until liquid has reduced by about one-half.

Put red peppers in a food processor; add wine reduction; and process 20 seconds or until smooth. Pour mixture back into the same pan and bring to a boil. Reduce and simmer 3 to 4 minutes, stirring often, or until sauce thickens.

Season fish with ½ teaspoon of the salt and ¼ teaspoon of the pepper. Grill fish with the lid closed, about 4 to 6 minutes on each side, or until fish is golden and separates with a fork.

Add butter to sauce, along with remaining salt and pepper; whisk until smooth. Spoon sauce onto serving plates containing yellow rice and peas; place fish on sauce; and top with pesto.

212   *Seafood*

GRILLED BLUEFISH WITH FRESH CORN SALSA

4 SERVINGS • PREP: 15 MIN. • GRILL: 4–6 MIN. + 6–10 MIN. IN OVEN

4 bluefish fillets (6 to 8 ounces each)
Salt and black pepper to taste
3 ears fresh or frozen corn, kernels removed
6 sprigs fresh cilantro, roughly chopped
2 teaspoons finely diced red onion
1 jalapeño, seeded and finely chopped
Juice of 2 limes
1 pinch cumin
1 teaspoon canola oil

Preheat grill to medium-high. Brush fillets with oil. Cook fish for 2 to 3 minutes on each side. Remove from grill and place in 225°F oven for 3 to 5 minutes. While fillets are in the oven, heat skillet until it is hot; add salsa; and cook approximately 2 minutes or until all ingredients are warm. Remove from heat. Arrange fish on plates and garnish with salsa.

RAINBOW TROUT STUFFED WITH LEMON, SHALLOTS & HERBS

2 SERVINGS • PREP: 10–15 MIN. • GRILL: 15–20 MIN.

Courtesy of Barry "CB" Martin, on Twitter: @BarryCBMartin.

2 12- to-14-inch rainbow trout, cleaned (head and tail removed if desired)
Salt and freshly ground pepper
2 tablespoons minced shallots
2 small lemons, sliced very thin
1 bunch dill, divided
1 bunch tarragon, divided
Canola oil spray
Seasoned wood chips if desired

Preheat grill to high. Season the cavity of each fish with salt and pepper; add 1 tablespoon of shallots to each; and rub all ingredients into the fish. Add lemon slices, dill, and tarragon. Secure stuffing by wrapping fish with kitchen twine or sealing with toothpicks if necessary.

Spray skin of each fish with canola oil. Place fish in grill basket and close.

Reduce heat of grill to medium. Place fish basket on the grill and cover with a piece of aluminum foil to retain heat and moisture. Close hood and cook for approximately 5 to 7 minutes. Lift basket off grill to check for grill marks; turn basket; and grill on other side, about 5 to 7 minutes.

Remove basket and place it in a pan to allow the fish to rest for a few minutes. Using two spatulas to support the fish on each end, remove from the basket and place on a plate.

To debone fish, insert the tip of a sharp boning knife into the top of the fish and "feel" your way to the spine. Run the knife gently along the spine, toward the tail. Use two forks to lift off this half of the fish, and then pinch the top end of the spine with two fingers and peel it away from the bottom half of the fish. Replace the top half.

For a quick sauce, briefly sauté thin lemon slices with pinches of the tarragon and dill in a touch of butter and olive oil until the lemon releases its aroma. Drizzle over each fish serving and place a lemon slice on top.

Clean as you go. Drink while you cook. Make it fun. It doesn't have to be complicated.

Gwyneth Paltrow

Use a fish basket to hold the stuffed fillets—it makes turning a breeze.

GRILLED CHESAPEAKE CROAKER

4 SERVINGS • PREP: 15 MIN. • MARINATE: 1 HR. GRILL: 10 MIN. PER IN. THICKNESS

4 whole croaker or other lean, white fish, dressed
¼ cup soy sauce
2 tablespoons brown sugar
1 clove garlic, minced
1 tablespoon freshly minced ginger
2 tablespoons finely julienned orange peel
2 tablespoons orange juice
¼ teaspoon crushed red pepper flakes
2 tablespoons melted butter
4 scallions, sliced

Place fish in a bowl. Combine remaining ingredients and pour over fish. Marinate for one hour in the refrigerator. Preheat grill to medium. Place fish on grill, about 5 inches from heat, and cook about 10 minutes per inch of thickness, turning once halfway through cooking time and basting often with the marinade. When fish is tender and flakes easily, remove from grill.

Atlantic croakers are usually caught in the Chesapeake Bay between June and August. Also known as "hardhead," croakers contain delicate white meat with a sweet flavor that ranges from mild to moderately pronounced. You can substitute croaker for any recipe that calls for catfish, perch, sea trout, spot, or striped bass.

SALMON SKEWERS

12 SERVINGS • MARINATE: 30 MIN. • GRILL: 8 MIN.

1 pound skinless salmon fillet

12 wooden skewers, soaked in water

¼ cup soy sauce

¼ cup honey

1 tablespoon rice vinegar

1 teaspoon minced fresh ginger root

1 clove garlic, minced

Pinch of pepper

12 lemon wedges

Lightly oil grill grate and preheat grill to medium-high heat. Slice salmon fillet lengthwise into 12 long strips and thread each strip on a soaked wooden skewer. Place skewers in a shallow baking dish. In a medium bowl, whisk together soy sauce, honey, vinegar, minced gingerroot, minced garlic, and pepper. Pour mixture over skewers in baking dish and let marinate at room temperature for 30 minutes. Pour remaining marinade into a small saucepan. Place saucepan over grill and bring mixture to a simmer. Thread 1 lemon wedge onto end of each skewer. Place marinated skewers over heated grill and cook for 4 minutes on each side, brushing often with simmering marinade mixture. Salmon is done when it flakes easily with a fork.

These burgers will be very soft. If the burgers aren't holding together on the grill, place a piece of aluminum foil on the grill and cook them on that. As the sliders begin to "set," transfer them off the foil to finish cooking.

SALMON SLIDER

8 SERVINGS • PREP: 10–15 MIN.
REFRIGERATE/SUFFUSE: 30 MIN.–OVERNIGHT • GRILL: 6–12 MIN.

1 pound salmon fillet
½ cup egg substitute or 2 whole eggs
¼ cup smoothly puréed roasted fennel
¼ cup Dijon mustard
¼ cup thinly sliced chives or green onions (scallions)
2 tablespoons dark chili powder
Salt and pepper to taste
Whole-wheat bread crumbs, couscous, or instant oatmeal as needed
Cooking spray as needed
Tomato and red onion, sliced, as needed
Romaine or iceberg lettuce as needed
Whole-wheat buns, bread, or English muffins (optional)

Place salmon, eggs, fennel, mustard, chives, chili powder, salt, and pepper in a food processor, and "pulse" blend until mixed but not puréed. (Mixture may be very soft and moist at this point.) Transfer mixture to a bowl and add the binder you choose (bread crumbs, etc.) a little at a time until mixture becomes malleable and you can form patties. Make eight slider-size burgers and let them rest for 30 minutes to overnight (in a refrigerator).

Preheat grill to medium-high. Lightly mist sliders with cooking spray to prevent sticking. Cook sliders to 145°F internal temperature or desired doneness. Place sliders on toasted buns or your bread of choice, and serve with your favorite burger condiments.

CEDAR-PLANK-GRILLED SALMON FILLETS WITH MUSTARD DILL AND CANNELLINI BEAN SAUCE

4 SERVINGS • PREP: 15–20 MIN. • GRILL: 10–15 MIN.

4 salmon fillets, 3-4 ounces each
4 pieces picked dill
Salt and pepper to taste
Cedar planks, soaked in water or
    white wine as needed

MUSTARD-DILL-AND-CANNELLINI-BEAN SAUCE

1 cup cannellini beans (white
    kidney beans)
¼ cup Dijon mustard
¼ cup extra-virgin olive oil
¼ cup roasted garlic
1 lemon, juiced
Salt and pepper to taste
Water as needed
¼ cup finely chopped dill, with
    most of the stems removed
¼ cup low-fat or fat-free
    Greek yogurt

Preheat one side of grill to high. For sauce, place all ingredients (except for dill and yogurt) in a blender and purée on high until smooth. Adjust consistency with water (if needed). Transfer to a grill-safe pan and warm through using indirect heat. Place cedar plank on grill; season salmon with salt and pepper; place a piece of dill on top of each piece of salmon; place salmon on top of cedar plank; and cover grill. Cook salmon to desired doneness and remove from heat.

To finish sauce, remove from the heat and stir in yogurt and dill.

To serve, place a piece of salmon on a plate and top with a tablespoon of bean sauce.

BLACKENED SALMON WITH GRILLED MAPLE BUTTERNUT SQUASH

4 SERVINGS • PREP: 10–15 MIN. • GRILL: 18–30 MIN. • REST: 10 MIN.

1½ pounds wild salmon fillet or Arctic char, skin on
1 large butternut squash, washed
1½ teaspoons salt
1½ tablespoons maple syrup
Cooking spray as needed

BLACKENED SEASONING

1 teaspoon ground white pepper
1 teaspoon garlic powder
1 teaspoon onion powder
1 teaspoon ground chili powder
1 teaspoon dried oregano
1 teaspoon paprika
1 teaspoon ground black pepper
1½ tablespoons canola oil (so salmon does not stick to grill)

Preheat grill to medium-high. Peel the squash and cut off the top and bottom. Slice in half lengthwise; scoop out pulp and seeds; and discard. (Keep the seeds and roast them for a snack!) Slice the squash into long slices from top to bottom about 1 inch thick; season with salt; spray with cooking spray; place on the grill; and grill each side for 5–10 minutes or until fork tender. Take the squash off the grill; cut it into ½-inch cubes; and drizzle it with maple syrup.

Combine and mix all of the ingredients for the blackened rub in a small bowl. Brush the salmon with 1 tablespoon of oil and rub the entire salmon fillet with the blackened seasoning. Before putting the salmon on the grill, brush the grill grates with the remaining oil. Place the salmon on the grill, skin side down.

Close the grill (so it acts like an oven for even cooking); grill for 4–5 minutes and then gently turn the salmon over and grill for another 4–5 minutes. Take the salmon off the grill and set it aside to rest for 10 minutes. If the salmon seems slightly raw in the center, don't worry; it will continue to cook while resting.

Remove the skin from the salmon before serving it with lemon slices.

ARCTIC CHAR WITH PEPPER GUACAMOLE

4 SERVINGS • PREP: 10–15 MIN. • GRILL: 6–10 MIN.

4 Arctic char fillets, 4 ounces
    each (or substitute salmon)
1 tablespoon chili pepper
Salt and pepper to taste
Cooking spray as needed

GUACAMOLE
1 ripe avocado
1 teaspoon diced shallots
2 tablespoons fresh lime juice
½ cup cilantro
½ cup small-diced tricolor
    bell peppers,
1 teaspoon ground cumin
1 teaspoon ground coriander
Salt and pepper to taste

Preheat grill to high. Coat the char with the chili pepper, salt, and pepper. Spray the grill lightly with the cooking spray and sear the fillets on a 45-degree angle with the grill, skin side up. After 2 minutes, turn the fillets 90 degrees, creating a diamond pattern on the fish. Flip to the skin side and cook to desired doneness.

For the guacamole, place all of the ingredients in a bowl and mash them together using a fork or whisk. Adjust the seasonings.

Serve the char with a heaping tablespoon of the guacamole on top.

SEA BASS WITH TROPICAL SALSA

4 SERVINGS • PREP: 25–30 MIN. • REFRIGERATE: 15 MIN.–2 HRS. • GRILL: 5–10 MIN.

4 sea bass fillets, 3–4 ounces each
Salt, pepper, and freshly ground
    cumin to taste
Cooking spray as needed

TROPICAL SALSA
½ cup finely diced tomatoes
¼ cup finely diced red bell pepper
¼ cup finely diced red onion
¼ cup finely diced cucumber,
    finely diced
2 tablespoons finely diced jalapeño
    pepper (optional)

2 tablespoons olive oil
½ cup medium-diced pineapple
¼ cup medium-diced mango
¼ cup chopped cilantro
2 tablespoons chopped mint
¼ cup lime juice
Salt and pepper to taste

Mix all of the salsa ingredients in a bowl and let it sit for 15 minutes to 2 hours under refrigeration.

Preheat grill to high. Season the fish and lightly spray with cooking spray. Carefully grill the bass until it reaches desired doneness. Serve topped with a generous portion of the tropical salsa.

GRILLED HALIBUT

4 SERVINGS • GRILL: 8–12 MIN.

1 ¼ pounds fresh or frozen
   halibut steaks or other fish
   (1 inch thick)
1 teaspoon olive oil
3 cloves garlic, minced
¼ teaspoon salt
¼ teaspoon black pepper
Cherry or yellow pear-shaped
   tomato halves, optional
Fresh chives, optional

Thaw fish if frozen. Rinse fish and pat dry with paper towels. Cut into four serving-size pieces if necessary. In a small bowl, combine oil, garlic, salt, and black pepper; mix well. Spread mixture evenly over fish, rubbing it in with fingers. To cook, lightly oil the grate and preheat grill to medium heat. Place fish on the grate and grill, uncovered, for 8 to 12 minutes or until fish flakes easily with a fork, turning once during cooking. Garnish with tomato halves and chives, if desired.

9

Cooking is a caring and nurturing act. It's kind of the ultimate gift for someone, to cook for them.

–Curtis Stone

Vegetables, Sides & Salads

ALL HANDS ON DECK!

AN OUT-OF-A-BAG SALAD AND stovetop veggies probably don't top the charts of everyone's favorite foods. But wait until you liven things up by moving to the grill for your sides and salads! Grown-ups and kids alike will enjoy the pumped-up flavors that grilling can reveal. Here's a sample recipe that everyone in the family can have fun making and eating!

PORTOBELLO PIZZA

4 SERVINGS • PREP: 5 MIN. • GRILL: 15 MIN.

4 large portobello mushrooms
¾ cup tomato sauce (can be homemade or your
   favorite store-bought brand)
2 ounces fresh mozzarella cheese (one slice
   per mushroom)

Preheat grill to medium-high. Clean the mushrooms with a wet paper towel. Remove the stem and clean out the "gills." Once you have prepped the mushrooms, fill them with desired amount of tomato sauce and then top each mushroom and sauce with the mozzarella. Place the mushrooms on the grill and lower the cover. Cook until mushroom is fully done and cheese is bubbling, about 15 minutes.

CHEF TASKS

COOKING RULES FOR ROOKIES & PROS!

- Wash your hands.
- Tie back long hair.
- Clean up any messes right away.
- Ask before you taste test.
- Always listen to the Head Chef!

KIDDO CHEF

- Gently scrub the mushrooms with a wet paper towel.
- Carefully add tomato sauce to each mushroom.
- Place cheese on top of each mushroom.

TEENAGE SOUS CHEF

- Cut the stems off the mushrooms.
- Rinse out the mushrooms' "gills."
- Carefully add tomato sauce to each mushroom.
- Place cheese on top of each mushroom.

HEAD CHEF (AKA THE GROWN-UP)

- Keep an eye on your helpers!
- Preheat the grill to medium-high.
- Grill the loaded mushrooms for about 15 minutes.

GRILLED CORN ON THE COB

4 SERVINGS • GRILL: 20–30 MIN.

4 ears of corn, husks intact
1 ½ tablespoons butter, melted
½ teaspoon ground cumin
¼ teaspoon chili powder
1 teaspoon fresh
   chopped cilantro

Preheat grill to medium heat. Pull back husks from ears of corn, leaving the husks attached. Remove 1 strip of husk from the inner side of each ear of corn and set aside.

In a small bowl, combine melted butter, ground cumin, chili powder and chopped cilantro. Brush melted butter mixture on corn. Bring husks up to cover corn and tie husks together with reserved strips of husk. Place corn on hot grate and grill for 20 to 30 minutes, turning occasionally.

HERB-STUFFED TOMATOES

4 TOMATOES • GRILL: 30 MIN.

4 large tomatoes
Ketchup to taste
1 cup herb-seasoned stuffing mix
¼ cup grated Romano cheese
2 tablespoons chopped
    green onion
2 tablespoons butter, melted
Dash black pepper
Salt to taste

Slice a thin portion off top of each tomato; scoop out pulp and reserve, discarding tops. Invert shells on paper towels to drain. In a medium bowl, combine pulp, ketchup, stuffing mix, cheese, onion, butter, and black pepper. Sprinkle tomato shells with salt; fill with stuffing mixture. Wrap bottom of each tomato in a piece of heavy-duty aluminum foil. Preheat grill to medium-high heat and grill tomatoes on foil about 30 minutes.

TOMATO SALAD ON THE GRILL

6–8 SERVINGS

1 tablespoon olive oil
1 tablespoon fresh lemon juice
2 cloves garlic, minced
3 dashes Worcestershire sauce

½ cup fresh chopped basil
5 large tomatoes, quartered
Salt and pepper to taste
½ loaf crusty bread, torn into pieces

Preheat grill to medium-high heat and cover the grate with aluminum foil. In a small bowl, whisk together olive oil, lemon juice, minced garlic, and Worcestershire sauce. Mix in chopped basil and set aside. In a medium bowl, combine quartered tomatoes, salt, and pepper. Drizzle additional olive oil over aluminum foil on grill. Turn tomatoes out onto aluminum foil on grill and heat, turning frequently, until browned. In a medium bowl, toss together grilled tomatoes and chopped basil mixture. Season with additional salt and pepper to taste. Serve tomato salad with pieces of crusty bread for dipping.

VEGGIES ON THE BARBIE

4 SERVINGS • GRILL: 15–20 MIN.

8 cherry tomatoes, halved

1 ½ cups corn kernels

1 sweet red pepper,
    sliced diagonally

½ sweet green pepper,
    sliced diagonally

1 small onion, peeled and sliced

1 tablespoon fresh chopped basil

¼ teaspoon grated lemon peel

Salt and pepper to taste

1 tablespoon plus 1 teaspoon
    butter, cut into pieces

Preheat grill to medium heat. In a large bowl, combine halved cherry tomatoes, corn, red and green pepper slices, onion slices, fresh chopped basil, grated lemon peel, salt, and pepper. Gently toss until well mixed. Cut two 12-inch square pieces of aluminum foil. Divide vegetable mixture in half and place each half in the center of one aluminum foil piece. Dot pieces of butter over vegetables and fold the foil to enclose vegetables in packets. Place packets on grill and cook for 15 to 20 minutes, or until vegetable are tender. Season with additional salt and pepper before serving.

BACON & CORN STUFFED PEPPERS

4 SERVINGS • GRILL: 18–25 MIN.

2 cups frozen corn, thawed
⅓ cup salsa
6 green onions, chopped

1 medium green bell pepper, halved, seeds and membranes removed
1 medium red bell pepper, halved, seeds and membranes removed

¼ cup shredded mozzarella cheese
2 bacon strips, cooked and crumbled
Additional salsa, optional

Preheat grill to medium heat. In a large bowl, combine corn, salsa and onions; spoon mixture into bell pepper halves. Coat heavy-duty aluminum foil with nonstick cooking spray. Place peppers on foil, folding foil over and sealing edges, allowing space inside for air circulation. Close grill lid for 15 to 20 minutes until peppers are tender. Sprinkle with cheese and bacon. Return to grill for 3 to 5 minutes or until cheese is melted. Serve with additional salsa, if desired.

BACON-WRAPPED ASPARAGUS

4–6 SERVINGS • GRILL: 8–12 MIN.

24 asparagus spears
Black pepper to taste
12 strips of bacon, cut in half crosswise

Place asparagus on a sheet of waxed paper; coat with cooking spray. Sprinkle with black pepper; turn to coat. Wrap bacon around each spear; secure ends with toothpicks. Grill bacon-wrapped asparagus uncovered for 4 to 6 minutes on each side or until bacon is crisp.

BLACK BEAN & RICE-STUFFED PEPPERS

6 SERVINGS • GRILL: 15–20 MIN.

1 (15-ounce) can black beans, drained and rinsed
¾ cup cooked white rice
4 medium green onions, sliced
¼ cup chopped fresh cilantro
2 tablespoon vegetable oil
2 tablespoon lime juice
1 clove garlic, finely chopped
¼ teaspoon salt
3 large bell peppers, cut in half lengthwise, seeds and membranes removed
1 Roma tomato, diced

Preheat grill to medium heat. Mix beans, rice, onions, cilantro, oil, lime juice, garlic, and salt. Spoon filling into peppers. Preheat grill to medium heat. Place peppers on foil, folding foil over and sealing edges, allowing space inside for air circulation. Close grill lid for 15 to 20 minutes until peppers are tender. Carefully open foil packets and sprinkle with tomato.

GRILLED EGGPLANT SOUP

6 SERVINGS • GRILL: 6–8 MIN. • COOK: 20 MIN.

2 (1½-pound) eggplants, sliced
1 tablespoon chopped
    fresh thyme
2 tablespoon chopped
    garlic, divided
¼ cup plus 3 tablespoon olive
    oil, divided
2 tablespoon balsamic vinegar
2 leeks, sliced
2 cups beef stock
2 cups chicken stock
Salt to taste
Black pepper to taste
Sour cream
Fresh thyme

Peel eggplant if desired (the skin can be eaten from small, immature eggplant) and cut eggplant into approximately ½-inch slices. These slices can be cut lengthwise, crosswise, or at a diagonal. Brush both sides of each slice lightly with oil and sprinkle with salt and black pepper.

Preheat grill to medium or high heat. In a small bowl, combine thyme, 1 tablespoon garlic, 3 tablespoons oil, and vinegar. Brush mixture on both sides of eggplant slices. Grill for about 6 to 8 minutes, turning once halfway through grilling time; set aside. In a saucepan, heat remaining ¼ cup oil; add 1 tablespoon garlic and leeks. When leeks are lightly brown, add the beef stock, chicken stock, and grilled eggplant. Simmer 20 minutes. Purée in food processor. Add salt and black pepper. To serve, ladle into bowls and top with sour cream and fresh thyme.

SIMPLE MARINATED MUSHROOMS

4 SERVINGS • MARINATE: 15 MIN.–2 HR. • GRILL: 12–16 MIN.

1 pound fresh mushrooms, stems
    removed and reserved
⅓ cup red wine vinegar
2½ tablespoons olive oil
Salt to taste
Black pepper to taste
1 clove garlic, crushed
Grated Parmesan cheese

Cut stems into thick slices and place slices and caps in a resealable plastic bag. In a small bowl, combine vinegar, oil, salt, black pepper, and garlic. Add marinade to mushrooms. Seal bag. Refrigerate at least 15 minutes, but no longer than 2 hours.

Preheat grill to medium heat. Place mushrooms and marinade on heavy-duty aluminum foil. Fold foil around mushrooms and seal edges, creating a packet. Place packet on the grill for about 12 to 16 minutes, turning every few minutes. Remove foil packet from grill and open carefully. Remove mushrooms and sprinkle with Parmesan cheese.

CRAB-STUFFED MUSHROOMS

12 MUSHROOMS

12 fresh small mushrooms
1 (8 ounces) package cream
   cheese, softened
1 cluster of steamed crab meat,
   cut into small pieces
3 cloves garlic, chopped
4 ounces shredded
   mozzarella cheese
4 ounces Asiago cheese

Preheat grill to medium heat. Remove and chop mushroom stems. In a large bowl, combine cream cheese, crab meat, garlic, and stems. Stuff mushrooms with cream cheese mixture. In a small bowl, combine mozzarella and Asiago cheeses; dip stuffed side of each mushroom into the mixture. Place mushrooms, stuffing side up, on a disposable foil pan or heavy-duty aluminum foil that has been sprayed with nonstick cooking spray. Grill with lid closed until cheese is melted.

You don't need a silver fork to eat good food.
–Paul Prudhomme

MUSHROOM KEBABS

4 SERVINGS • GRILL: 4–6 MIN.

¾ cup fresh mushrooms
2 red bell peppers, seeded and
   cut into 1-inch pieces
1 green bell pepper, seeded and
   cut into 1-inch pieces
¼ cup olive oil
2 tablespoons lemon juice
1 clove garlic, minced
2 teaspoons chopped fresh thyme
1 teaspoon chopped
   fresh rosemary
¼ teaspoon salt
¼ teaspoon black pepper

Brush grate with oil and preheat grill to medium heat. Thread mushrooms, red and green bell peppers alternately on skewers*. In a small bowl, mix oil, lemon juice, garlic, thyme, rosemary, salt, and black pepper. Brush mushrooms and bell peppers with oil mixture and place kebabs on grill. Baste frequently with oil mixture during grilling. Cook about 4 to 6 minutes or until mushrooms are tender and thoroughly cooked.

* If using wooden skewers, be sure to soak in water at least 30 minutes before using to prevent burning.

MINI MUSHROOM MAC 'N' CHEESE

4 SERVINGS

2 cups (4 ounces) uncooked cavatappi (or other spiral, tube-shaped pasta)

1 pound assorted mushrooms, cut into ½-inch pieces

1 tablespoon olive oil

¼ cup butter

¼ cup flour

½ teaspoon salt

2 cups milk

6 ounces fresh goat cheese

½ cup shredded mozzarella cheese

2 tablespoons minced fresh rosemary

1 tablespoon minced fresh thyme

Preheat grill to medium heat. Cook pasta according to package directions. Grill mushrooms in a disposable foil pan with oil until mushrooms brown on one side. Turn mushrooms and grill until the other side is brown. In a large saucepan, melt butter and stir in flour. Cook to lightly toast flour. Stir in salt and whisk in milk. Bring to a low boil over medium-high heat, stirring occasionally to slightly thicken sauce, about 5 minutes. Remove sauce from heat, add goat cheese, mozzarella cheese, rosemary, and thyme; stir until cheeses melt. Stir in mushrooms and pasta and place into a 4- to 6-cup foil pan that has been sprayed with nonstick cooking spray. Cover pan with aluminum foil and place on grill; close lid. Bake until cheese bubbles around edges, about 15 to 20 minutes. Remove from grill and let rest about 5 minutes. Serve warm.

GRILLED POTATO PLANKS

4 SERVINGS • PREP: 5 MIN. • GRILL: 18 MIN.

Courtesy of www.christopherranch.com

1½ pounds (about 3 large) unpeeled baking potatoes, cut into ½-inch-thick slices
3 tablespoons olive oil
2 teaspoons finely chopped fresh rosemary
1 garlic clove, minced
½ teaspoon salt

Preheat grill to medium-high. Combine oil, rosemary, garlic, and salt in dish. Add potato slices and turn until well-coated. Grill potatoes for about 8 minutes. Turn, and continue grilling 10 minutes longer or until cooked. Remove from grill and serve.

Grilling is an easy tradition to start at any age! To get started, one only needs a modest investment in equipment and a little bit of outdoor space.

–Barton Seaver

CHEESY POTATOES WITH BACON

4–6 SERVINGS • GRILL: 20–30 MIN.

1½ to 2 pounds potatoes, peeled
   and thinly sliced
8 strips bacon, cooked
   and crumbled
1 large onion, chopped
1½ cups mozzarella cheese
½ cup grated Parmesan cheese
2 teaspoons salt
1 teaspoon black pepper
6 tablespoons butter

Preheat grill to medium heat. Spray a large sheet of heavy-duty aluminum foil with nonstick cooking spray. On foil, combine potatoes, bacon, and onion; sprinkle with mozzarella and Parmesan cheeses, salt, and black pepper. Dot with butter. Fold foil, sealing all edges to make a packet. Grill over medium heat, with grill lid closed, 20 to 30 minutes or until tender.

EASY HERBED POTATOES

4–6 SERVINGS

2 tablespoons olive oil

1 tablespoon balsamic vinegar

1 teaspoon garlic salt

1 teaspoon dried rosemary

¼ teaspoon pepper

2 small Vidalia onions, peeled
and chopped

3 large carrots, peeled and
sliced diagonally

2 red potatoes, cut into wedges

Preheat grill to high heat. In a 9 x 13-inch metal baking dish, combine olive oil, vinegar, garlic salt, dried rosemary, and pepper. Add onion, carrot slices, and potatoes. Toss until evenly coated. Place baking dish directly over grill. Cover grill and cook, turning occasionally, until vegetables are tender.

GRILLED POTATO SALAD

6 SERVINGS • GRILL: 10–16 MIN.

1½ pounds potatoes (not small new potatoes), sliced

¾ cup plus 2 tablespoons olive oil, divided

Salt to taste

Black pepper to taste

2 teaspoons Dijon mustard

¾ cup apple-cider vinegar

1 tablespoon finely chopped fresh rosemary

½ cup chopped black olives

Spray grate with nonstick cooking spray. Preheat grill to medium heat. Slice potatoes into ¼-inch thick slices. In a large bowl, combine 2 tablespoons of the oil, salt, and black pepper. Add potatoes, tossing to coat. Place potato slices on the grate and grill 5 to 8 minutes per side.

Meanwhile, in a small bowl, whisk together mustard, vinegar, remaining ¾ cup oil, salt, and black pepper to make a vinaigrette. Stir in rosemary and olives. When potatoes are tender, transfer them back to the large bowl, cutting them into smaller pieces, if desired. Pour vinaigrette over potatoes and toss well while still warm. The potatoes will absorb the vinaigrette.

QUICK SWEET POTATOES 'N' APPLES

6 SERVINGS • GRILL: 15–20 MIN.

1 can (18 ounces) sweet
    potatoes, drained
¼ cup apple butter
2 tablespoons brown sugar
¼ teaspoon ground cinnamon
1 tablespoon butter

Preheat grill to medium heat. Cut one large piece of heavy-duty aluminum foil; spray with nonstick cooking spray. Slice sweet potatoes on foil. In a small bowl, combine apple butter, brown sugar, 1 tablespoon water, and cinnamon. Spoon over potatoes; dot with butter. Fold in sides of foil and seal well. Grill packet, seam side up, for 15 to 20 minutes or until heated through.

PECAN-GLAZED SWEET SPUDS

4 SERVINGS • GRILL: 20 MIN.

4 medium sweet potatoes
½ cup pecan halves
½ cup brown sugar
¼ cup butter

Parboil sweet potatoes until tender. Cut into ½-inch slices. Place slices on heavy-duty aluminum foil and arrange pecans on top. Sprinkle with brown sugar and dot with butter. Bring up sides of foil and double-fold top and ends to seal, leaving room for heat circulation inside. Bake on preheated hot grill for about 20 minutes.

TENDER CARROT SLICES

4 SERVINGS

4 large carrots, peeled
2 tablespoons olive oil

Cover the grate of the grill with aluminum foil. Preheat grill or place grilling grate over campfire. Using a sharp knife, cut carrots in half lengthwise. Brush carrots with olive oil and lay carrots over aluminum foil on grill. Cook carrots to desired tenderness, turning every few minutes.

INDIAN-SPICE-GRILLED CAULIFLOWER

4 SERVINGS • PREP: 15 MIN. • GRILL: 5 MIN.

4 tablespoons butter
¼ teaspoon cinnamon
¼ teaspoon dried coriander
½ teaspoon grated fresh ginger
⅛ teaspoon crushed saffron
    threads (optional)
¼ teaspoon ground cardamom
1 tablespoon minced garlic
1 head cauliflower, cut into florets

In a skillet, cook the butter over medium heat until golden brown. Combine the cinnamon, coriander, ginger, saffron, cardamom, and garlic; stir this mixture into the butter. Add the cauliflower, stirring to coat the florets with sauce, and cook for 3 to 4 minutes, stirring occasionally. Transfer the cauliflower florets to a grill basket, saving any remaining sauce for basting. Grill the vegetables over high heat, basting and turning them frequently. Cook for 5 minutes or until they are crunchy-tender. Be careful not to overcook. Serve.

BBQ BAKED BEANS

15–20 SERVINGS • GRILL: 1½ HR.

2 pounds hamburger, browned
and drained
1 (1 ounce) pkg. dry onion
soup mix
1 (12-ounce) bottle
barbecue sauce
¼ cup prepared yellow mustard
1 tablespoon vinegar
¼ cup brown sugar
2 (15-ounce) cans pork
and beans

Preheat grill to medium heat. In a large bowl, combine hamburger, soup mix, barbecue sauce, 1 cup cold water, mustard, vinegar, brown sugar, and beans. Pour into a heatproof pan and grill with grill lid closed, about 1½ hours.

OUTSTANDING ONION RINGS

4 SERVINGS • PREP: 30 MIN. • COOK: 10 MIN.

1 giant sweet onion
1½ cups flour
1 teaspoon salt
¼ teaspoon freshly ground
    black pepper
⅛ teaspoon cayenne pepper
1½ cups buttermilk
Vegetable oil for frying
Popcorn salt to taste

Peel the onion, removing the tough outer layer of the onion with the skin. Cut into horizontal slices about ½ inch thick. Separate the slices into individual rings.

Combine the flour, salt, black pepper, and cayenne in a shallow bowl; stir to mix. Pour the buttermilk into a separate bowl. Coat the onion rings, a few at a time, in the flour mixture, shaking off the excess, and place them in a baking dish. One or two at a time, dip the onion rings into buttermilk. Remove, and coat them again in the flour mixture, shaking off any excess. Transfer the rings back to the baking dish. Repeat the process with all the remaining onion rings.

Pour the oil to a depth of ½ to 1 inch in a cast-iron skillet or deep fryer, and heat over medium-high heat. When the temperature reaches 375°F, add onion rings a few at a time. Allow enough room for each of the onion rings to fry without touching one another. Cook, turning once, until deep golden brown on both sides, about 3 minutes. Remove the onion rings from the oil and drain. While the onion rings are hot, salt them to taste. Be sure the oil returns to 375°F before frying additional rings. Serve at once, or place the onion rings on an ovenproof dish and keep them warm in a 200°F oven until ready to serve.

GRILLED RATATOUILLE

½ large red onion, quartered
1 package cherry tomatoes
2 zucchini, sliced
1 package sliced mushrooms
2 large yellow squash, sliced
1 red pepper, julienned
1 yellow pepper, julienned
1 green pepper, julienned
¾ cup balsamic vinegar
¼ cup Worcestershire sauce
1 tablespoon olive oil
1 tablespoon Creole seasoning
1 teaspoon seasoned salt

Combine ingredients in a large bowl and then in a plastic storage bag. Marinate in the refrigerator for at least 2 hours. Preheat grill to medium-high. Grill the mixture in a grill wok or a basket until the vegetables are tender, stirring occasionally. The vegetables are best when somewhat charred.

PINEAPPLE SALSA

4 SERVINGS • PREP: 5 MIN.

3 medium tomatoes, diced
1 large onion, finely chopped
¼ fresh pineapple, cut into chunks
1 clove garlic, minced
1 bunch of cilantro, chopped
Salt and pepper
Olive oil
Chili flakes

Combine tomatoes, onion, pineapple chunks, garlic, and cilantro in a medium bowl. Season with salt, pepper, olive oil, and chili flakes to taste.

Cooking is like painting or writing a song. Just as there are only so many notes or colors, there are only so many flavors— it's how you combine them that sets you apart.

–Wolfgang Puck

ASIAN SUPER SLAW

8 SERVINGS • MARINATE: 30 MIN. • PREP: 15 MIN.

6 tablespoons rice vinegar

6 tablespoons vegetable oil

5 tablespoons creamy peanut butter

3 tablespoons soy sauce

3 tablespoons golden brown sugar, packed

2 tablespoons minced fresh ginger

1½ tablespoons minced garlic

5 cups thinly sliced green cabbage

2 cups thinly sliced red cabbage

2 large red or yellow bell peppers, cut into matchstick-size strips

2 medium carrots, peeled and cut into matchstick-size strips

8 large scallions, cut into matchstick-size strips

½ cup chopped fresh cilantro

Whisk together the first seven ingredients in a small bowl until blended. Cover and let chill. (The dressing can be made 1 day ahead.) Let the dressing stand at room temperature for 30 minutes before continuing.

Combine the remaining ingredients in a large bowl. Add the dressing and toss to coat. Season the salad with salt and pepper, and serve.

ONE-BEER SKILLET BREAD

12 SERVINGS • PREP: 15 MIN. • GRILL: 1 HR.

3 cups self-rising flour
¼ cup sugar
Pinch salt
1 can beer
1 egg, beaten

Preheat grill to medium low. Mix flour, sugar, salt, and beer, and lightly knead into a dough. Pour dough into a well-seasoned cast-iron skillet, or add a bit of bacon grease to the bottom and sides of a pan. Brush the top of the dough with the beaten egg; then top with the onions, corn, or other additions.

Place skillet on grill over indirect heat. Close lid. After about 50 minutes, move the skillet over direct heat and continue cooking for 10 minutes.

Skillet bread is done when toothpick inserted in the center comes out clean. Flip bread over onto a cooling rack. Serve in wedges.

OPTIONAL ADDITIONS

Sliced onions, corn, bacon bits, bell pepper, jalapeño, or chopped herbs

GRILLED POLENTA

6 SERVINGS • PREP: 1 HR. • CHILL: 1 HR.–OVERNIGHT • GRILL: 10 MIN.

3 cups water
1 teaspoon salt
2 tablespoons unsalted butter
¾ cup polenta or coarse-ground
    yellow cornmeal
¾ cup freshly grated
    Parmesan cheese
¼ teaspoons cayenne pepper
Olive oil

Combine the water, salt, and butter in a saucepan and bring to a boil. Gradually add the polenta, whisking constantly to avoid lumps. Reduce heat and continue cooking, stirring constantly, until mixture is very thick, 10 to 15 minutes. Remove the pan from the heat and stir in Parmesan cheese and cayenne pepper.

Line a 9-inch pie plate with plastic wrap, letting it extend over the edges. Spread the polenta evenly over plastic wrap and smooth the top. Cover tightly with plastic wrap, and chill until firm, at least 1 hour.

Preheat the grill to medium. Invert the pie plate to allow molded polenta to be removed. Peel off the plastic wrap. Cut the polenta into six wedges. Brush each wedge lightly on both sides with oil. Arrange the polenta wedges on the cooking grate. Grill, turning 2 or 3 times, until golden, about 10 minutes.

YOU WON'T KNOW IT'S NOT POTATO SALAD

16½-CUP SERVINGS • PREP: 15 MIN. • COOK: 8–10 MIN. • CHILL: 30 MIN.–1½ HR. +

2 1-pound bags frozen
  cauliflower florets
1 10-ounce bag frozen peas
  and carrots
1¾ cups reduced-fat mayonnaise
  or salad dressing
1 teaspoon granulated sugar
1 teaspoon salt
¼ teaspoon pepper
¼ teaspoon paprika
1 tablespoon cider vinegar
1 teaspoon yellow mustard
1 cup chopped celery (2½ stalks)
⅔ cup chopped onion (about
  1 medium)
4 hard-boiled eggs, peeled,
  chopped, and cooled

Place cauliflower, peas, and carrots in a large microwavable bowl; cover with microwavable waxed paper. Cook on high 8 to 10 minutes or until tender, pausing halfway to stir, and then continue to cook. Drain in colander and rinse with cold water to stop cooking process. Place colander with vegetables over same bowl; refrigerate at least 30 minutes.

In a small bowl, make the dressing by combining the next seven ingredients; set aside.

Remove vegetables from refrigerator and pat dry with paper towels; discard any liquid in bowl. Chop large florets into ¾-inch chunks. Return to bowl with the other vegetables and add the celery, onion, and chopped eggs.

Coat with the dressing. If desired, cover and refrigerate at least 1 hour or until well chilled before serving.

GRILLED SALMON SALAD WITH VINAIGRETTE

4 SERVINGS • PREP: 30 MIN. • GRILL: 10–15 MIN.

SALAD DRESSING

⅓ cup extra-virgin olive oil
¼ cup tarragon vinegar
1 tablespoon Dijon mustard
1 clove garlic, pressed

SALAD

4 salmon steaks or fillets (4 to 6
    ounces each), fresh, thawed,
    or frozen
1 large apple, cored and chopped
1 ripe avocado, peeled
    and chopped
1 tablespoon lemon juice
1 package (10 ounces) prepared
    salad greens
1 navel orange, peeled
    and chopped
¼ medium red onion, sliced
    very thin
⅓ cup slivered almonds
⅓ cup raisins
2 teaspoons olive, canola, peanut,
    or grape-seed oil
Salt and pepper

Rinse any ice from frozen fish under cold water; pat dry with paper towel. Preheat grill to medium-high. Brush both sides of salmon with oil. Place salmon on grill and cook about 3 to 4 minutes until good sear marks appear. Turn salmon, and season with salt and pepper. Reduce heat to medium and close grill lid. Cook an additional 6 to 8 minutes for frozen salmon or 3 to 4 minutes for fresh or thawed fish. Cook just until fish is opaque throughout.

Mix dressing ingredients in a small bowl; set aside. Place chopped apple and avocado in a large salad bowl. Drizzle with lemon juice. Add salad greens, orange, onion, almonds, and raisins; mix.

Divide salad among four plates; place salmon portion on top. Drizzle with vinaigrette dressing and serve.

10

Desserts

THE MOST ANTICIPATED PART of a meal for kids—and adults—may be eating a yummy dessert. Get excited about making those sweet treats, too! Step outside and see what your grill can do with simple ingredients to create mouthwatering desserts.

CHOCOLATE PEANUT BUTTER CUPS

4 SERVINGS • PREP: 20 MIN. • GRILL: 10–15 MIN.

4 miniature graham cracker pie crusts
1 ripe banana
12 miniature chocolate peanut butter cups
1 package miniature marshmallows

Preheat grill or place grilling grate over campfire. Place miniature graham cracker pie crusts in a 9 x 13-inch metal baking dish. Slice banana into pieces. Layer 3 to 4 banana slices in each pie crust. Place 3 miniature peanut butter cups over top of bananas in each crust. Sprinkle several miniature marshmallows over peanut butter cups in each pie crust. Cover baking dish with aluminum foil. Place baking dish over grill for 10 to 15 minutes. Using a hot pad or oven mitt, carefully remove pie crusts from baking dish.

CHEF TASKS

COOKING RULES FOR ROOKIES & PROS!

- Wash your hands.
- Tie back long hair.
- Clean up any messes right away.
- Ask before you taste test.
- Always listen to the Head Chef!

KIDDO CHEF

- Peel the banana and slice it into small pieces.
- Place the banana pieces in each pie crust.
- Place the mini chocolate peanut butter cups over the banana pieces.
- Sprinkle a few marshmallows over the peanut butter cups.

TEENAGE SOUS CHEF

- Place the pie crusts in the metal baking dish.
- Help the Kiddo Chef as needed!
- Cover the baking dish with aluminum foil.
- Carefully remove the pie crusts from the baking dish when done.

HEAD CHEF (AKA THE GROWN-UP)

- Keep an eye on your helpers!
- Preheat the grill.
- Place the baking dish on the grill and cook for 10–15 minutes.

APPLE CAKE
WITH CINNAMON SUGAR

6–8 SERVINGS • GRILL: 35–40 MIN.

5 tablespoons cold butter plus
   more for greasing pie plate
1¼ cups flour
1¼ teaspoons baking powder
½ cup sugar
½ teaspoon salt
½ teaspoon ground
   cinnamon, divided
⅛ teaspoon ground cloves
½ cup milk
2 eggs, at room temperature
½ teaspoon vanilla extract
2 large Granny Smith apples
2 tablespoons brown sugar

Preheat grill to medium heat. Generously grease a disposable foil pie plate with butter. In a large bowl, sift the flour and baking powder. Add sugar, salt, ¼ teaspoon cinnamon, and cloves; mix well. Cut 5 tablespoons butter into small pieces and add to the bowl, mixing until coarse and crumbly. In a small bowl, whisk together milk, eggs, and vanilla; add to flour mixture. Mix well. The batter should be well combined but still have some small lumps. Pour batter evenly into pie plate.

Core and slice apples lengthwise into ⅛-inch-thick slices. Arrange slices on top of the batter, overlapping slightly. In a small bowl, mix brown sugar and remaining ¼ teaspoon cinnamon. Sprinkle evenly over apples. Grill over indirect heat with the lid closed for 20 minutes. Rotate pan 90 degrees. Continue grilling with the lid closed until a skewer inserted in the center comes out clean, about 15 to 20 minutes more. Cool on a wire rack 15 minutes before serving.

GRILLED APPLE CRISP

12 SERVINGS • GRILL: 20–25 MIN.

10 cups (about 8 medium) thinly
    sliced, peeled apples
1 cup old-fashioned oats
1 cup brown sugar
¼ cup flour

1 tablespoon ground cinnamon
1 teaspoon ground nutmeg
¼ teaspoon ground cloves
¼ cup cold butter

Place apple slices on a double thickness of heavy-duty aluminum foil
(about 12 x 24 inches) that has been sprayed with nonstick cooking
spray. In a small bowl, combine oats, brown sugar, flour, cinnamon,
nutmeg, and cloves; cut in butter until mixture is crumbly. Sprinkle over
apples. Fold foil around apple mixture and seal tightly. Grill, covered,
over medium heat 20 to 25 minutes or until apples are tender.

HOT-FROM-THE-GRILL APRICOT PIE

1 PIE • GRILL: 40 MIN.

1 unbaked, rolled refrigerated
    pie crust
¼ cup brown sugar
2 teaspoons flour
⅛ teaspoon ground cardamom
⅛ teaspoon chili powder, optional

1 pound apricots, halved and
    pitted or 2 (15-ounce) cans
    apricot halves in light syrup,
    drained
¾ cup granola with raisins
2 tablespoons pecan halves

Bring pie crust to room temperature. Preheat grill to medium heat. In
a medium bowl, combine brown sugar, flour, cardamom, and chili
powder. Add apricots and gently toss to coat; set aside. In a small
bowl, combine granola and nuts; set aside. Lightly grease a disposable
foil loaf pan (about 5 x 8 inches). Ease crust into pan, allowing edges
to hang over pan. Add apricot mixture; sprinkle with granola mixture.
Fold in crust edges, covering part of the filling. Grill, using indirect heat,
in a covered grill for 40 minutes or until crust is golden brown, fruit is
tender, and filling is bubbly. Let cool 45 minutes before serving.

BLUEBERRY COBBLER

4–6 SERVINGS • GRILL: 30 MIN.

2 cups fresh blueberries
2 tablespoons honey
¼ cup brown sugar
½ cup flour

½ cup quick-cooking oats
¼ teaspoon salt
¼ cup butter

Preheat grill to medium heat. Place berries on an 8 x 12-inch piece of heavy-duty aluminum foil with shiny side facing up; drizzle with honey. In a small bowl, combine brown sugar, flour, oats and salt; sprinkle over berries. Cut butter into small pieces and place on top. Seal foil around berries. Grill for about 30 minutes. Cool slightly before serving.

BLUEBERRY-RHUBARB CRUMBLE

6 SERVINGS • GRILL: 20–25 MIN.

3 cups fresh or frozen blueberries
2 cups fresh or frozen diced rhubarb
½ cup sugar
¼ cup plus 2 tablespoons
    flour, divided
½ cup quick-cooking oats

½ cup brown sugar
¼ teaspoon ground nutmeg
¼ teaspoon ground cinnamon
¼ cup butter
Whipped topping, optional

In a medium saucepan over medium heat, combine blueberries, rhubarb, sugar, and 2 tablespoons flour. Cook, stirring constantly, until bubbly and thickened. Pour mixture into an 8-inch square metal or foil baking pan and set aside. To make topping, in a medium bowl, combine oats, brown sugar, remaining ¼ cup flour, ground nutmeg, and ground cinnamon; mix well. Using a pastry blender, cut in butter until mixture resembles coarse crumbs. Sprinkle topping mixture over fruit mixture in baking dish. Cover pan tightly with aluminum foil. At the tailgate, preheat grill to medium heat. Place metal or foil pan over grill and heat for 20 to 25 minutes, or until topping is lightly browned. If desired, serve warm with whipped topping.

GRILLED BANANAS

8 SERVINGS • PREP: 3–5 MIN. • REST: 5 MIN. • GRILL: 7 MIN.

4 bananas (not too ripe),
   unpeeled
2 tablespoons sugar
2 teaspoons ground cinnamon
Pinch fine-grain sea salt
Cooking spray as needed

DIY Grilled Banana Split: Serve grilled bananas with a variety of frozen yogurt, sorbet, low-fat ice cream, or homemade ganache and caramel sauce, nuts, and toppings. Let everyone customize his or her own sundae.

"N'awlins" Variation: Serve the grilled bananas on top of vanilla ice cream, and drizzle with bourbon and toasted pecans before serving.

Slice the bananas, in their skins, in half lengthwise. Set them aside on a clean platter. In a small bowl, combine the sugar, cinnamon, and salt. Sprinkle the cinnamon-sugar on the cut sides of the bananas. Let the bananas sit for 5 minutes.

Preheat grill to medium-low and mist the grates with cooking spray to prevent sticking. Place the bananas, cut-side down, on the center of a clean cooking grate, and cover. Grill for 2 minutes or until grill marks appear. Using a pair of long-handled tongs, turn the banana pieces over and cook 5 more minutes or until the skin pulls away from the bananas.

Remove the bananas from the grill and serve them immediately. Serve them on their own or with your favorite accompaniment.

GRILLED PINEAPPLE

4 SERVINGS • PREP: 5 MIN. • GRILL: 6–10 MIN.

1 ripe pineapple, peeled and quartered lengthwise
2 tablespoons clover honey
¼ cup dark rum
1 teaspoon canola oil
1 tablespoon fresh lime juice
½ teaspoon ground cinnamon

Preheat grill to high. Combine the honey, rum, oil, lime juice, and cinnamon in a bowl, and pour this mixture over the pineapple quarters. Grill the pineapple until it's marked on all sides. Remove it from the heat and let it cool.

When the pineapple is cool enough to handle, dice it into ¼- to ½-inch chunks. To assemble for serving, place the chunks of pineapple in hollowed-out pineapple rinds for family style or in small bowls for individual servings.

Cooking is at once child's play and adult joy. And cooking done with care is an act of love.

–Craig Claiborne

GRILLED FRUIT PARFAIT

4 SERVINGS • PREP: 10–15 MIN. • GRILL: 6–10 MIN.

4 low-fat oatmeal cookies
2 cups low-fat or fat-free Greek
   yogurt, vanilla flavored
2 tablespoons maple syrup
   (optional)
1 banana, sliced lengthwise
2 nectarines, halved
1 cup sliced strawberries (about
   ⅛ inch thick)
1 tablespoon sugar (optional)
4 fresh spearmint sprigs

Preheat grill to medium. Grill the fruit on each side until marked, about 3–5 minutes. Remove the fruit from the grill, and dice the banana and nectarine halves into uniform medium-size pieces. Leave the strawberries as slices. If the fruit pieces are not sweet enough on their own, sprinkle them with sugar. If the yogurt isn't sweet enough, add a little maple syrup to sweeten it.

In a stemmed drinking glass that is taller than it is wide, add a little yogurt, being extra careful not to drip any down the side of the glass. Then add a little of the fruit, again making sure not to dirty the side of the glass. Then add one-half oatmeal cookie, crumbled. Repeat this procedure until you reach the top of the glass (make sure you portion enough for 4 servings if you are using a large glass). Garnish with a sprig of mint.

SPICY POPCORN ON THE GRILL

4 CUPS • GRILL: 8–10 MIN.

2 tablespoons vegetable oil
3 tablespoons popping corn
1 teaspoon chili powder
1 teaspoon garlic salt

Preheat grill to medium heat. In an 8 x 8-inch disposable foil pan, combine oil, popping corn, chili powder, and garlic salt. Place pan inside another disposable pan of same size to double its thickness. Invert a third disposable pan of same size over the top to act as a lid. Wrap one long strip (at least 30 inches) of aluminum foil, folded in half lengthwise, to fit crosswise around pan, folding over to secure pans together and form a handle at the top. Place pan in center of grate. Grill 8 to 10 minutes or until popping stops, shaking pan occasionally.

Note: Chili powder may darken with heat, giving it an overcooked appearance. This shouldn't affect taste.

CHEESY POPCORN

4 CUPS • GRILL: 8–10 MIN.

2 tablespoons vegetable oil
3 tablespoons popping corn

½ cup grated Parmesan cheese
Cayenne pepper to taste

Preheat grill to medium heat. In an 8 x 8-inch disposable foil pan, combine oil, popping corn, cheese, and cayenne pepper. Place pan inside another disposable pan of same size to double its thickness. Invert a third disposable pan of same size over the top to act as a lid. Wrap one long strip (at least 30 inches) of aluminum foil, folded in half lengthwise, to fit crosswise around pan, folding over to secure pans together and form a handle at the top. Place pan in center of grate. Grill 8 to 10 minutes or until popping stops, shaking pan occasionally.

GRILLED DESSERT FRENCH TOAST

6 SERVINGS • GRILL: 6 MIN.

1 cup sliced strawberries or
   whole raspberries
1 tablespoon sugar
2 eggs
⅓ cup milk

½ teaspoon vanilla extract
6 slices pound cake, at least
   ½ inch thick
Powdered sugar

In a small bowl, mash berries with sugar to form sauce; set aside.

Spray grate with nonstick cooking spray. Preheat grill to medium heat. In a flat, shallow bowl, whisk together eggs, milk, and vanilla. Using two spatulas, dip pound cake slices into egg mixture for about 10 seconds per side. Gently transfer to grill; cook over medium heat for about 3 minutes per side or until lightly toasted. Serve immediately with a dusting of powdered sugar and strawberry sauce.

CREAM-FILLED POUND CAKE

4 SERVINGS • GRILL: 4–6 MIN.

4 tablespoons pineapple-flavored
   cream cheese
8 (½-inch-thick) slices pound cake

Sweetened whipped cream
Fresh strawberries and blueberries

Preheat grill to medium-high heat. Spread pineapple cream cheese evenly over one side of four pound cake slices. Top with remaining pound cake slices. Place on grill, close lid, and grill 2 to 3 minutes on each side. Serve immediately, topped with whipped cream and berries.

PEANUT BUTTER S'MORES

4 SERVINGS • GRILL: 2 MIN.

4 whole graham crackers, halved
4 teaspoon peanut butter
2 milk-chocolate candy bars

Preheat grill to low heat. Spread four graham cracker squares each with 1 teaspoon of peanut butter. Top with half a candy bar. Top with remaining cracker squares. Heat on a foil-covered grate for about 2 minutes. Carefully remove from grill. Chocolate will be hot!

COOKOUT CARAMEL S'MORES

4 SERVINGS

8 large marshmallows
2 teaspoons chocolate syrup
4 whole graham crackers, halved
2 teaspoons caramel ice cream topping

Preheat grill to medium-high heat. Using a long-handled fork, toast marshmallows over grill until golden brown, turning occasionally. Drizzle chocolate syrup over four graham cracker squares; top each with two toasted marshmallows. Drizzle with caramel topping. Cover with remaining graham crackers.

GRILLED ANGEL FOOD CAKE S'MORES

8 SERVINGS • PREP: 5 MIN. • GRILL: 8–10 MIN.

8 ½-inch-thick slices angel food cake
4 1-ounce chocolate bars, preferably 35 percent or more cocoa
8 large marshmallows (about 3 ounces)
4 pinches salt

Preheat grill to medium. Make four s'mores sandwiches consisting of two slices of angel food cake, a piece of chocolate, and two marshmallows, sprinkled with a small pinch of salt. Wrap each sandwich in aluminum foil and place on the grill, on an upper rack, or cook the sandwich using indirect heat. In 5 minutes, check one to make sure it is starting to melt.

Remove sandwiches from the foil and grill quickly on each side to mark them. Place the sandwiches diagonally to the grates until marked; turn 90 degrees; and mark again to create diamond shapes. Serve the sandwiches, sliced in half, with a glass of milk.

Strength is the capacity to break a chocolate bar into four pieces with your bare hands—and then eat just one of the pieces.

–Judith Viorst

11

Learning to season in cooking is like learning to stickhandle in hockey; it's absolutely fundamental.
–Rob Feenie

Marinades, Sauces & Rubs

ALL HANDS ON DECK!

MEAT AND VEGGIES ARE GREAT
as they are, but there's another level of tastiness when you souse, douse, and rub in more flavor. Kids and teens can be intrepid explorers of ways to create exciting new tastes for everyday meals. With your guidance, let them experiment with herbs, sauces, and rubs to make their own masterpieces to share with the family!

EZ DR PEPPER® BBQ SAUCE

YIELD: 3 CUPS • PREP: 10 MIN. • COOK: 10 MIN.
USE WITH: RIBS, CHICKEN, PORK

Courtesy of Barry "CB" Martin, on Twitter: @BarryCBMartin.

12 ounces regular Dr Pepper
1 cup tomato ketchup
¼ cup apple-cider vinegar
¼ cup Worcestershire Sauce
⅛ teaspoon hot pepper sauce
2 tablespoon Basic Dry Rub (see page 286)
2 teaspoons paprika

Combine Dr Pepper, ketchup, vinegar, Worcestershire, and hot pepper sauce in a saucepan on your grill's side burner; bring mixture to just below a boil. Stirring gently, mix in dry ingredients. Bring to a boil. Brush mixture on during grilling or serve as a dipping sauce.

Use this as a mop sauce, glaze, or dipping sauce for ribs, chicken, and all manner of pork!—CB

CHEF TASKS

COOKING RULES FOR ROOKIES & PROS!

- Wash your hands.
- Tie back long hair.
- Clean up any messes right away.
- Ask before you taste test.
- Always listen to the Head Chef!

KIDDO CHEF

- Measure each of the ingredients.
- Place all but the dry ingredients in a saucepan.

TEENAGE SOUS CHEF

- Stir the wet ingredients in the saucepan on the grill's side burner.
- Add the dry ingredients to the saucepan and bring to a boil.

HEAD CHEF (AKA THE GROWN-UP)

- Keep an eye on your helpers!
- Light the grill's side burner.
- Brush the mixture on the meat during grilling.

MAÎTRE D' BUTTER

YIELD: 2 CUPS • PREP: 10 MIN. • REFRIGERATE: 1 HR.
OR OVERNIGHT • USE WITH: VEGETABLES

1 pound (4 sticks) unsalted
   butter, softened
3 tablespoons lemon juice
   (about 1 lemon)

¼ cup chopped Italian (flat-leaf)
   parsley, or other herbs or spices
   as desired

In a large bowl, mash the butter. Add lemon juice and parsley and,
using a wooden spoon, blend.

Spread a 1-foot-square piece of plastic wrap across a work surface
and scoop the butter mixture on top. Gently wrap the plastic film
around the butter, forming a cylinder. Tie off the ends of the wrap with
string or a twist tie. Chill or freeze until needed.

**Maître d' Butter is simply softened butter with seasonings,
which is rolled and chilled. You can serve it in slices
on top of vegetables. Experiment by combining
your favorite herbs and spices.**

ADOBO MARINADE

YIELD: 1 CUP • PREP: 5–10 MIN. • MARINATE: 2 HR.–
OVERNIGHT • USE WITH: CHICKEN

½ cup fresh orange juice
2 tablespoons lime juice
2 tablespoons wine vinegar
3 canned chipotle chiles
3 garlic cloves

2 teaspoons oregano
½ teaspoon black pepper
½ teaspoon salt
½ teaspoon ground cumin

In the bowl of a food processor, place all ingredients; purée. Place
chicken in self-sealing plastic bag; add marinade.

**_Adobo_ means "seasoning" or "marinade" in Spanish.
This dark-red marinade is often used in Filipino
and Puerto Rican cooking.–CB**

CHIPOTLE MARINADE

YIELD: ½ CUP • PREP: 5–10 MIN.
MARINATE: 2 HR.–OVERNIGHT • USE WITH: CHICKEN

⅓ cup fresh lime juice
¼ cup fresh chopped cilantro
1 tablespoon packed brown sugar

2 teaspoons minced chipotle chiles in adobo sauce
2 tablespoons adobo sauce (from chiles)
2 cloves garlic, minced

Combine ingredients well and then pour marinade over poultry. Marinate in a plastic zippered bag or covered dish in the refrigerator.

QUICK CHIMICHURRI MARINADE

YIELD: 1½ CUPS • PREP: 5–10 MIN. • MARINATE: 2 HR.–OVERNIGHT
USE WITH: POULTRY

¾ cup prepared, noncreamy Caesar dressing
½ cup chopped fresh parsley

¾ teaspoon crushed red pepper
Salt and pepper

Combine ingredients well and then pour marinade over meat. Marinate in a plastic zippered bag or covered dish in the refrigerator.

GARLIC-YOGURT MARINADE

YIELD: 1 CUP • PREP: 5 MIN. • MARINATE: 2–4 HR. • USE WITH: STEAK

1 cup plain yogurt
¼ cup chopped fresh parsley
2 tablespoons lemon juice

1 tablespoon sweet paprika
1 tablespoon minced garlic
1 teaspoon salt

In a bowl, whisk together all ingredients until completely emulsified. Marinate meat in a sealable plastic bag or covered container in the refrigerator.

KOREAN KALBI MARINADE

YIELD: APPROX. 1 CUP • PREP: 5 MIN.
MARINATE: OVERNIGHT • USE WITH: SHORT RIBS

1 tablespoon soy sauce

¼ cup sugar

2 tablespoons honey

¼ cup Chinese rice wine

2 teaspoons Korean toasted-
sesame oil

2 green onions, minced

4 teaspoons (1 to 2 cloves)
garlic, chopped

2 tablespoons roasted
sesame seeds

2 tablespoons water

1 teaspoon ginger root, grated

Mix ingredients in nonreactive bowl. Use some as an overnight marinade for meat—placed in a sealable plastic bag or covered container in the refrigerator—and reserve some for glazing during the final 5 to 7 minutes of cooking.

The recipe is a classic one used for most Korean kalbi (grilled short ribs).

SPICY GRILLED-VEGGIE MARINADE

YIELD: 1 ½ CUPS • PREP: 5 MIN. • MARINATE: 1 HR.
USE WITH: VEGETABLES

⅔ cup white wine vinegar

½ cup soy sauce

2 tablespoons minced fresh ginger

2 tablespoons olive oil

2 tablespoons sesame oil

2 large cloves garlic, minced

2 teaspoons Tabasco® sauce

In a bowl, whisk together all ingredients until completely emulsified. Marinate in a sealable plastic bag or covered container in the refrigerator.

MARINADE TRIO

YIELD: 1 CUP • PREP: 5 MIN. • MARINATE: 4–12 HR. • USE WITH: POULTRY

CLASSIC MARINADE

1 cup prepared Italian-style vinaigrette

1 teaspoon minced garlic

¼ teaspoon coarsely ground black pepper

MEXICAN VARIATION

To classic marinade, add

1 tablespoon fresh lime juice

1 teaspoon ground cumin

1 teaspoon chipotle chili powder

½ teaspoon salt

ASIAN VARIATION

To classic marinade, add

2 tablespoons reduced-sodium soy sauce

2 tablespoons minced fresh ginger

1 tablespoon packed brown sugar

1 tablespoon sesame seeds, toasted

1½ teaspoons dark sesame oil

In a bowl, whisk together all ingredients until completely emulsified. Marinate meat in a sealable plastic bag or covered container in the refrigerator.

TERIYAKI-STYLE SAUCE

YIELD: ¾ CUP • PREP: 5–10 MIN. • USE WITH: CHICKEN, VEGETABLES

Courtesy of Barry "CB" Martin, on Twitter: @BarryCBMartin.

½ cup firmly packed dark brown sugar

½ cup soy sauce

¼ cup of hot water (or more to taste)

1 tablespoon Asian sesame oil

1 teaspoon dry Chinese-style mustard

1 teaspoon ground ginger

1 teaspoon orange zest

Combine ingredients in saucepan. Heat and then brush on meat during final minutes of grilling.

BASIC BEER SAUCE

YIELD: 3 CUPS • PREP: 15 MIN. • USE WITH: POULTRY

Courtesy of Barry "CB" Martin, on Twitter: @BarryCBMartin.

1 12-ounce can or bottle of ale or dark beer

½ cup apple cider

½ cup water

¼ cup peanut oil

2 medium shallots, chopped

3 garlic cloves, chopped

1 tablespoon Worcestershire sauce

1 teaspoon hot sauce

Combine ingredients in a saucepan. Heat mixture and then brush it on the meat during the final minutes of grilling.

NORTH CAROLINA BBQ SAUCE I

YIELD: 2 CUPS • PREP: 15 MIN. • MARINATE: 2 HR. • USE WITH: CHICKEN

2 cups cider vinegar
¼ cup brown sugar
1 tablespoon crushed red pepper
3 teaspoons salt

1½ teaspoons ground cayenne pepper
1 teaspoon freshly ground black pepper
1 teaspoon ground white pepper

Combine all ingredients in a large bowl; mix well; and let stand for 2 hours to blend the flavors.

NORTH CAROLINA BBQ SAUCE II

YIELD: 2 CUPS • PREP: 15 MIN. • MARINATE: 2 HR. • USE WITH: CHICKEN

2 cups cider vinegar
¼ cup brown sugar
1 tablespoon crushed red pepper
3 teaspoons salt
1½ teaspoons ground cayenne pepper

1 teaspoon freshly ground black pepper
1 teaspoon ground white pepper
1 cup ketchup
1 teaspoon Worcestershire sauce
½ teaspoon cinnamon

Combine all ingredients in a large bowl; mix well; and let stand for 2 hours to blend the flavors.

TEXAS BBQ SAUCE

YIELD: 3 CUPS (ENOUGH FOR 6 POUNDS OF MEAT) • PREP: 15 MIN.
COOK: 20 MIN. • USE WITH: POULTRY

1 tablespoon salt
1 teaspoon barbecue seasoning mix
½ teaspoon pepper
3 tablespoons brown sugar
¼ cup ketchup
½ cup Worcestershire sauce

3 tablespoons Dijon mustard
1 tablespoon liquid smoke
1 cup brewed, strong coffee
½ cup vinegar
1 cup olive oil

Mix ingredients in order listed, using a handheld mixer when adding oil. Simmer slowly until thickened. Keep hot. Use to baste poultry.

MEMPHIS BBQ SAUCE

YIELD: 3 CUPS • PREP: 15 MIN. • COOK: 25 MIN.
USE WITH: CHICKEN

¼ cup apple-cider vinegar
½ cup prepared mustard
2 cups ketchup
3 tablespoons
    Worcestershire sauce
1 tablespoon finely ground
    black pepper
¼ cup brown sugar

2 teaspoons celery salt
2 tablespoons chili powder
1 tablespoon onion powder
2 teaspoons garlic powder
¼ to ½ teaspoon cayenne pepper
    (optional)
2 teaspoons liquid smoke (optional)
2 tablespoons canola oil

Combine all ingredients, except the oil, in a saucepan. Bring them
to a boil, stirring to dissolve the sugar. Reduce the heat and simmer
for 25 minutes, stirring occasionally. With a whisk, blend in oil
until incorporated.

SOUTH CAROLINA RED BBQ SAUCE

YIELD: 2 CUPS • PREP: 20 MIN. • USE WITH: CHICKEN

1½ cups apple-cider vinegar
½ cup ketchup
1 tablespoon brown sugar

1 teaspoon salt
½ teaspoon crushed red pepper

Combine all ingredients; stir until sugar and salt dissolve. Taste, and
adjust the sauce by adding more ketchup and brown sugar to reduce
the tangy flavor. Sauce can be prepared up to 3 days ahead, covered,
and refrigerated.

REVEREND STEPHEN'S TEMPTATION BBQ SAUCE

YIELD: 3½ CUPS • PREP: 15 MIN. • COOK: 20 MIN.
USE WITH: SMOKED OR BARBECUED CHICKEN

*This recipe was sent to CB by a BBQ fan
known as Reverend Stephen.*

½ onion, minced
4 garlic cloves, minced
¾ cup bourbon
½ teaspoon ground black pepper
½ tablespoon salt
2 cups ketchup
¼ cup tomato paste

⅓ cup apple-cider vinegar
2 tablespoons liquid smoke
¼ cup Worcestershire sauce
¼ cup packed brown sugar
½ teaspoon hot pepper sauce (or
   to taste)

In a large skillet over medium heat, combine onion, garlic, and bourbon.
Simmer for 10 minutes or until onion is translucent. Mix in ground
black pepper, salt, ketchup, tomato paste, vinegar, liquid smoke,
Worcestershire sauce, brown sugar, and hot pepper sauce. Bring this
to a boil. Reduce heat to medium-low and simmer for 20 minutes. If
you prefer a smoother sauce, pour mixture through a strainer.

MOROCCAN SAUCE

YIELD: APPROX. 1 CUP • PREP: 5 MIN.
COOK: 12–13 MIN. • USE WITH: COD, HALIBUT,
SALMON, CRAB, SCALLOPS

1½ tablespoons garlic, minced
½ cup olive oil
½ cup unsalted butter
2 tablespoons harissa
1½ tablespoons fresh lemon juice or
   1 to 2 tablespoons sherry

Coarse salt to taste
Black pepper, cracked, to taste
2 tablespoons Italian (flat-leaf)
   parsley, chopped
2 tablespoons salted almonds,
   chopped (optional)

Place garlic, olive oil, and butter in a small saucepan over low heat.
Cook until garlic begins to soften, about 10 minutes. Add harissa and
lemon juice, blending with a whisk; continue cooking 2 to 3 minutes
more. Season to taste with salt and pepper. Garnish with parsley and,
if desired, almonds.

*Note: If harissa is not available, substitute 1 tablespoon of pimenton
(smoked Spanish paprika).*

JALAPEÑOS IN ADOBO SAUCE

YIELD: 3 CUPS • PREP: 10–15 MIN. • USE WITH: POULTRY

10 jalapeño peppers, smoked or grilled, split, and seeded

1 can (18 ounces) tomatoes, diced

10 large garlic cloves, crushed and minced

6 tablespoons olive oil

2 tablespoons chopped fresh coriander or cilantro

2 tablespoons apple-cider vinegar

1 tablespoon crushed red pepper

1 teaspoon cumin

1 teaspoon oregano

1 teaspoon coarse salt

Juice from ½ large lime

Juice from ½ large lemon

Pinch of brown sugar, if necessary

After preparing jalapeño peppers, mix all ingredients and seal in nonreactive container. Sauce can be kept in refrigerator for several weeks.

FILIPINO ADOBO SAUCE

YIELD: 3+ CUPS • PREP: 5 MIN. • COOK: 30–40 MIN. (UNTIL SAUCE THICKENS)
USE WITH: CHICKEN, PORK

Courtesy of Barry "CB" Martin, on Twitter: @BarryCBMartin.

1 cup soy sauce

½ cup rice-wine vinegar (may substitute apple-cider vinegar)

1 tablespoon garlic, minced

1 tablespoon fresh ginger, minced

2 cups coconut milk

1 teaspoon smoked paprika

1 small jalapeño, diced

1 cup water

Whole chicken, cut into eighths, or 2-pound pork loin, cubed

1 tablespoon lime juice, freshly squeezed

Combine soy sauce, vinegar, garlic, ginger, ½ cup of coconut milk, paprika, jalapeño, and water in a deep pot, and slowly simmer on low for about 5 to 10 minutes until ingredients are blended and sauce is heated evenly.

Add meat; cook for about 15 to 20 minutes. When it starts to get firm, remove meat from pot; pat dry with a paper towel; and reserve to finish on grill.

Turn up heat a bit and add remaining coconut milk. Reduce until sauce has consistency of runny cake batter. Add lime juice, and strain before serving.

LEMON-GARLIC BUTTER SAUCE

YIELD: ¼ CUP PER SERVING • PREP: 15 MIN.
COOK: 5 MIN. • USE WITH: CHICKEN, VEGETABLES

Courtesy of Barry "CB" Martin, on Twitter: @BarryCBMartin.

PER SERVING

2 tablespoons clarified butter (see note below)
½ fresh lemon, juiced
2 tablespoons light olive oil or canola oil

1 garlic clove, crushed
¼ teaspoon lemon zest

Combine ingredients in a saucepan. Heat mixture, and brush it on food during final minutes of grilling and on serving plate.

Clarified butter has a higher smoke point than regular butter.
Place 1 pound of unsalted butter in a saucepan at the back of the stove; cover;
and allow the butter to melt while you're cooking. Skim off the solids that have risen
to the surface. Use immediately or pour into a glass container to freeze.–CB

TARRAGON BUTTER SAUCE

YIELD: ¼ CUP PER SERVING • PREP: 10 MIN.
USE WITH: CHICKEN, VEGETABLES

Courtesy of Barry "CB" Martin, on Twitter: @BarryCBMartin.

PER SERVING

2 tablespoons clarified butter (see note above)
2 tablespoons light olive oil or canola oil
1 tablespoon chopped fresh tarragon

Combine all ingredients in a saucepan. Heat mixture and brush it on chicken or vegetables during final minutes of grilling.

GEORGIA-STYLE MUSTARD SAUCE

YIELD: 2½ CUPS • PREP: 10 MIN. • COOK: 20–30 MIN.
USE WITH: CHICKEN

Courtesy of Barry "CB" Martin, on Twitter: @BarryCBMartin.

2 tablespoons vegetable oil
½ cup minced Vidalia or other
    sweet onion
1 cup prepared mustard
½ cup fresh lemon juice
    (or lemonade)

¼ cup firmly packed dark
    brown sugar
¼ cup apple-cider vinegar
1 teaspoon celery seed
1 teaspoon kosher salt
1 teaspoon powdered ginger

Heat oil in a nonreactive saucepan over medium heat. Add onions and sauté until translucent, about 3 to 4 minutes. Add remaining ingredients; blend well. Bring mixture to a boil and then reduce heat and simmer for 15 to 20 minutes.

CREAMY GORGONZOLA SAUCE

YIELD: 2+ CUPS • PREP: 5 MIN. • CHILL: 30 MIN. TO
1 HR. • USE WITH: STEAKS, VEGETABLES

1 cup reduced-fat cream
    cheese, softened
1 cup plain nonfat yogurt

½ cup Gorgonzola
    cheese, crumbled
¼ cup onion, minced
1 teaspoon pepper

Combine all ingredients in a small bowl; mix well. Chill for 30 minutes to 1 hour before serving.

ROASTED GARLIC

YIELD: ABOUT ¼ CUP • PREP: 5–10 MIN. • COOK: 30–40 MIN. ON GRILL, 35–45 MIN. IN OVEN • USE WITH: CHICKEN, GRILLED CORN, OR AS A SPREAD ON GRILLED BRUSCHETTA

1 whole garlic bulb
1 teaspoon canola oil
1 small rosemary sprig (optional)

Freshly ground black pepper to taste
Salt to taste (optional)

Cut ½ inch off top of garlic bulb so that individual cloves are exposed. Cut an 8-inch-square sheet of heavy-duty aluminum foil. Place garlic bulb on foil; add oil to cut end of garlic bulb. Place herb sprig across bulb, and season with pepper and salt. Wrap foil around bulb.

Preheat grill to high. When ready, place wrapped bulb on grill and cook for 30 to 40 minutes, turning carefully several times.

Remove bulb from grill; let cool. Squeeze cooked garlic bulb by hand, and delicious, soft pulp will come forth. If desired, garlic can be roasted in oven at 375°F for 45 minutes to 1 hour until soft.

ROASTED-GARLIC MAYO

YIELD: 1 CUP • PREP: 20 MIN. • USE WITH: CHICKEN, VEGETABLES

2 whole heads roasted garlic (See recipe above.)
1 cup prepared mayonnaise

½ teaspoon lemon juice

Squeeze garlic pulp from cloves into work bowl of a food processor; pulse three or four times until smooth. Add mayonnaise and lemon juice, and blend until smooth and well combined. Use this mayonnaise immediately, or cover and refrigerate for up to 2 days.

BETTER-THAN-HOMEMADE MAYO

YIELD: 1 CUP • PREP: 20 MIN. • USE WITH: CHICKEN

1 cup prepared mayonnaise
1½ tablespoons olive oil
¼ teaspoon fresh lemon juice

¼ teaspoon minced garlic
Tabasco® sauce to taste

Whisk ingredients together. This mayonnaise can be used immediately, or covered and refrigerated for 2 to 3 weeks.

ROASTED RED-PEPPER MAYO

YIELD: 1 ¼ CUPS • PREP: 20 MIN.
USE WITH: CHICKEN, VEGETABLES

2 red peppers, roasted
and chopped
1 garlic clove, chopped

1 cup prepared mayonnaise
¼ teaspoon cayenne pepper

Combine peppers and garlic in a food processor; blend until smooth.
Add mayonnaise and cayenne until combined. Use this mayonnaise
immediately, or cover and refrigerate for up to 2 days.

ORANGE AIOLI

YIELD: 1 ¼ CUPS • PREP: 10 MIN.
USE WITH: CHICKEN, VEGETABLES

Courtesy of Barry "CB" Martin, on Twitter: @BarryCBMartin.

1 cup mayonnaise
¼ cup orange juice
1 tablespoon hot-pepper sauce
½ teaspoon sugar

½ teaspoon chopped garlic
½ teaspoon prepared horseradish
2 tablespoons chopped scallions

Stir all ingredients together and refrigerate until ready to use. Because
it only keeps for a few days, make just enough to use in about 24 hours.

Aioli is a word that has been popping up on restaurant menus all over the place.
It's really just flavored mayonnaise. So whether you make your own mayo
or purchase it in jars like most folks, experiment with some new flavors and
impress your friends when you call it aioli. (A-OH-LEE!)–CB

GUACAMOLE

YIELD: ABOUT 2 CUPS • PREP: 15 MIN.,
PLUS 1 HR. REFRIGERATION
USE WITH: TACO CHIPS, RAW VEGETABLES

3 to 4 large, ripe avocados
5 cloves roasted garlic
Juice of 1 lime
2 tablespoons chopped cilantro

½ teaspoon red pepper flakes
Salt and pepper to taste
1 large tomato, diced

Peel avocados; discard pits; and remove any bad spots. Cut them
into ½-inch cubes. In a food processor, blend together avocado, garlic,
lime juice, cilantro, red pepper, and salt and pepper. Move to a serving
dish. Stir in chopped tomato. Cover, and refrigerate for 1 hour.

CLASSIC PARMESAN-BASIL PESTO

YIELD: ABOUT 2 CUPS • PREP: 5–10 MIN.
USE WITH: CHICKEN BREAST, VEGETABLES

1⅓ cups basil leaves
1½ teaspoons chopped garlic
¼ cup pine nuts, toasted

½ cup grated Parmesan cheese
¼ cup olive oil
Salt and pepper to taste

Combine first four ingredients in a food processor; pulse three or four times. With motor running, slowly drizzle in olive oil until mixture blends into a paste. Season with salt and pepper to taste.

SUN-DRIED TOMATO PESTO

YIELD: ABOUT 2 CUPS • PREP: 5–10 MIN.
USE WITH: CHICKEN BREAST, VEGETABLES

1½ cups sun-dried tomatoes, packed in oil, drained
6 garlic cloves, peeled
1 cup grated Parmesan cheese

1 cup fresh basil leaves
½ cup olive oil
2 tablespoons balsamic vinegar

Combine all ingredients in a food processor or blender; blend until mixture is smooth and well combined.

GREEN-CHILE PESTO

YIELD: APPROX. 2 CUPS • PREP: 15 MIN. • USE WITH: MEAT, POULTRY, FISH

6 large, long green chiles or 4 medium poblano chiles, roasted, peeled, and seeded
¾ cup pine nuts
2 cups lightly packed fresh basil, leaves and stems
6 garlic cloves, peeled and chopped

1 cup extra-virgin olive oil
¾ cup Parmesan cheese, grated
½ cup Romano cheese, grated
½ teaspoon salt
½ teaspoon black pepper, ground

Chop the chiles and set aside.

In a skillet over medium heat, toast pine nuts and then let them cool to room temperature.

In a food processor, combine chiles, pine nuts, basil, and garlic. Process, scraping down sides of bowl once or twice, until smooth. Drizzle in olive oil. Transfer mixture to a bowl and blend in cheese, salt, and pepper. Use immediately, or cover and refrigerate for up to 3 days; freeze (without cheese) for up to 3 months.

DRIED-CHERRY CHUTNEY

YIELD: 3 CUPS • PREP: 10 MIN. • COOK: 23–25 MIN.
USE WITH: PORK

1½ cups port or sherry
1½ cups dried cherries
1 large shallot, minced
2 cloves garlic, minced
1 teaspoon peppercorns, crushed
4 whole cloves, crushed, or ¼
    teaspoon ground cloves

4 to 5 allspice berries, crushed, or
    ¼ teaspoon ground allspice
1 teaspoon whole cumin
    seeds, crushed
1 teaspoon coriander
    seeds, crushed
2 tablespoons to ¼ cup
    fruit preserves

Heat wine in a microwave on high for 30 seconds; make sure wine is not boiling and then pour it into a bowl over cherries. Let it sit for 1 hour.

Over medium-high heat, sauté shallots and garlic until transparent. Add wine, cherries, and spices. Reduce heat to medium; simmer for 3 or 4 minutes; add preserves; and cook until thickened, about 20 minutes.

BASIC "WET" RUB

YIELD: ½ CUP • PREP: 10 MIN. • MARINATE: 20 MIN.
USE WITH: CHICKEN, VEGETABLES

Courtesy of Barry "CB" Martin, on Twitter: @BarryCBMartin.

1 tablespoon minced garlic
¼ cup brown sugar
⅛ teaspoon coarse salt

⅛ teaspoon fresh ground
    black pepper
1 tablespoon Worcestershire sauce
⅛ cup balsamic vinegar

Combine dry ingredients; add wet ingredients; mix again. Apply to meat about 20 minutes before slow cooking. Note: Use plastic gloves or plastic sandwich bags over your hands to prevent irritation from spices. Wet rub may be stored in refrigerator for up to 3 days.

BASIC DRY RUB

YIELD: 1 CUP • PREP: 10 MIN. • MARINATE: 1 HR.–OVERNIGHT • USE WITH: CHICKEN

Courtesy of Barry "CB" Martin, on Twitter: @BarryCBMartin.

½ cup garlic powder

⅛ cup kosher salt

⅛ cup powdered ginger

⅛ cup dry mustard

3 tablespoons coarsely ground black pepper

1 tablespoon cumin powder

½ tablespoon curry powder

Combine ingredients in a bowl; mix thoroughly with a wire whisk. Pour rub mixture into a clean, dry jar and tightly seal. Massage 2 to 3 tablespoons of rub into meat. Store remaining rub away from light and heat.

INDIAN SPICE RUB

YIELD: ½ CUP • PREP: 10 MIN. • USE WITH: CHICKEN, VEGETABLES

Courtesy of Barry "CB" Martin, on Twitter: @BarryCBMartin.

1 tablespoon cumin seeds

1 tablespoon coriander seeds

1 tablespoon fennel seeds

1 tablespoon kosher salt

½ tablespoon curry powder

¼ to ½ teaspoon cayenne pepper

4 large garlic cloves

¼ cup fresh lemon juice

½ tablespoon vegetable oil

In a small, heavy skillet, toast cumin, coriander, and fennel seeds over high heat, stirring until fragrant and lightly browned (about 2 minutes). Cool on a plate. Place seeds in blender and whirl until finely ground. Add salt, curry powder, cayenne, and garlic; blend to a paste. Add lemon juice and oil; blend to combine.

DRY SUGAR RUB

YIELD: ¼ CUP • PREP: 10 MIN. • USE WITH: CHICKEN

Courtesy of Barry "CB" Martin, on Twitter: @BarryCBMartin.

2 tablespoons sugar

1 tablespoon chili powder

1 teaspoon black pepper

½ tablespoon ground cumin

½ tablespoon paprika

½ tablespoon salt

¼ teaspoon dry mustard

Dash cinnamon

Combine ingredients in a bowl; mix thoroughly with a wire whisk. Pour the rub mixture into a clean, dry jar and tightly seal. Massage 2 to 3 tablespoons of rub into meat. Store remaining rub away from light and heat.

SOUTHWEST-STYLE RUB

YIELD: 1 CUP • PREP: 10 MIN. • MARINATE: 20 MIN.
USE WITH: CHICKEN

Courtesy of Barry "CB" Martin, on Twitter: @BarryCBMartin.

DRY INGREDIENTS

¼ cup chili powder
¼ cup packed brown sugar
⅛ cup ground cumin
⅛ cup kosher salt
⅛ cup black pepper
1 teaspoon ground cinnamon

WET INGREDIENTS

1 tablespoon Worcestershire sauce
⅛ cup apple-cider vinegar
1 tablespoon minced fresh garlic (or
    1 tablespoon garlic powder)
1 teaspoon hot sauce

Mix dry ingredients; add wet ingredients; mix again. Store mixture in refrigerator for up to 3 days. Apply rub to meat; let meat rest for about 20 minutes before slow cooking. Note: Use plastic gloves or plastic sandwich bags over your hands to prevent irritation from spices.

HERBED POULTRY RUB

PREP: 5 MIN. • USE WITH: CHICKEN, TURKEY

Courtesy of Barry "CB" Martin, on Twitter: @BarryCBMartin.

Equal parts fresh parsley, sage, rosemary, and thyme, finely chopped
½ part coarse salt

Blend ingredients in a spice mill or with a mortar and pestle until mixture becomes a coarse paste.

LAVENDER RUB FOR LAMB

PREP: 5 MIN. • USE WITH: LAMB

Courtesy of Barry "CB" Martin, on Twitter: @BarryCBMartin.

3 parts lavender flowers
1 part fresh lemon sage,
   finely chopped

1 part fresh rosemary, chopped
½ part coarse salt
½ part cumin, ground

Blend ingredients in a spice mill or with a mortar and pestle until mixture becomes a coarse paste.

PACIFIC NORTHWEST SEASONING FOR GAME

PREP: 5 MIN. • USE WITH: DUCK, PHEASANT, CHUKAR, QUAIL

Courtesy of Barry "CB" Martin, on Twitter: @BarryCBMartin.

2 parts dried cherries or cranberries
1 part rosemary

1 part orange zest
½ part coarse salt

Blend ingredients in a spice mill or with a mortar and pestle until mixture becomes a coarse paste.

WET SALT RUB FOR FISH

PREP: 5 MIN. • USE WITH: FISH

Courtesy of Barry "CB" Martin, on Twitter: @BarryCBMartin.

1 part coarse salt
1 part fresh lemon thyme,
   finely minced

½ part anchovy paste
2½ parts dry white vermouth

Whisk together all ingredients until blended.

AVOCADO CREAM

YIELD: 1½ CUPS • PREP: 30 MIN. • USE WITH: GARLIC-
LIME ALASKA PRAWNS (SEE PAGE 208)

2 avocados, 1½ pounds total
½ cup sour cream
2 tablespoons mayonnaise
2 tablespoons lime juice

1 teaspoon ground dried ancho
   chiles or chili powder
½ teaspoon salt

Peel ripe avocados; cut into chunks; and put in the work bowl of a food processor. Add sour cream, mayonnaise, lime juice, ancho chiles or chili powder, and salt; blend until smooth. Taste, and add more lime juice and salt if desired. Scrape into small bowl.

HORSERADISH SAUCE

YIELD: 1½ CUPS • PREP: 15 MIN.
USE WITH: SMOKED PRIME RIB

1 3-ounce package cream cheese
1 cup sour cream
1 teaspoon grated onion
2 tablespoons horseradish

¼ teaspoon sugar
¼ teaspoon salt
¼ teaspoon pepper

Combine all ingredients in a blender.

PROVENCAL CITRUS-TARRAGON SAUCE

YIELD: 1½ CUPS • PREP: 5 MIN. • USE WITH: HALIBUT, SALMON, CRAB, SCALLOPS

¼ cup apple-cider vinegar
2 tablespoons Dijon mustard
⅓ cup olive oil
2 tablespoons honey

⅓ cup fresh tarragon leaves
1 can (11 ounces) mandarin orange
   slices, drained, or 2 fresh

mandarin oranges, peeled,
   sectioned, and seeded
½ teaspoon coarse salt

Combine vinegar and mustard in a blender or food processor, and pulse until smooth; slowly add olive oil until fully incorporated. Add the honey, tarragon, and oranges; blend or pulse again until almost smooth. Salt to taste.

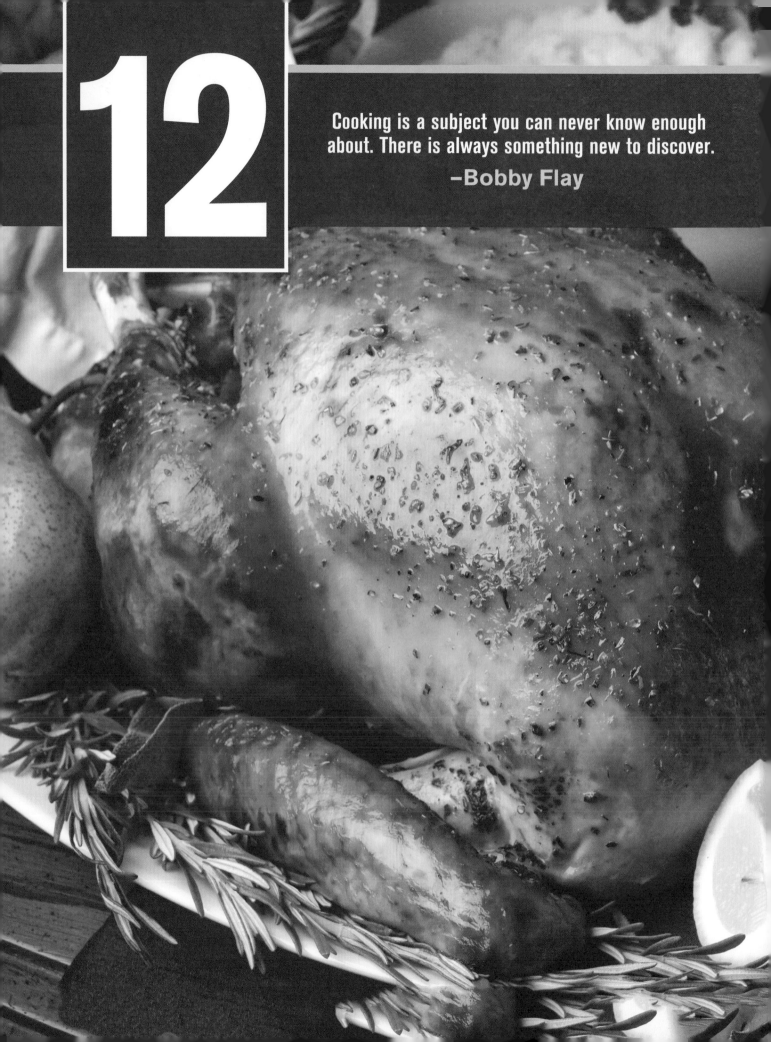

12

Cooking is a subject you can never know enough about. There is always something new to discover.

–Bobby Flay

Cooking with The Big Easy®

FOOD FOR FAMILY & FRIENDS

INFRARED COOKING AND THE BIG EASY®
OIL-LESS TURKEY FRYER

Infrared is a natural form of radiant heat we've all experienced in our daily lives. The warm rays of the sun are transferred to your skin by infrared heat waves. And if you've ever made "sun tea," you've brewed it using the sun's infrared heat.

Charcoal has been used to cook food for centuries and is still prized by some folks today for the flavor it imparts to food. But it's probably a safe bet that many people don't realize it's the infrared heat produced by a charcoal fire that helps the food retain its juiciness and flavor. And charcoal fires require a little more time and effort to adequately prepare them for grilling.

With the introduction of an affordable line of gas grills equipped with infrared cooking systems, Char-Broil® has made the technology used for decades by professional chefs available to backyard grillers. You'll find this exciting technology in Char-Broil's best grills, as well as The Big Easy®, Char-Broil's infrared turkey fryer that cooks without using a drop of oil.

Accessories for The Big Easy® add even more possibilities. The Easy Load Kabob Holder and Skewers (left) makes cooking kabobs easy. The Leg Racks (center) are perfect for chicken or turkey drumsticks. The Rib Hooks (right) allow you to cook ribs in the fryer basket.

The Bunk-Bed Basket divides The Big Easy® fryer basket into two compartments, so you can cook meat and vegetables or two chickens at the same time.

The Stackable Oven works much like a Dutch oven, and you can fit up to three in The Big Easy®.

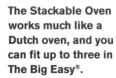

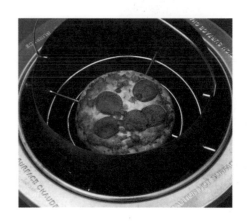

NO-OIL "DEEP FRYING"

Deep-fried turkey is the juiciest, tastiest, most crisp-skinned bird you'll ever eat. The Big Easy® is an oil-less way to "fry" a turkey using infrared technology. Turkeys cooked in The Big Easy® are prepped the same way as for traditional fryers. One of the many bonuses of The Big Easy®, however, is that you can use dry rubs and seasonings on the outside of the bird.

1. Brine bird up to 24 hours for extra flavor.

2. Spray cooking basket with vegetable oil.

3. Place bird–breast facing up–in basket.

4. Allow bird to rest for 20 to 30 minutes.

FIRST THINGS FIRST

We suggest you take a few moments to read the Product Guide that arrived with The Big Easy® and ensure that your fryer is assembled correctly and completely and that you are familiar with both its construction and operation before using it for the first time.

You will find that most of the product assembly has been completed for you at the factory. Complete any remaining steps and reference all safety and usage information found in the Product Guide.

Another important step is to register your cooker so that we can be more helpful when you need us. Please complete the warranty registration card found on the last page of your Product Guide or save a stamp and visit us at *www.support.charbroil.com*.

After you register, be sure to go to *www.charbroil.com/community* for new tips, tricks, recipes, party ideas, and exclusive subscriber offers. We never sell or distribute your contact information! We want your Char-Broil® experience to be a great one, and this is one way we can stay in touch.

Seasoning

Just like grandma's cast iron skillet, the stainless steel cooking chamber in The Big Easy® needs to be seasoned prior to use. **This is most important** because it will allow the cooking chamber to work properly. In addition, it will make cleaning easier and inhibit rusting.

To season, coat all interior surfaces of the cooking chamber with vegetable oil. If you use a vegetable spray, wipe down the cooking chamber after spraying to ensure an even coat. Start The Big Easy® and let it burn until the vegetable oil burns off and stops smoking. The shiny finish of the stainless steel cooking chamber should now have a very dark brown or bronze color.

You are now ready to cook. The more you use your Big Easy®, the better it will cook. The darker—more seasoned—the cooking chamber becomes, the hotter and more evenly it will cook. A light coat of vegetable oil after each use will keep the surfaces seasoned and help prevent any rusting—again, just like grandma's cast iron skillet.

It will be tempting to start cooking right away with your Big Easy® fryer, but make sure you take some time to familiarize yourself with it and all of its parts and accessories before you try out your first recipe.

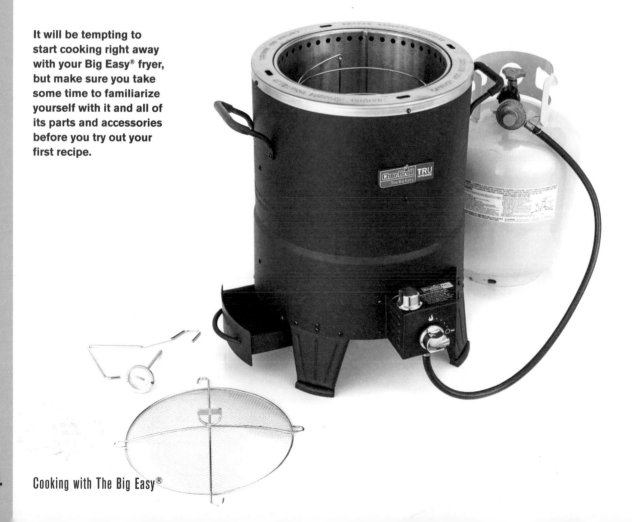

FREQUENTLY ASKED QUESTIONS

1. How does this thing work? You'll think it's magic, but it's really simply using two methods of heat transfer. First, the propane burner heats the air between the cooking chamber and the outside wall of the cooker. This hot air, or convective heat, warms the cooking chamber. The cooking chamber absorbs the heat and radiates it to the inside as TRU-Infrared® heat. By converting the hot air, or convective heat, into TRU-Infrared®, radiant heat, food cooked in The Big Easy® is moist and juicy.

2. How should I prepare the turkey? The turkey must be completely thawed, and you should always remove the giblets, neck, and anything from inside the cavity before cooking. Remove the metal or plastic tie that may be used to bind the legs together before putting the turkey in the cooking basket. Opening the legs will allow the turkey to cook evenly and maintain its position inside the basket. Always set the turkey inside the basket with the breast side up and the legs down so that it can cook evenly.

3. Can I cook a turkey with stuffing inside? The USDA recommends cooking stuffing separately for optimal safety and uniform doneness. Visit *www.isitdoneyet.gov* for more information on cooking turkey safely.

4. Can I use injectable marinades? Absolutely. But if you are really into making it easy, use a dry rub on the outside. One of our favorites to use is a Creole seasoning with salt, red pepper, garlic, and other spices found readily at any grocery store. Try to avoid rubs with high sugar content because the sugar can burn. You can also rub the skin with peanut or canola oil before using a dry rub. The TRU-Infrared® heat will keep your turkey moist and juicy on the inside.

5. How long will it take to cook my turkey? With The Big Easy®, food is done once it reaches proper internal temperature. Cook times will vary depending on outdoor weather conditions, but generally you can expect 10 minutes per pound for turkey, 15 minutes per pound for chicken, and 30 minutes per

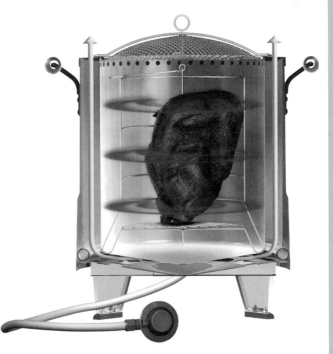

The Big Easy® uses infrared heat. The propane burner heats the air between the cooking chamber and the outside wall of the cooker. This hot air warms the cooking chamber, which absorbs and radiates the heat to the inside of the fryer.

Make sure you use a food thermometer to check your meat's internal temperature and ensure it is cooked properly.

USDA RECOMMENDED SAFE MINIMUM INTERNAL TEMPERATURES

TEMPERATURE	MEAT
165°F	Whole poultry
165°F	Poultry breasts
165°F	Ground poultry
160°F	Ground meats
145°F and allow to rest at least 3 minutes	Beef, pork, lamb, and veal (steaks, roasts, and chops)

www.isitdoneyet.gov

pound for pork or beef roasts. Always use a food thermometer to check doneness. Use the included food thermometer for larger cuts of meat where at least three-quarters of the stem length can be inserted into the turkey, chicken, or roast. For smaller foods, use an instant-read thermometer that measures temperatures closer to the tip of the stem. Always follow the instructions for use from the manufacturer. See www.charbroil.com for instant-read and other food thermometer purchase options. Finally, remember these USDA guidelines for proper use:

- Insert the probe into the thickest part of the food—not touching bone, fat, or gristle—before lowering into the cook chamber.
- After cooking, check the temperature in several places to make sure the food is evenly heated.
- Compare your thermometer reading to the USDA guidelines above to determine if your food has reached a safe temperature.
- Make sure to clean your food thermometer with hot, soapy water before and after each use.
- Visit www.isitdoneyet.gov for more information on food safety.

6. How is The Big Easy faster than an oil fryer? A traditional oil fryer requires up to 3 gallons of peanut oil that can take up to 45 minutes to preheat to the proper temperature. After preheating, cook time is about 3 minutes per pound, but it can take several hours for the oil to cool down before you can clean up and recycle it. With The Big Easy®, there is no preheat time required, and it will cool off about 15 minutes

after turning off the regulator and shutting off the propane flow. The oil-frying process, from start to finish, will take twice as long as frying without oil in The Big Easy.

7. When do I use the wire mesh lid? Use the wire mesh lid only when you are cooking in colder outdoor temperatures or on extremely windy days, or toward the end of your cook time if extra browning is desired. The lid will reflect infrared heat back into the cooking chamber and can burn the exterior of your food before it is done if used for the entire cook time.

8. Can I use the drippings for gravy? Yes—if they are properly prepared. Before cooking the turkey, you must insert a food-safe aluminum liner into the removable grease tray to catch the drippings. After cooking the turkey, the drippings must be heated on a stovetop to the proper temperature for doneness (180°F). Never serve the drippings directly from the removable grease tray. Additional food-safe aluminum liners are available for purchase at www.charbroil.com.

9. What is the easiest way to remove a cooked turkey from the basket? Patience is a virtue. When you remove the basket with the turkey from the cooking chamber, you will be tempted to immediately remove the turkey. Instead, set the basket and the turkey on a tray or platter and allow it to rest for 10 to 15 minutes. Once the basket has cooled, gently separate any places where the turkey has attached itself to the basket during the cooking process. Turn the basket on its side to remove the turkey.

10. **How do I clean The Big Easy®?** After each use, burn off any excess grease and food debris remaining on the cooking basket or that has accumulated in the bottom of the cooking chamber by allowing the unit to cool for approximately 15 minutes with the wire mesh lid on. After the unit has cooled, a grill brush can be used to loosen any remaining material in the bottom of the cook chamber.

After brushing/scraping the bottom of the cook chamber, it can then be lifted out and emptied. The wire basket can be brushed and treated similarly to the cooking grates on a gas grill. It can also be washed in a sink or dishwasher if desired.

The disposable food-safe aluminum liners for the grease tray make cleanup much easier. If any drippings spill onto the grease tray when removing it, clean with soap and water. The grease tray has a painted finish and should be cleaned in a dishwasher. Likewise, the painted exterior surfaces can be cleaned with soap and water as desired.

Minimize cleaning between uses with a custom-fit cover for The Big Easy®, available from Char-Broil®.

Once your food has finished cooking, give it plenty of time to rest and cool down before removing it from the fryer basket.

THE BIG EASY® FRIED TURKEY

8–10 SERVINGS • PREP: 10 MIN. • COOK: 2 HR.

10- to 12-pound turkey
Coarse salt
Favorite no-sugar rub
Vegetable oil

Thaw the turkey in the fridge for several days. Remove the giblets and neck from both cavities, as well as any metal or plastic ties used to bind the legs. Cut the wing tips from the turkey, as well as the small tail, as they may get caught in the fryer basket. Rinse the turkey well with cold water and thoroughly pat it dry with paper towels. Coat the back of the turkey with coarse salt and your favorite rub. Place the turkey in the fryer basket of The Big Easy®, breast side up. Set the basket on its side so the front of the turkey is up and season with coarse salt and the rub. Insert a meat thermometer in the breast. Place the fryer basket with turkey in The Big Easy® and begin cooking. After 30 to 40 minutes, drizzle the oil over the turkey and put the lid on. Cook the turkey for approximately 10 minutes per pound or until the thermometer registers 160°F–165°F (about 2 hours for a bird this size). Carefully remove the turkey from the basket and allow to rest for 15 to 20 minutes to let the juices redistribute through the turkey. Slice and serve.

SAVORY ROASTED TURKEY

8–10 SERVINGS • PREP: 20 MIN. • COOK: 2 HR.

12-pound turkey
1 stick butter, room temperature
2 tablespoons minced
    fresh thyme
2 tablespoons minced
    fresh parsley
2 teaspoons minced shallots
Vegetable oil
Salt and pepper

Remove the giblets and neck from both cavities, as well as any metal or plastic ties used to bind the legs. Cut the wing tips from the turkey, as well as the small tail, as they may get caught in the fryer basket. Rinse the turkey well with cold water and thoroughly pat it dry with paper towels. Use your fingers to separate the breast skin from the meat, slowly inching your way down the breast to avoid breaking the skin.

Combine the butter, thyme, parsley, and shallots in a small bowl, mixing thoroughly. Using your hands, spread the butter mixture under the breast skin. Press down on the skin as you go to move the butter down the breast. Brush the turkey with vegetable oil and liberally salt and pepper the bird.

Place the turkey in the fryer basket of The Big Easy®, breast side up; insert the meat thermometer in the breast. Cook the turkey for approximately 10 minutes per pound or until the thermometer registers 160°F–165°F. Carefully remove the turkey from the basket and place on a platter. Allow the turkey to rest for 15 to 20 minutes before carving.

HOT tip! Oil the fryer basket of The Big Easy® before adding the turkey to help prevent sticking.

SOUTHERN THANKSGIVING TURKEY

8–10 SERVINGS • PREP: 15 MIN. • MARINATE: 2 HR.–OVERNIGHT • COOK: 2–2½ HR.

10- to 12-pound natural turkey
   (not self-basting)
⅔ cup vinaigrette dressing
⅓ cup dry sherry
2 teaspoons lemon-
   pepper seasoning
1 teaspoon garlic powder
1 teaspoon onion powder
1 teaspoon cayenne pepper

Remove the giblets and neck from both cavities; rinse the turkey well with cold water; and thoroughly pat it dry with paper towels. In a medium bowl, mix the vinaigrette, sherry, and seasonings together. Strain the marinade and and inject the mixture into the turkey breast, thighs, and legs using a marinade injector. Place the bird in a large plastic bag; refrigerate; and let marinate for at least 2 hours. Turn the bag, massaging the turkey occasionally.

Drain the marinade from the turkey; discard the marinade. Place the turkey in the fryer basket of The Big Easy®, breast side up; insert the meat thermometer in the breast. Cook the turkey for approximately 10 minutes per pound or until the thermometer registers 165°F. Carefully remove the turkey from the basket and place on a platter. Allow the turkey to rest for 15 to 20 minutes before carving.

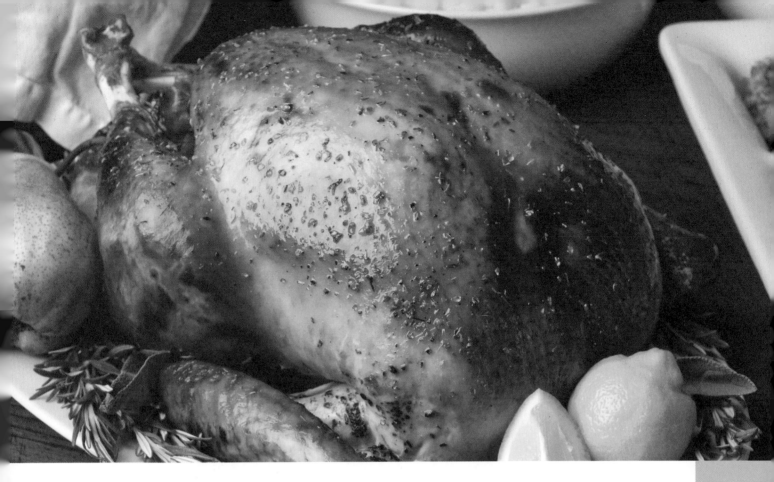

LOUISIANA-STYLE FRIED TURKEY

8–10 SERVINGS • PREP: 15 MIN. • COOK: 2 HR.

10- to 12-pound turkey
3 tablespoons peanut oil
Brine (optional)
Creole seasoning dry rub (low
    sugar content)
Cajun-style marinade to inject
    turkey (optional)

Remove the giblets and neck from both cavities, as well as any metal or plastic ties used to bind the legs. Cut the wing tips from the turkey, as well as the small tail, as they may get caught in the fryer basket. Brine overnight if desired. Remove from brine about 1 hour prior to cooking. Rinse the turkey well with cold water and thoroughly pat it dry with paper towels. Apply dry rub between the skin and the meat if desired (rub on the outside of the turkey will flavor the skin, not the meat). At this time, you may also inject the turkey with marinade if desired. Lightly spray or brush peanut oil on the outside of the turkey.

Place the turkey in the fryer basket of The Big Easy®, breast side up; insert the meat thermometer in the breast. Cook the turkey for approximately 10 minutes per pound or until the thermometer registers 160°F–165°F. Carefully remove the turkey from the basket and place on a platter. Allow the turkey to rest for 15 to 20 minutes before carving.

SPICY ITALIAN TURKEY

12 SERVINGS • PREP: 20 MIN. • MARINATE: OVERNIGHT • COOK: 2 HR.

10- to 12-pound turkey
1 cup Italian salad
    dressing, strained
1 cup white wine
1 box (26 ounces), free-
    flowing salt
3 tablespoons pepper
¼ cup cayenne pepper
2 tablespoons garlic powder
2 tablespoons chili powder

In a small bowl, combine the strained Italian dressing and the white wine. In a separate bowl, combine the salt, pepper, cayenne pepper, garlic powder, and chili powder. Mix until well blended and sprinkle half of the salt mixture over the Italian dressing mixture. Stir thoroughly and constantly so the dressing and wine do not separate.

Remove the giblets and neck from both cavities, as well as any metal or plastic ties used to bind the legs. Cut the wing tips from the turkey, as well as the small tail, as they may get caught in the fryer basket. Rinse the turkey well with cold water and thoroughly pat it dry with paper towels. Place the turkey in a large roasting pan and, using a poultry injector, season the turkey by injecting marinade 2 to 3 times on each side of the breast and upper thighs. If desired, inject any additional marinade into the meaty parts of the turkey. Rub the remaining half of the salt mixture over the outside and inside cavity of the turkey. Cover the roasting pan and turkey with a plastic bag and place overnight in the refrigerator.

Place the turkey in the fryer basket of The Big Easy®, breast side up; insert the meat thermometer in the breast. Cook the turkey for approximately 10 minutes per pound or until the thermometer registers 160°F–165°F. Carefully remove the turkey from the basket and place on a platter. Allow the turkey to rest for 15 to 20 minutes before carving.

Cooking with The Big Easy®

MAPLE-PECAN GLAZED TURKEY

12 SERVINGS • PREP: 15 MIN. • COOK: 2 HR.

10- to 12-pound turkey
¼ cup maple syrup
3 tablespoons butter
2 tablespoons Dijon mustard
2 tablespoons whiskey
¼ cup finely chopped
    pecans, toasted
Salt and pepper

Remove the giblets and neck from both cavities, as well as any metal or plastic ties used to bind the legs. Cut the wing tips from the turkey, as well as the small tail, as they may get caught in the fryer basket. Rinse the turkey well with cold water and thoroughly pat it dry with paper towels.

Place the turkey in the fryer basket of The Big Easy®, breast side up; insert the meat thermometer in the breast. Cook the turkey for approximately 10 minutes per pound or until the thermometer registers 160°F–165°F. Carefully remove the turkey from the basket and place on a platter.

While the turkey is cooking, in a medium saucepan over medium heat, combine the maple syrup, butter, Dijon mustard, whiskey, and chopped toasted pecans. Bring the mixture to a boil, stirring frequently. Reduce the heat and let simmer for 2 to 3 minutes. After the turkey has cooked, spoon the glaze over the hot turkey. Allow the turkey to rest for about 15 minutes before carving. Season with salt and pepper.

ASIAN TURKEY

8–10 SERVINGS • PREP: 15 MIN. • BRINE: 8 HR.–OVERNIGHT • COOK: 2–2½ HR.

10- to 12-pound natural turkey,
   (not self-basting)
2 tablespoons salt
1 tablespoon freshly ground
   black pepper
3 tablespoons wasabi powder

BRINE
1 cup low-sodium soy sauce
⅔ cup sugar
⅔ cup salt

Remove the giblets and neck from both cavities. Rinse the turkey with cold water. Cut off the wing tips and tail, as they may be caught in the fryer basket. Combine the soy sauce, sugar, and salt in a 40- to 60-quart pot. Submerge the turkey in brine. Add enough water to cover it. Stir the liquid to distribute the seasonings evenly. Cover, and refrigerate the turkey for 8 to 24 hours.

Remove the turkey from the brine and then rinse it well, removing all sugar and salt. Pat the interior and exterior dry with paper towels. Drain the brining liquid.

Stir together the salt, black pepper, and wasabi powder. Rub the spice mixture all over the turkey, inside and out. Place the turkey in the fryer basket, breast side up; insert the meat thermometer in the breast. Cook the turkey for approximately 10 minutes per pound or until the internal temperature reaches a minimum of 165°F. Carefully remove the turkey from the basket. Allow the turkey to cool for 15 to 20 minutes before carving.

DOUBLE SPICY TURKEY

12 SERVINGS • PREP: 20 MIN. • COOK: 2 HR.

10- to 12-pound turkey
½ cup liquid garlic
½ cup liquid onion
½ cup liquid celery
1 tablespoon cayenne pepper
2 tablespoons salt
2 tablespoons Tabasco® sauce
2 tablespoons liquid crab boil or
    1 teaspoon Old Bay® seasoning

To make the marinade, in a medium frying pan over medium-high heat, combine the liquid garlic, liquid onion, liquid celery, cayenne pepper, salt, Tabasco® sauce, and crab boil (or Old Bay® seasoning). Sauté the ingredients until the cayenne pepper and salt are completely dissolved.

Remove the giblets and neck from both cavities, as well as any metal or plastic ties used to bind the legs. Cut the wing tips from the turkey, as well as the small tail, as they may get caught in the fryer basket. Rinse the turkey well with cold water and thoroughly pat it dry with paper towels. Place the turkey in a large roasting pan and, using a poultry injector, season the turkey by injecting marinade 2 to 3 times on each side of the breast and upper thighs. If desired, inject any additional marinade into the meaty parts of the turkey.

Place the turkey in the fryer basket of The Big Easy®, breast side up; insert the meat thermometer in the breast. Cook the turkey for approximately 10 minutes per pound or until the thermometer registers 160°F–165°F. Carefully remove the turkey from the basket and place on a platter. Allow the turkey to rest for 15 to 20 minutes before carving.

ONION-STUFFED TURKEY WITH HONEY BEER SAUCE

12 SERVINGS • PREP: 20 MIN. • COOK: 2 HR.

10- to 12-pound turkey
1 medium yellow onion, cut into
  ¼-inch slices
2 tablespoons beer
2 tablespoons honey
2 tablespoons Dijon mustard
1 teaspoon fresh chopped thyme

Remove the giblets and neck from both cavities, as well as any metal or plastic ties used to bind the legs. Cut the wing tips from the turkey, as well as the small tail, as they may get caught in the fryer basket. Rinse the turkey well with cold water and thoroughly pat it dry with paper towels. Use your fingers to separate the breast skin from the meat, slowly inching your way down the breast to avoid breaking the skin. Gently lift the skin and slide the onion slices under the skin.

Place the turkey in the fryer basket of The Big Easy®, breast side up; insert the meat thermometer in the breast. Cook the turkey for approximately 10 minutes per pound or until the thermometer registers 160°F–165°F. Carefully remove the turkey from the basket and place on a platter.

While the turkey is cooking, in a small bowl, combine the beer, honey, Dijon mustard, and fresh chopped thyme. Mix well. After the turkey has cooked, spoon the honey and beer mixture over the hot turkey. Allow the turkey to rest for about 15 minutes before carving.

GINGER-ROSEMARY TURKEY

8–10 SERVINGS • PREP: 15 MIN. • COOK: 2–2½ HR.

10- to 12-pound natural turkey (not self-basting)

¼ cup fresh ginger, peeled and sliced

2 tablespoons fresh rosemary, crushed

6 cloves fresh garlic, peeled

¼ cup fresh garlic, minced

2 tablespoons kosher salt

2 teaspoons freshly ground black pepper

Remove the giblets and neck; rinse the turkey well with cold water; and thoroughly pat it dry with paper towels. Take care to dry both the inside and outside. Fill the cavity with the ginger, rosemary, and garlic cloves. Mix together the minced garlic, salt, and pepper, and rub this on the exterior of the bird. Do not truss or tie the legs together. Cut off the wing tips and the small tail, as they may get caught in the fryer basket. Cover the pan and place it in the refrigerator overnight.

Place the turkey in the basket, breast side up; insert a meat thermometer in the breast. Cook the turkey for approximately 10 minutes per pound or until the internal temperature is a minimum of 165°F. Carefully remove the turkey from the basket. Allow the turkey to rest for 15 to 20 minutes before carving.

CIDER-BRINED TURKEY

6 SERVINGS • PREP: 15 MIN • BRINE: UP TO 24 HR • COOK: 2 HR., 30 MIN

12- to-14-pound fresh turkey
Onions, fresh herbs for stuffing

BRINE
4 quarts fresh apple cider, divided
1½ cups coarse kosher salt
¼ cup whole allspice
8 bay leaves
4 quarts cold water

This recipe requires advance preparation, as the turkey must be brined and then air-dried in the refrigerator before cooking. If you don't have room in the refrigerator to brine the turkey, put the turkey in a large oven bag in a large cooler. Pour the brine into the bag and seal tightly. Place ice or reusable ice packs around the turkey; close the lid; and let the turkey brine, adding more ice packs as needed to keep the temperature at 40°F or below.

To brine: Simmer 1 quart of apple cider, salt, allspice, and bay leaves in a large stockpot for 5 minutes. Cool, and add remaining cider and the cold water. Leave the brine in the pot, or pour into a large food-safe container. After removing the giblets, neck, and pop-up thermometer, add the turkey to the brine; refrigerate overnight or up to 24 hours.

Day of cooking: One hour before cooking, remove the turkey from the brine; rinse well with cold water; and pat dry with paper towels. Place the turkey in a large roasting pan. If desired, cut the skin between the leg and the rib cage to improve heat penetration. Loosely stuff any aromatics—onions, herbs—into the cavity of the turkey. Truss legs to keep aromatics inside the cavity during cooking.

Place the prepared turkey in the fryer basket, legs down, and centered as much as possible. Place the basket into the cooker and turn on the unit according to instructions. Plan your cooking to approximately 10 minutes per pound of turkey. Turkey is done when an instant-read thermometer inserted in the thickest part of the thigh registers 180°F and 165°F in the breast. Carefully remove the turkey basket from the cooking chamber. Place the turkey on a serving platter; tent with foil; and allow the bird to rest for 20 to 30 minutes before carving.

THE BIG EASY®
ROTISSERIE CHICKEN

4–6 SERVINGS • PREP: 10 MIN. • COOK: 2½ HR.

5- to 6-pound chicken
Herb seasoning or lemon-pepper
   dry rub

Remove the giblets and neck from both cavities, as well as any metal or plastic ties used to bind the legs. Season the outside of the chicken with your favorite low-sugar dry rub. Place the chicken in the fryer basket of The Big Easy®, breast side up. Cook the chicken for approximately 15 minutes per pound or until the internal temperature registers 165°F in the breast and 175°F in the thighs. If desired, use the wire mesh lid during the last few minutes of cooking to help crisp up the skin. Allow the chicken to rest for 5 to 10 minutes before carefully removing from the basket, slicing, and serving.

HOT tip! Cook two chickens at the same time using The Big Easy® cooking racks available at *www.charbroil.com*.

BEER-CAN CHICKEN

6 SERVINGS • PREP: 15 MIN. • MARINATE: 1 HR.–OVERNIGHT • GRILL: 1½–2 HR.

1 whole chicken (4 to 5 pounds)
2 teaspoons vegetable oil
1 16-ounce can beer

RUB

1 teaspoon dry mustard
¼ cup onion, minced
1 teaspoon paprika
1 teaspoon kosher salt
4 small cloves garlic, minced
½ teaspoon ground coriander
⅓ teaspoon ground cumin
½ teaspoon freshly ground
    black pepper

In a small bowl, combine the rub ingredients. Wash the chicken and pat it dry. Rub the entire chicken with vegetable oil and season it with the rub, inside and out.

Take the can of beer (make sure it is warm), opened, and place the chicken (legs down, breast up) over the can of beer and then place it in the fryer basket of The Big Easy®. Try to make sure some of the beer can is exposed so the infrared heat will hit the can and warm it. Cook the chicken for approximately 15 minutes per pound or until the internal temperature registers 165°F in the breast and 175°F in the thighs. After cooking, place the chicken on a pan or tray—most of the beer should be evaporated—tent with foil, and rest for 15 to 20 minutes before slicing and serving.

ROASTED THAI CHICKEN

4–6 SERVINGS • PREP: 4 HR. • BRINE: 2–4 HR. • COOK: 2½ HR.

Courtesy of Chris Grove, "Nibble Me This"

5- to 6-pound roaster chicken
1 teaspoon salt
¾ teaspoon black pepper

BRINE

2 quarts water
5 tablespoons salt
1 teaspoon red pepper flakes
1 teaspoon dried minced garlic

COMPOUND BUTTER

1 stick unsalted butter,
 room temperature
1 tablespoon sambal oelek
1 teaspoon minced fresh ginger
1 teaspoon chopped cilantro
2 cloves garlic, peeled
 and chopped
8 basil leaves, sliced into strips

Remove the giblets and neck from both cavities, as well as any metal or plastic ties used to bind the legs. Mix the brine by stirring 1 quart of water, salt, red pepper flakes, and dried garlic together in a pot large enough to hold your bird. Bring to a boil and allow to sit for 5 minutes. Add the remaining cool water and place in the fridge to chill the brine down to 40°F before use. Place the chicken in the brine and let sit for 2 to 4 hours. While the bird brines, make the compound butter by stirring together the butter, sambal oelek, ginger, cilantro, garlic, and basil. Keep refrigerated until ready for use.

Remove the chicken from the brine, rinse well with cold water, and thoroughly pat it dry with paper towels. Work the compound butter under and on top of the chicken skin. Season with salt and pepper and place the chicken in the fryer basket of The Big Easy®, breast side up. Cook the chicken for approximately 15 minutes per pound or until the internal temperature registers 165°F in the breast and 175°F in the thighs. If desired, use the wire mesh lid during the last few minutes of cooking to help crisp up the skin. Allow the chicken to rest for 5 to 10 minutes before carefully removing from the basket, slicing, and serving.

YARDBIRD WINGS

4 SERVINGS • PREP: 4 HR. INCLUDING MARINATING • COOK: 10 MIN.

Around 24 chicken wings
½ cup canola or vegetable oil
½ cup or more lemon juice
½ cup favorite seasoning
    or rub for chicken wings
Salt and pepper to taste

Mix seasoning ingredients together in a nonreactive container. Wash and cut off the wing tips, and then the drum, from each 2-bone wing. Add prepped chicken parts to container and allow them to marinate at least two hours or overnight.

Place all of the wings in The Big Easy® cooking basket. (Use either the EZ Out Cooking Rack or the Half Racks to fit all the wings in the basket.)

Place the loaded cooking basket into The Big Easy®; cover with the lid; and set heat to high. Let wings cook for at least 5 to 10 minutes. Pay close attention to the wings, turning the basket and using tongs to move the wings around for even cooking. Serve the wings with your favorite dipping sauce.

THE BIG EASY® BEEF ROAST

8–10 SERVINGS • PREP: 10 MIN. • COOK: 2½ HR.

3- to 5-pound beef roast
Kosher salt
Fresh cracked pepper
Creole rub (optional)

Season the entire cut of meat with the salt and pepper or a creole rub for added spice. Place the roast vertically in The Big Easy® basket (using skewers to hold it in place), or place the roast horizontally using The Big Easy® Bunk-Bed Basket inside the main cooking basket. Cook the roast approximately 30 minutes per pound or until the internal temperature registers 145°F for medium rare. Allow the roast to rest for 5 to 10 minutes before carefully removing from the basket and slicing.

HOT tip! Try cooking roasted red potatoes and corn above the roast using The Big Easy® cooking rack.

THE BIG EASY® PRIME RIB

8–10 SERVINGS • PREP: 10 MIN. • COOK: 2½ HR.

5-pound rib roast
1 tablespoon sea salt
1 tablespoon freshly ground
   black pepper

Season the entire cut of meat with the salt and pepper. Place the roast vertically in The Big Easy® basket (using skewers to hold it in place), or place the roast horizontally using a cooking rack inside the main cooking basket. Cook the roast approximately 30 minutes per pound or until the internal temperature registers 145°F for medium rare. Carefully remove the roast from the basket and place on a platter. Cover the roast with aluminum foil and a kitchen towel. Allow the roast to rest for 15 to 20 minutes before slicing.

FAVORITE PRIME RIB

8–10 SERVINGS • PREP: 15 MIN. • COOK: 2½ HR.

5-pound rib roast
1 tablespoon garlic powder
1 tablespoon sea salt
1 tablespoon onion powder
2 teaspoons cayenne pepper
2 teaspoons dried rosemary
2 teaspoons dried thyme

Mix all the dry ingredients together in a large mixing bowl using a fork or whisk. Place the rib roast in the bowl and use your hands to work the rub into all areas of the meat. Note: Rubber gloves can come in handy to prevent the spices from coating your hands. Place the roast vertically in The Big Easy® basket (using skewers to hold it in place), or place the roast horizontally using The Big Easy® Bunk-Bed Basket inside the main cooking basket.). Cook the roast approximately 30 minutes per pound or until the internal temperature registers 145°F for medium rare. Allow the roast to rest for 5 to 10 minutes before carefully removing from the basket and slicing.

COFFEE-BRINED BEEF ROAST

10–12 SERVINGS • PREP: 12 HR. (INCLUDES BRINING OVERNIGHT)
COOK: 1 HR., 30 MIN.

Sirloin tip beef roast
    (5 to 7 pounds)
1 tablespoon flour
½ tablespoon butter

COFFEE BRINE

4 cups warm water, or enough to
    cover roast
2 cups brewed coffee
½ cup salt
¼ cup white sugar
¼ cup brown sugar
3 tablespoons oil
2 teaspoons white pepper
2 teaspoons black pepper
¼ cup Worcestershire sauce
2 tablespoons onion flakes

Mix brine ingredients and let mixture cool to room temperature. Place roast in a large pan or container; pour brine over meat. Cover meat and refrigerate for a minimum of 8 hours.

Remove meat from brine about 1 hour before cooking; set in shallow pan or bowl to allow brine to drip off. Do not rinse.

Line drip tray with aluminum foil or use The Big Easy® foil drip pans. Place meat vertically in The Big Easy® basket (using skewers to hold it in place), or place the roast horizontally using The Big Easy® Bunk-Bed Basket inside the main cooking basket; lower basket into the cooking chamber; and cover with mesh lid. Set control knob to high; ignite.

After approximately 30 minutes, remove the lid and turn the control knob to about halfway between high and off. Continue cooking for approximately 1 hour or until meat reaches an internal temperature of 145°F for medium rare.

Lift the cooking basket from the cooker; carefully remove the meat from the basket; and wrap with foil. Place in a shallow bowl or tray to rest for 30 minutes. Pour drippings from the drip tray into a measuring cup. Skim off fat and solids, and add remaining juices to saucepan. Add one teaspoon of flour and ½ tablespoon of butter. Cook, stirring occasionally, until sauce is reduced by about half, approximately 5 minutes. Slice roast; arrange on platter; and serve.

The key to good grilling is to recognize that you are setting yourself up to cook in a whole new environment. This is actually one of the main purposes of grilling—to get yourself outside.

–Barton Seaver

BLOODY MARY LONDON BROIL

6 SERVINGS • PREP: 20 MIN. • MARINATE 2 HR.–OVERNIGHT • COOK: 15–30 MIN.

1 London broil, about 3½ pounds

2 cups tomato juice

¼ cup Worcestershire sauce

3 tablespoons
  prepared horseradish

3 tablespoons dry sherry

2 teaspoons dried
  marjoram, crushed

1 teaspoon dried basil, crushed

1 teaspoon freshly ground
  black pepper

Combine the tomato juice, Worcestershire sauce, horseradish, sherry, and seasonings in a bowl. Place the steak in a baking dish. Spoon the tomato juice mixture over the meat, spreading to cover. Turn the meat to coat the other side. Cover and refrigerate for at least 2 hours or set aside at room temperature for 30 minutes.

Place the meat in the fryer basket of The Big Easy®. Cook until the internal temperature registers 145°F for medium rare. Allow the roast to rest for 5 to 10 minutes before carefully removing from the basket and slicing.

THE BIG EASY® FRESH HAM

8 SERVINGS • PREP: 2 HR. • BRINE: UP TO 24 HR. • COOK: 4 HR.

14-pound fresh uncured ham
Brine for ham
Glaze for ham

Try a bourbon, honey, or molasses glaze.

It's recommended that you remove the skin from the ham, but leave as much fat on as possible. Brine the ham for 24 hours (or overnight). Remove from brine about 1 hour prior to cooking. Rinse the ham well with cold water and thoroughly pat it dry with paper towels. If desired, add a mustard and rub combo, but keep in mind to limit the mustard and rub material because the long cook time might cause these to burn.

Using a cooking rack, place the ham in the fryer basket of The Big Easy® so it rests on the shelf one level above the bottom of the basket. Cook the ham approximately 30 minutes per pound or until the internal temperature registers 145°F. Carefully remove the ham from the basket and place on a platter. Cover the ham with aluminum foil and a kitchen towel and place it in an insulated container. Allow the ham to rest in the container for about 30 minutes before slicing.

THE BIG EASY® BBQ

8–10 SERVINGS • PREP: 10 MIN. • COOK: 1½ HR.

3- to 5-pound pork roast or
    Boston Butt
Low-sugar dry rub
Barbecue sauce

Season the entire cut of meat using your favorite low-sugar barbecue dry rub. Place the roast vertically in The Big Easy® basket (using skewers to hold it in place), or place the roast horizontally using The Big Easy® Easy-Out Cooking Rack within the main cooking basket. Cook the roast approximately 30 minutes per pound or until the internal temperature registers 145°F for medium rare. Carefully remove the roast from the basket and cover with your favorite barbecue sauce. Wrap the roast with two layers of heavy-duty aluminum foil and return it to the cooking basket for an additional 15 to 30 minutes. Allow the roast to rest for 5 to 10 minutes before carefully removing from the basket. Serve chopped, sliced, or cubed.

HOT tip! For pulled pork, cook the roast inside the aluminum foil until the internal temperature reaches 195°F–200°F.

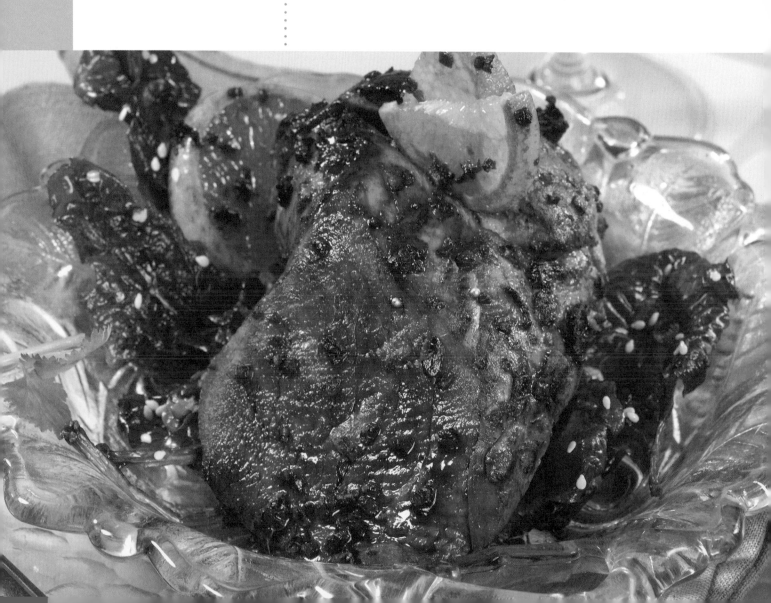

BABY BACK RIBS

10–12 SERVINGS • PREP: 10 MIN. • MARINATE: UP TO 24 HR. • COOK: 2 HR.

4–6 racks of baby back pork ribs
Steak seasoning
Favorite sauce

Season the ribs with steak seasoning and allow to marinate for 24 hours (or overnight). Use rib hooks to hang the ribs in the fryer basket of The Big Easy®. Cook the ribs on high for about 20 minutes and then reduce the heat to low. Continue to cook until done (usually about 2 hours). Carefully remove the ribs from the basket. Cover half of the racks with your favorite sauce and leave the remaining half plain. Wrap each rack in foil and a kitchen towel. Let the ribs rest for 2 hours in an insulated container before serving.

My sisters and I can still recite Dad's grilling rules: Rule No. 1: Dad is in charge. Rule No. 2: Repeat Rule No. 1.
–Connie Schultz

THE BIG EASY®
PORK TENDERLOINS

6–8 SERVINGS • PREP: 10 MIN. • COOK: 30 MIN.

2 pork tenderloins
Kosher salt
Fresh cracked pepper

Season the tenderloins with the salt and pepper. Place the pork loins in the fryer basket of The Big Easy®. Cook until the internal temperature registers 145°F. (Note: The tenderloins will cook fast; check the internal temperature after 30 minutes.) Allow the tenderloins to rest for 5 to 10 minutes before carefully removing them from the basket and slicing. Serve with your favorite sauce and side dishes.

HOT tip! Skewer one end of each tenderloin and allow them to hang vertically inside the cooking chamber.

MUSHROOM DUXELLES-STUFFED PORK LOIN

6 SERVINGS • PREP: 15 MIN. • COOK: 45 MIN.

Courtesy of Catherine Mayhew, "The South in My Mouth"

2-pound pork loin

8 ounces fresh mushrooms, diced

¼ cup onion, diced

2 tablespoons butter

Salt and pepper

1 teaspoon dried thyme

2 tablespoons Madeira

Butterfly the pork loin by slicing a 1-inch opening through the top half. Next, slice the bottom lengthwise to create a single, flat piece of pork.

Squeeze the mushrooms inside a clean kitchen towel to remove all excess water. Combine the mushrooms, onions, butter, salt, pepper, and thyme in a skillet and sauté until the onions are translucent. Add the Madeira and continue to sauté until the liquid has evaporated. Cool completely.

Spread the cooled mushroom mixture over the flattened pork loin, leaving about 1 inch around the ends and sides. Roll the pork loin back into its original shape, with the fat cap on the top. Using three pieces of kitchen twine or silicone ties, wrap the roast at each end and in the middle to secure it in place. Liberally salt and pepper the roast.

Place the pork loin in the fryer basket of The Big Easy®. Cook until the internal temperature registers 145°F. (Note: The loin will cook fast; check the internal temperature after 30 minutes.) Allow the loin to rest for 5 to 10 minutes before carefully removing from the basket and slicing.

THE BIG EASY® LEG OF LAMB

6–10 SERVINGS • PREP: 20 MIN. • MARINATE: 4–24 HR. • COOK: 3½ HR.

Courtesy of Scott Thomas, "Grillin' Fools"

1 bone-in leg of lamb
    (7 to 8 pounds)
½ cup olive oil
⅓ cup red wine
1 teaspoon Dijon mustard
1 teaspoon fresh rosemary,
    rough chopped
1 teaspoon fresh thyme leaves
3 cloves fresh garlic, minced
10 turns of a black pepper mill
10 turns of a white pepper mill
    (optional)
2 cloves garlic, sliced into slivers
2 tablespoons rosemary sprigs

For the marinade, combine the olive oil, red wine, mustard, rosemary, minced garlic, thyme, black pepper, and white pepper. With a slender knife, make slits in the lamb and insert slivers of garlic or rosemary or both. Place the lamb in a resealable plastic bag and coat with the marinade on both sides. Place the marinating leg of lamb in the fridge for 4 to 24 hours. Remove from the bag and coat the lamb with salt and black pepper.

Place the leg of lamb in the fryer basket of The Big Easy®, thick side down. Cook until the internal temperature registers 125°F (approximately 3 hours) and then sear on a conventional grill. If no conventional grill is available and you want the lamb to be beyond rare, leave it in The Big Easy®, checking it periodically with a probe thermometer.

Remove the lamb from the grill or fryer and allow to rest for at least 20 minutes. Slice and serve.

SHRIMP PACKETS

1 SERVING • PREP: 10 MIN. • COOK: 10–15 MIN.

1 pound shrimp, peeled
   and deveined
¼ cup butter or margarine, cut
   into pieces

1 clove garlic, minced
½ teaspoon pepper
1 teaspoon salt
1 cup parsley flakes

Lay the shrimp out on a large piece (or pieces) of aluminum foil. Top with the butter pieces, minced garlic, pepper, salt, and parsley flakes. Wrap the aluminum up and over the ingredients to seal the packet. Wrap the packet in another layer of aluminum foil. Place the packet in the fryer basket of The Big Easy® and cook for 10 to 15 minutes until the shrimp is fully cooked. Carefully remove the packet from the basket, unwrap, and enjoy.

You don't need a Dutch oven or a campfire for these recipes. Cook them right in The Big Easy® Fryer!

HONEY MUSTARD CHICKEN PACKETS

4 SERVINGS • PREP: 10 MIN. • COOK: 20–30 MIN.

4 boneless, skinless chicken breasts
4 potatoes, quartered lengthwise
1 green or red bell pepper, cut into strips
8–12 tablespoons honey mustard barbecue sauce

Set out 4 large pieces of aluminum foil. Divide the chicken breasts, potatoes, and bell pepper strips onto each piece. Drizzle 2 to 3 tablespoons of honey mustard barbecue sauce over each packet. Wrap the aluminum up and over the ingredients to seal each packet. Wrap each packet in another layer of aluminum foil. Place the packets in the fryer basket of The Big Easy® and cook for 20 to 30 minutes until the chicken is fully cooked. Carefully remove the packets from the basket, unwrap, and enjoy.

DEEP-DISH PIZZA

10–12 SERVINGS • PREP: 1½ HR. • COOK: 15–25 MIN.

1¼ teaspoons active dry yeast

2 teaspoons sugar

1 teaspoon salt

¼ teaspoon garlic powder

1 tablespoon olive oil

1½–2 cups bread flour

½ cup prepared pizza sauce

Favorite pizza toppings

1–1½ cups shredded
    mozzarella cheese

1 tablespoon grated Parmesan
    cheese

Freshly ground pepper

Chopped fresh basil, optional

In a medium bowl, combine the yeast, sugar, and ½ cup very warm water; stir to dissolve and let stand until foamy (about 10 minutes). Stir in the salt, garlic powder, oil, and just enough flour to make a dough that pulls away from the sides of the bowl. Turn the dough out on a lightly floured surface and knead for 5 minutes. Cover and let rest 30 to 60 minutes.

Spray the rack of the Stackable Oven for The Big Easy® with nonstick cooking spray. Roll out the dough in a circle about 1 inch larger on all sides than the bottom of the oven. Place the dough circle in the oven, pressing it up the sides to form a rim. If necessary, place an aluminum pie plate in the bottom of the oven first to ensure that the dough stays in place. Spread the sauce over the dough. Sprinkle with your desired toppings, finishing with the mozzarella and Parmesan cheeses. Sprinkle with pepper. Cover the Stackable Oven and place it in the cooking chamber of The Big Easy®. Cook for 15 to 25 minutes or until the crust is golden brown and the cheese is melted. Sprinkle with fresh basil if desired.

ITALIAN GARLIC ROLLS

10–12 SERVINGS • PREP: 1 HR. • COOK: 25 MIN.

1 package Pillsbury Hot Roll
  Mix, 16 ounces
2 tablespoons plus 4 tablespoons
  butter, softened, divided
1 egg

⅔ cup grated Parmesan cheese
1½ teaspoons garlic powder
2 teaspoons Italian seasoning
½ teaspoon dried oregano
Flour for kneading

Following the directions on the roll mix package, mix the contents of the box and yeast in a large bowl. Stir in 1 cup hot water, 2 tablespoons butter, and egg until the dough forms. On a floured surface, shape the dough into a ball and knead until smooth (about 5 minutes). Meanwhile, in a small bowl, stir together the Parmesan cheese, garlic powder, Italian seasoning, and oregano; set aside.

Roll the dough into an 8 x 18-inch rectangle. Spread the remaining 4 tablespoons butter over the dough. Sprinkle the dough evenly with the cheese mixture. Starting at one long edge, roll up the dough, cinnamon-roll fashion, and pinch the long edge to seal. Slice into rolls about 1½ inches thick.

Spray the rack of the Stackable Oven for The Big Easy® with nonstick cooking spray. Arrange the rolls in a single layer in the oven. Cover the oven with the lid and let the rolls rise in a warm place until doubled in size (about 30 to 40 minutes). Place the Stackable Oven with rolls in the cooking chamber of The Big Easy® (no cooking basket needed). Cook for 18 to 25 minutes or until lightly browned. Allow the rolls to cool in the oven for several minutes before removing.

POTATO & EGG FOIL PACKETS

1 SERVING • PREP: 10 MIN. • COOK: 45–60 MIN.

1 baked potato
1 egg

Butter
Salt and pepper

Coat the outside of the potato with butter; wrap it tightly in heavy-duty aluminum foil. Place the wrapped potato in the fryer basket of The Big Easy® and cook for 45 to 60 minutes or until tender. Carefully remove the potato from the basket and unwrap it. Slice the potato partway through and open it slightly. Place some butter inside and then break the egg into the potato. Rewrap the potato in the foil. Return the wrapped potato and egg to the fryer and cook until the egg is set. Season with salt and pepper.

GARLIC-ROASTED SWEET POTATOES WITH ARUGULA

6 SERVINGS • PREP: 15 MIN. • GRILL: 40–45 MIN.

2 pounds sweet potatoes, peeled and cut into 2-inch pieces

4 garlic cloves, peeled and sliced

2 tablespoons extra-virgin olive oil

½ teaspoon salt

½ teaspoon black pepper, ground

2 Bartlett pears, cored and cut into 2-inch pieces

1 5-ounce package arugula

½ teaspoon lemon peel, grated

Preheat grill or oven to medium-high. In a large roasting pan, combine potatoes, garlic, oil, salt, and pepper, and toss to coat well. Roast for 30 minutes, tossing occasionally, until tender and browned. Add pears and roast another 10 minutes.

Place the arugula in a large bowl. Add the cooked potatoes and pears, and toss until the arugula wilts. Sprinkle with the lemon peel.

I've long believed that good food, good eating, is all about risk.

–Anthony Bourdain

CREAMY ZUCCHINI & GARLIC

3–4 SERVINGS • PREP: 5 MIN. • COOK: 5–10 MIN.

2½ tablespoons butter
6 garlic cloves, minced
6 medium zucchini, grated
2½ tablespoons garlic powder
1 teaspoon thyme, chopped
2½ tablespoons sour cream
Fresh pepper

Melt butter in a heavy-bottom skillet over medium heat. Lower heat; add minced garlic; and sauté for about 1 to 2 minutes. (Do not let garlic burn.) Add grated zucchini, garlic powder, and thyme.

Cook, stirring frequently until zucchini is tender. Remove from heat and stir in sour cream. Season with fresh pepper. Serve immediately.

Try these delicious side dishes for the grill. They will pair beautifully with any meat you cook in The Big Easy®.

CRANBERRY-PECAN RICE PILAF

4 SERVINGS • PREP: 10 MIN.• COOK: 18–20 MIN.

2 tablespoons butter or margarine

1 cup uncooked rice

1 can (14½ ounces) chicken broth

1 cup Parmesan cheese, grated

½ cup dried cranberries

½ cup pecans, chopped and toasted*

¼ cup green onions, sliced

Salt and black pepper, ground, to taste

Melt butter in 2-quart saucepan over medium heat. Add rice and cook, stirring, 2 to 3 minutes. Add broth, and heat to boiling, stirring once or twice. Reduce heat; cover; and simmer 15 minutes or until liquid is absorbed.

Remove from heat. Stir in cheese, cranberries, pecans, and onions. Season to taste with salt and pepper.

*To toast pecans, spread nuts on small baking sheet. Bake 5 to 8 minutes at 350°F, or until golden brown, stirring frequently.

ROASTED ASPARAGUS WITH CHERRY TOMATOES, GARLIC & OLIVE OIL

4 SERVINGS • PREP: 10 MIN. • GRILL: 20–25 MIN.

2 pounds pencil asparagus, woody ends trimmed

2 cups cherry tomatoes, washed and stemmed

12 garlic cloves, peeled and smashed

¼ cup extra-virgin olive oil

1 teaspoon coarse salt

½ teaspoon black pepper, freshly ground

¼ cup fresh lemon juice, reserve lemon halves

Preheat grill to medium-high. In a large bowl, combine asparagus, tomatoes, and garlic. Drizzle with olive oil and season with coarse salt and pepper. Toss to coat and then transfer to a large aluminum baking sheet. Drizzle lemon juice over asparagus; add lemon halves to pan; and place on grill. Roast until asparagus stalks are tender and tomatoes begin to caramelize, about 20 to 25 minutes. Remove from grill and serve hot or at room temperature.

LIVEFIRE'S HOLIDAY POTATO TORTE

6 SERVINGS • PREP: 20 MIN. • GRILL: 35–40 MIN.

Courtesy of Curt McAdams, www.livefireonline.com

3 to 4 russet potatoes, scrubbed
    but not skinned
Olive oil
Salt and black pepper to taste
2 tablespoons fresh
    rosemary, chopped
V-slicer or mandolin

Preheat grill to medium-high. Generously butter a well-seasoned 10-inch cast-iron or other heavy skillet. Using a V-slicer or mandolin, thinly slice each potato, placing slices in the skillet as you go to prevent oxidation.

Because you will invert the torte after it is cooked, the bottom layer of potatoes will be the top of the torte, so make sure to arrange the slices in an attractive pattern. As you add each layer, brush it with olive oil, and sprinkle with salt and pepper and about ½ teaspoon of rosemary. When you're finished, you should have about 7 layers of potatoes.

Place the skillet on the grill and cook until the potatoes are sizzling nicely, about 12 to 15 minutes. Using heat-resistant gloves or potholders, remove the skillet from the grill and drain off excess oil. Carefully invert the torte onto a clean plate and then slide the potatoes, bottom side up, back into the skillet. Return to the grill and cook, with lid closed, for about 20 to 25 minutes or until potatoes are browned and crispy and inner layers are tender.

ROASTED-GARLIC MASHED POTATOES

4 SERVINGS • PREP: 10 MIN. • COOK: 20–30 MIN.

4 Russet potatoes
1 cup milk
½ cup buttermilk
¼ cup unsalted butter

2 heads of roasted garlic
¼ cup extra-virgin olive oil
1 tablespoon dried thyme
Salt and pepper to taste

Peel potatoes and cut them into quarters. Boil them in salted water for 20 to 30 minutes or until tender. Meanwhile, heat the milk, buttermilk, and butter in a pot. When the potatoes are done, drain and return them to the same pot. Squeeze the garlic cloves out of their skins and then add the milk and butter a little at a time; mash potatoes until the desired consistency is achieved. Season the potatoes with salt and pepper to taste. Serve hot.

GRILLED PEAR & GORGONZOLA SALAD

2–4 SERVINGS • PREP: 5 MIN. • GRILL: 5–10 MIN.

2 ripe pears, cored and cut
    in eighths
Canola oil
3 to 4 leaves of Bibb or other tender
    lettuce, washed and dried

2 tablespoons extra-virgin olive oil
1 wedge Gorgonzola or bleu cheese
4 tablespoons salted roasted
    almonds, chopped

Preheat grill to medium-high. Spray pear slices with canola oil and sear over direct heat, turning to ensure both sides become fairly dark brown but not blackened.

Arrange the seared pear slices on the lettuce leaves. Drizzle with olive oil; crumble cheese over them; and sprinkle with the roasted almonds.

MARINATED PORTOBELLO MUSHROOMS WITH ROASTED-PEPPER VINAIGRETTE

6 SERVINGS • PREP: 10 MIN. • MARINATE: 1 HR. • GRILL: 4–6 MIN.

Courtesy of christopherranch.com

1 pound fresh Portobello
    mushrooms, stems trimmed
Olive oil for skillet

MARINADE

4 tablespoons balsamic vinegar
6 garlic cloves, minced
2 tablespoons fresh thyme
    leaves, chopped
⅓ cup olive oil

VINAIGRETTE

1 red pepper, roasted, peeled,
    seeded, and chopped coarsely
1 Poblano chile, roasted, peeled,
    seeded, and chopped coarsely
4 garlic cloves, peeled
2 tablespoons red wine vinegar
1 lemon, squeezed for juice
¼ cup olive oil
Coarse salt
Black pepper, freshly ground

In a small bowl, whisk together marinade ingredients. Arrange mushroom caps in a single layer in a nonreactive shallow pan. Pour marinade over mushrooms; cover; and marinate for 1 hour, turning mushrooms several times. In a blender, combine vinaigrette ingredients until smooth. Taste for seasoning.

Heat an oiled grill skillet. Remove mushrooms from marinade; place them in pan; and use a food press or a heavy can to press down on them. Sear them about 2 to 3 minutes on each side or until tender. Transfer mushrooms to a cutting board; slice thin; and drizzle with red-pepper vinaigrette.

BASIC BRINE RECIPE

YIELD: 4 CUPS BRINE • PREP TIME: 10 MIN.
BRINING TIME: 4 HR.–OVERNIGHT
USE FOR: TURKEY, CHICKEN, BEEF BRISKET, SALMON

¼ cup kosher salt
¼ cup packed brown sugar
4 cups hot water

In a medium bowl, combine salt, sugar, and water. Whisk vigorously until salt and sugar have dissolved. Allow mixture to cool. Pour brine over meat, poultry, or fish. Marinate for several hours or overnight in refrigerator. Before cooking, rinse meat's surface and pat it dry.

Note: The meat should be fully submerged in the brine; make more brine by converting the recipe as needed.

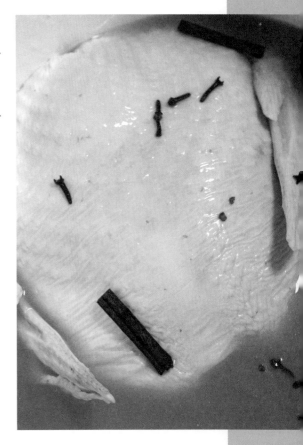

SAVANNAH SMOKER'S SPECIAL PORK BRINE

YIELD: 2+ GAL.• PREP: 5 MIN. • USE WITH: PORK

Courtesy of "Sizzle on the Grill" contributor "Savannah Smoker."

2 gallons water
2 cups dark brown sugar
2 cups coarse salt
¼ cup ground ginger
¼ cup garlic powder
½ cup apple-cider vinegar
¼ cup ground cumin

4 large sprigs fresh rosemary
¼ cup black pepper, coarsely ground
2 tablespoons Worcestershire sauce
2 tablespoons Tabasco® sauce
2 medium-size lemons chopped, squeezed, and smashed

Fill a large pot with water; add remainder of ingredients; and stir. Brine meat overnight or for 24 hours.

FILIPINO ADOBO SAUCE

YIELD: 3+ CUPS • PREP: 5 MIN.
COOK: 30–40 MIN. (UNTIL SAUCE THICKENS)
USE WITH: CHICKEN, PORK

1 cup soy sauce
½ cup rice-wine vinegar (may
    substitute apple-cider vinegar)
1 tablespoon garlic, minced
1 tablespoon fresh ginger, minced
2 cups coconut milk
1 teaspoon smoked paprika

1 small jalapeño, diced
1 cup water
Whole chicken, cut into eighths, or
    2-pound pork loin, cubed
1 tablespoon lime juice,
    freshly squeezed

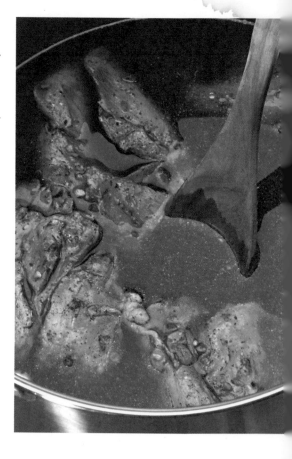

Combine the soy sauce, vinegar, garlic, ginger, ½ cup of the coconut milk, paprika, jalapeño, and water in a deep pot, and slowly simmer on low for about 5 to 10 minutes until ingredients are blended and sauce is heated evenly.

Add the meat; cook for about 15 to 20 minutes. When it starts to get firm, remove the meat from pot; pat dry with a paper towel; and reserve to finish.

Turn up the heat a bit, and add the remaining coconut milk. Reduce until the sauce has the consistency of runny cake batter. Add lime juice, and strain before serving.

CHILI-CINNAMON RUB FOR CHICKEN

YIELD: APPROX. ¼ CUP • PREP: 5 MIN.
USE WITH: CHICKEN

2 teaspoons ancho chili powder
2 teaspoons cinnamon, ground
2 teaspoons cumin, ground

4 teaspoons fresh thyme
2 teaspoons salt
2 teaspoons brown sugar

Blend spices, salt, and sugar in a small bowl.

Ancho chili powder works well in this recipe, but you can use chipotle or other, milder, chili powders.

JAN'S DRY RUB

YIELD: APPROX. 3 CUPS • PREP: 5 MIN.
USE WITH: PORK RIBS, CHICKEN

1¼ cups sugar
¼ cup Lawry's® Seasoned Salt
¼ cup garlic salt
¼ cup + 1½ teaspoon celery salt
¼ cup onion salt
½ cup paprika
3 tablespoons chili powder

2 tablespoons black pepper
1 tablespoon lemon pepper
2 teaspoons celery seed
2 teaspoons dry sage, ground
1 teaspoon dry mustard
½ teaspoon dry thyme, ground
½ teaspoon cayenne pepper

Blend all ingredients in a large bowl.

"Sizzle on the Grill" contributor KyNola says his wife, Jan,
came up with this recipe to match a secret version
at a local BBQ restaurant. It has "only" 14
ingredients and makes a bunch.

PLUM MARINADE

YIELD: APPROX. ¾ CUP • PREP: 5 MIN.
MARINATE: 4–6 HR. • USE WITH: STEAK, CHICKEN

½ cup plum preserves
3 tablespoons green onion, minced
2 tablespoons white vinegar
2 tablespoons hoisin sauce

2 teaspoons fresh ginger, minced
1 teaspoon dry mustard
½ teaspoon ground red pepper
Green onion, minced (optional)

In a bowl, whisk together all ingredients until completely emulsified.
Marinate meat in a sealable plastic bag or covered container
in refrigerator.

CAPTAIN JESSIE'S JAMAICAN JERK MARINADE

YIELD: 1 CUP • PREP: 10 MIN. • MARINATE: 4 HR.–
OVERNIGHT • USE WITH: MEAT AND POULTRY

1 white onion, chopped
½ cup scallions, chopped
2 teaspoons fresh thyme or
    1 teaspoon dried thyme
1 whole Scotch Bonnet or habanero
    pepper, seeded and chopped
1 teaspoon coarse salt
2 teaspoons light brown sugar

1 teaspoon allspice
½ teaspoon ground nutmeg
½ teaspoon ground cinnamon
1 teaspoon black pepper
1 tablespoon soy sauce
1 tablespoon Worcestershire sauce
1 tablespoon vegetable oil
1 tablespoon apple-cider vinegar

In a food processor or blender, add onion, scallions, thyme, and peppers. Stir in other spices, and pulse until mixture becomes a light slurry. Marinate meat in a sealable plastic bag or covered container in refrigerator.

Note: When working with fresh peppers, use food-safe gloves; do not touch your eyes, mouth, or nose until you have washed your hands with soap and water.

**Spices from the Caribbean give this marinade
a kick to heat up your mouth!**

SAVANNAH SMOKER'S MOHUNKEN RUB

YIELD: 3+ CUPS • PREP: 5 MIN. • USE WITH: PORK

½ cup brown sugar
1 cup white sugar
1 cup paprika
¼ cup garlic powder
¼ cup coarse salt
2 tablespoons chili powder
2 teaspoons cayenne pepper

4 teaspoons black pepper
2 teaspoons dried oregano
    or Italian seasoning
2 teaspoons cumin
1 tablespoon mustard power
Yellow mustard to taste

Blend all ingredients in a small bowl.

Resources

This list of manufacturers and associations is meant to be a general guide to additional industry and product-related sources. It is not intended as a listing of all of the products and manufacturers presented in this book.

COMPANIES AND ASSOCIATIONS

The Alaska Seafood Marketing Institute (ASMI)

www.alaskaseafood.org
Alaska's official seafood marketing agency offers a consumer recipe database on its website.

Butterball

www.butterball.com
The company provides recipes, tips, and ideas, and product information on its website.

Cattlemen's Beef Board

www.beefboard.com
The beef industry offers tips, food safety information, and recipes for preparing beef through its website.

Char-Broil

www.charbroil.com
This is the official website for the Char-Broil® company.

Christopher Ranch

www.christopherranch.com
Christopher Ranch provides product information and recipes on its website.

Litehouse Foods

www.litehousefoods.com
The company's website features recipes and product information.

Louisiana Seafood Promotion & Marketing Board

http://louisianaseafood.com
The organization's website features news, information, and recipes.

Mann's Fresh Vegetables

www.veggiesmadeeasy.com
The company's website features product information and recipes.

Marie's

www.maries.com
The company's website features product information and recipes.

National Pork Board

www.porkbeinspired.com
The National Pork Board-sponsored website features information, nutrition, and recipes.

National Turkey Federation

www.eatturkey.com
The National Turkey Federation-sponsored website offers recipes, information, and merchandise.

Nourish with Lamb

www.nourishwithlamb.com
The Tri-Lamb Group offers nutritional information, preparation and cooking tips, and recipes on its website.

Ocean Mist Farms

www.oceanmist.com
Ocean Mist Farms provides recipes, videos, and nutrition information on its website.

The Other White Meat

www.theotherwhitemeat.com
The National Pork Board-sponsored website features information, nutrition, and recipes.

Perdue

www.perdue.com
Perdue provides recipes, information, and tips on its website.

Pillsbury

www.pillsbury.com

The company's website features recipes, holiday cooking guides, and product information.

Potatoes USA

www.potatogoodness.com

Potatoes USA features recipes and information about healthy eating on its website.

Sizzle on the Grill

www.charbroil.com/cook

Char-Broil sponsors this newsletter and website, which features grilling tips and recipes.

Tabasco

www.tabasco.com

The company's website features product information, recipes, and merchandise.

Tyson Foods

www.tyson.com

Tyson's website provides recipes and product information.

United States Department of Agriculture (USDA) Food Safety and Inspection Service

www.fsis.usda.gov

The website offers consumer safety information on buying, storing, preparing, and cooking meat and poultry.

USA Rice Federation

www.usarice.com

The organization's website features information, news, and recipes.

USDA Meat & Poultry Hotline

888-MPHotline

This hotline answers questions about safe storage, handling, and preparation of meat and poultry products.

Virginia Seafood

www.virginiaseafood.org

This website features news, information, and recipes from the Virginia Marine Products Board.

Index

Note: Page numbers in **bold** indicate recipe category lists.